PEACEBUILDING, CONFLICT AND COMMUNITY DEVELOPMENT

Rethinking Community Development

Series Editors: **Mae Shaw**, University of Edinburgh,
Rosie R. Meade, University College Cork and
Sarah Banks, University of Durham

Rethinking Community Development is an international book series that offers the opportunity for a critical re-evaluation of community development – to rethink what community development means in theory and practice. It is intended to draw together international, cross-generational and cross-disciplinary perspectives.

Series titles:

Young People, Radical Democracy and Community Development
Edited by **Janet Batsleer**, **Harriet Rowley** and **Demet Lüküslü**

Arts, Culture and Community Development
Edited by **Rosie Meade** and **Mae Shaw**

Populism, Democracy and Community Development
Edited by **Sue Kenny**, **Jim Ife** and **Peter Westoby**

Environmental Justice, Popular Struggle and Community Development
Edited by **Anne Harley** and **Eurig Scandrett**

Ethics, Equity and Community Development
Edited by **Sarah Banks** and **Peter Westoby**

Funding, Power and Community Development
Edited by **Niamh McCrea** and **Fergal Finnegan**

Find out more at

policy.bristoluniversitypress.co.uk/rethinking-community-development

PEACEBUILDING, CONFLICT AND COMMUNITY DEVELOPMENT

Edited by
John Eversley, Sinéad Gormally
and Avila Kilmurray

First published in Great Britain in 2023 by

Policy Press, an imprint of
Bristol University Press
University of Bristol
1–9 Old Park Hill
Bristol
BS2 8BB
UK
t: +44 (0)117 374 6645
e: bup-info@bristol.ac.uk

Details of international sales and distribution partners are available at
policy.bristoluniversitypress.co.uk

© Bristol University Press 2023

British Library Cataloguing in Publication Data
A catalogue record for this book is available from the British Library

ISBN 978-1-4473-5933-3 hardcover
ISBN 978-1-4473-5934-0 paperback
ISBN 978-1-4473-5935-7 ePub
ISBN 978-1-4473-5936-4 ePdf

The right of John Eversley, Sinéad Gormally and Avila Kilmurray to be identified as editors of this work has been asserted by them in accordance with the Copyright, Designs and Patents Act 1988.

All rights reserved: no part of this publication may be reproduced, stored in a retrieval system, or transmitted in any form or by any means, electronic, mechanical, photocopying, recording, or otherwise without the prior permission of Bristol University Press.

Every reasonable effort has been made to obtain permission to reproduce copyrighted material. If, however, anyone knows of an oversight, please contact the publisher.

The statements and opinions contained within this publication are solely those of the editors and contributors and not of the University of Bristol or Bristol University Press. The University of Bristol and Bristol University Press disclaim responsibility for any injury to persons or property resulting from any material published in this publication.

Bristol University Press and Policy Press work to counter discrimination on grounds of gender, race, disability, age and sexuality.

Cover design: Liam Roberts Design
Front cover image: Ian Shaw

Contents

Series editors' preface		vii
List of figures and tables		viii
Notes on contributors		ix
Preface		xv

1	Introduction *John Eversley, Sinéad Gormally and Avila Kilmurray*	1
2	Everyday peace as a community development approach *Anthony Ware, Vicki-Ann Ware and Leanne Kelly*	25
3	Peacebuilding with youth: experience in Cúcuta, Colombia *Nohora Constanza Niño Vega*	40
4	Dialogues to develop civil movements in the Caucasus *Larissa Sotieva and Juliet Schofield*	59
5	Working for social justice through community development in Nigeria *Samir Halliru*	79
6	Memory, truth and hope: long journeys of justice in Eastern Sri Lanka *Sarala Emmanuel and P.B. Gowthaman*	98
7	Brazil: public security as a human right in the favelas *Eliana Sousa Silva and Lidiane Malanquini*	117
8	Nepal: working with community-based women to influence inclusion and peacebuilding *Susan Risal*	134
9	Palestinian storytelling: authoring their own lives *Patricia Sellick*	151
10	Community-based action in Northern Ireland: activism in a violently contested society *Monina O'Prey*	168

11	Everyday peace: after ethnic cleansing in Myanmar's Rohingya conflict	191
	Vicki-Ann Ware, Anthony Ware and Leanne Kelly	
12	Conclusion: Drawing the threads together	209
	John Eversley, Sinéad Gormally and Avila Kilmurray	
Index		233

SERIES EDITORS' PREFACE

Rethinking Community Development

Communities are a continuing focus of public policy and citizen action worldwide. The purposes and functions of work with communities of place, interest and identity vary between and within contexts and change over time. Nevertheless, community development – as both an occupation and as a democratic practice concerned with the demands and aspirations of people in communities – has been extraordinarily enduring.

This book series aims to provide a critical re-evaluation of community development in theory and practice, in the light of new challenges posed by the complex interplay of emancipatory, democratic, self-help and managerial imperatives in different parts of the world. Through a series of edited and authored volumes, Rethinking Community Development will draw together international, cross-generational and cross-disciplinary perspectives, using contextual specificity as a lens through which to explore the localised consequences of global processes. Each text in the series will:

- *promote critical thinking*, through examining the contradictory position of community development, including the tensions between policy imperatives and the interests and demands of communities;
- *include a range of international examples*, in order to explore the localised consequences of global processes;
- *include contributions from established and up-and-coming new voices*, from a range of geographical contexts;
- *offer topical and timely perspectives*, drawing on historical and theoretical resources in a generative and enlivening way;
- *inform and engage a new generation of practitioners*, bringing new and established voices together to stimulate diverse and innovative perspectives on community development.

If you have a broad or particular interest in community development that could be expanded into an authored or edited collection for this book series, contact:

Mae Shaw	Rosie Meade	Sarah Banks
mae.shaw@ed.ac.uk	r.meade@ucc.ie	s.j.banks@durham.ac.uk

List of figures and tables

Figures

1.1	Overlapping boundaries between conflict prevention, peacemaking, peacekeeping, peacebuilding and peace enforcement	6
1.2	Lederach's pyramid	8
1.3	Smith's palette	10
1.4	United Nations Sustainable Development Goals for 2030	11
1.5	Conflict escalation and de-escalation model	16
3.1	Map of Colombia showing Cúcuta	42
4.1	Map of the Caucasus	61
5.1	Map of Nigeria	80
6.1	Map of Sri Lanka	100
7.1	Map of Brazil	119
7.2	Map of Redes da Maré favela in Rio de Janeiro	120
8.1	Map of Nepal	135
9.1	Territories occupied by Israel since June 1967	153
9.2	Rebecca Bubb's illustration of growing up in a cave	160
10.1	Map of Great Britain, Northern Ireland and Ireland	169
10.2	Map of Northern Ireland	173
11.1	Map of Myanmar	195

Tables

1.1	What makes a community and how it impacts on conflict, violence and peacebuilding	3
1.2	Community development values	5
1.3	Defining key terms in peace activities	7
1.4	Levels of conflict, risk factors and potential interventions	13
1.5	Community development interventions at different stages of conflict	17
2.1	Types of social practice that constitute everyday practice	32
7.1	Impact of police operations on Maré's favelas	125
7.2	Violent death rates in police operations and conflicts between armed groups in Maré	126
8.1	The foundational principles of Nagarik Aawaz	140
10.1	Some community approaches adopted in Northern Ireland	178
10.2	Factors and indicators of weak community infrastructure	182

Notes on contributors

Sarala Emmanuel is a feminist activist and researcher living and working in Batticaloa, Sri Lanka. She worked with the Suriya Women's Development Center (2005–18), and currently is a part of several community-based as well as national and international feminist networks. Her work and research focus on women's economic rights, labour rights, rights of queer communities, violence against women and girls, and peace with accountability and justice and food security in the COVID-19 context.

John Eversley began his working life in Northern Ireland as youth worker and social researcher during the Troubles in the early 1970s. He spent most of the next four decades working in London in variety of community work, policymaking and management roles. His experience spans the voluntary sector, higher education and director-level posts in the National Health Service and local government. John has wide experience in the public sector of promoting social justice using community development approaches to policy and practice, particularly in the fields of public health, primary and social care. He has published extensively in the area of public policy, social justice and social change, including most recently *Social and Community Development: An Introduction* (Red Globe Press, 2018).

Sinéad Gormally is Senior Lecturer in Community Development, School of Education, at the University of Glasgow. She is a qualified community and youth worker, and her current research is twofold – one area focuses on social justice and equality, challenging the deficit, pathologising discourse perpetuated at the most marginalised in society and analysing how youth and community practitioners can create a positive counter-narrative. Her other area of interest focuses on the impact of violence and conflict on individuals and communities.

P.B. Gowthaman is a development practitioner with a keen interest and experience working on community development in conflict settings. He was the country director for Oxfam Australia (2004–10) and headed their programmes responding to complex emergencies. Since then, he has been involved as a consultant in evaluations and assessments of development and humanitarian response interventions in protracted conflict areas. Currently he is managing a civil society support programme based out of Colombo.

Samir Halliru is Lecturer in the Department of Adult Education and Community Services, Bayero University, Kano (BUK), Nigeria. Samir's research interest focuses on lifelong learning, social justice and social change.

He is interested on seeing how education empowers individuals and groups from the shackles of poverty, illiteracy and dehumanisation. He is interested in seeing how social justice brings about peaceful communities.

His research and teaching covers adult education, social justice, social work, women's empowerment, community studies and youth work, at undergraduate and postgraduate level. Samir obtained a Diploma in Public and Private Law (HUK Polytechnic), a BEd Adult Education and Community Development (BUK), MEd Community Development (BUK), MSC Adult and Continuing Education (University of Glasgow, UK) and PhD in Education (University of Glasgow, UK). He is a member of the board of the Standing Conference on the University Teaching and Research on the Education of the Adults (SCUTREA), UK.

Leanne Kelly has worked in community development and social service non-profits for nearly two decades. As well as working directly with community members affected by intercommunal conflict, Leanne has evaluated the impact of peacebuilding approaches on attitudes, behaviours and social harmony. She has published over two dozen academic papers on development and evaluation related topics and two books: *Evaluation in Small Development Non-Profits: Deadends, Victories and Alternative Routes* (Palgrave Macmillan, 2021) and *Internal Evaluation in Non-Profit Organisations: Practitioner Perspectives on Theory, Research, and Practice* (with Alison Rogers, Routledge, 2022). She is a postdoctoral research fellow at Deakin University and evaluation lead in emergency services at the Australian Red Cross.

Avila Kilmurray is currently working with the Social Change Initiative (Northern Ireland) on peacebuilding, refugee protection and migrant rights. She has worked extensively in the community and voluntary sectors in Northern Ireland since the mid-1970s and was Director of the Community Foundation for Northern Ireland (1994–2014) when it was active in the reintegration of political ex-prisoners and support for victims/survivors of the conflict as well as funding community-based activism. She was a founder member of the Northern Ireland Women's Coalition and a member of its negotiating team during the 1996–8 peace talks. Avila is a Board Member of the International Fund for Ireland and the St. Stephen's Green Trust. She is author of *Community Action in a Contested Society: The Story of Northern Ireland* (Peter Lang, 2017).

Lidiane Malanquini is a social worker and PhD candidate at the Postgraduate Program in Social Work at the Federal University of Rio de Janeiro. At present, she coordinates the Centre for Rights to Public Security and Access to Justice at Redes da Maré and has experience in research and social and political mobilisation on the topics of public security, favelas and peripheral communities, and human rights.

Nohora Constanza Niño Vega is a psychologist from the Universidad Nacional de Colombia with a PhD in Research in Social Sciences and Sociology from Facultad Latinoamericana de Ciencias Sociales, Mexico. Her research interest is in childhood, youth, violence, peacebuilding, borders and forced migration. She has research experience in Colombia and Mexico, working with communities affected by the armed conflict in Colombia and forcibly displaced communities in need of international protection in both countries.

Nohora has worked on research projects that investigate the connections between the different forms of violence experienced by children and young people and the strategies they develop to cope with it; peacebuilding processes through arts and culture and, the forced migration of Mexicans and Venezuelans from the experience of children and young people.

Monina O'Prey is a peacebuilding activist from Northern Ireland, with over 30 years' expertise in developing and delivering grassroots peacebuilding, community development and social justice programmes and campaigns. Her work has included anti-poverty campaigns, work with lone parents, and extensive engagement with excluded Loyalist and Republican communities. She has combined work at the grassroots with roles as a policy advocate and as a funder. Through her fellowship with the Social Change Initiative (Northern Ireland), Monina co-authored the publication *Activism Across Division: Peacebuilding Strategies & Insights from Northern Ireland* (2020). Monina currently works as Management Agent with the International Fund for Ireland on addressing peace barrier issues.

Renata Peppl translated Eliana and Lidiana's contribution. She is Research Programme Manager at Queen Mary University of London. Renata is from Brazil and has been working for over eight years as Senior Research and Programme Manager for International Research on the topics of gender-based violence, mental health, urban violence and wellbeing, and arts and homelessness. Since 2016, she has been partnering with Redes da Maré on a number of international research and community engagement programmes to support the production of knowledge on gender inequalities, public security and mental health there. She is also International Coordinator supporting Women of the World (WOW) Festival, Rio de Janeiro. She recently joined as Programme Manager at the Unit of Social and Community Psychiatry at Queen Mary University of London, managing PIECEs, a four-year programme testing arts and social interventions to improve community-based care of people with severe mental health illness in India and Pakistan.

Susan Risal is Chief Executive Officer of Nagarik Aawaz (Citizen's Voices), a peacebuilding organisation in Nepal which works with conflict-affected youth and women which she joined in 2003 as an admin/finance officer. She became a programme manager there in 2009 and in 2011 became Chief Executive Officer. Susan is a peace practitioner based in Kathmandu, Nepal. Susan holds a PhD degree in applied conflict transformation studies from a collaborative programme between the Center for Peace Studies and Pannasatra University, Cambodia. She also holds two master's degrees: a Master's in Business Administration from Tribhuvan University of Nepal and a Master's in Applied Conflict Transformation Studies from Pannasastra University of Cambodia. Her PhD topic was 'Defining dignity and justice through gendered peace building: A case study of gender-based violence during armed conflict in Nepal'.

Patricia Sellick is Visiting Researcher at the Centre for Trust, Peace and Social Relations, Coventry University. She is a practitioner academic, who has zig-zagged between working with people affected by conflict and researching issues of peace and conflict. She has worked for both the British and the US American Quakers in the Middle East, based first in Hebron and then in East Jerusalem. Her primary interest is in the ways in which people connect across generations to make change without recourse to violence.

Larissa Sotieva and **Juliet Schofield** are co-founders of Independent Peace Associates (Indie Peace), a conflict transformation organisation specialising in research, training and facilitation of dialogue to build confidence between communities affected by conflict.

Larissa has over 25 years' experience managing humanitarian, conflict transformation and civic engagement programmes in the former Soviet Union and has a wealth of expertise in political and conflict analysis, facilitation of research, and cross-conflict dialogue processes, including high-level policy dialogues. Larissa has worked for a number of international organisations in Russia in the North Caucasus and also in the South Caucasus, Central Asia and Ukraine. Between 2006 and 2019, Larissa worked as senior adviser for the Eurasia region with International Alert, after which she founded Independent Peace Associates.

Juliet has over 20 years' experience managing conflict transformation and civic engagement programmes in the former Soviet Union and western Balkans, working with organisations VSO and International Alert, bringing a wealth of expertise in programme management, design, monitoring and evaluation. She has managed research, dialogue, public education and advocacy initiatives, bringing together conflicting sides, fostering youth engagement, critical thinking and promoting social justice. Juliet also has a degree in psychosocial studies and recently has been exploring the use of arts and culture-based approaches for social change inspired by her engagement with cultural dialogue between writers, artists, musicians and public figures from across the Caucasus.

Eliana Sousa Silva grew up in the favela of Redes da Maré, Rio de Janeiro, Brazil. When she was 21, she established the now flourishing community initiative. She is Director of Redes da Maré (Maré Development Networks), curator/director, WOW Rio de Janeiro (Women of the World Festival) and an advisory board member of Women of the World Global Foundation. She is Visiting Professor at the University of Sao Paulo, holding the Olavo Setubal Chair in Arts, Culture and Science, and the leader of the CNPq Research Group at the Center for Violence Prevention, Access to Justice and Education in Human Rights. Until 2017, she was Director of the University & Community Department at the Federal University of Rio de Janeiro. She is also the author of the book *Testimonies of Maré* (2015).

Anthony Ware is Associate Professor of International and Community Development at Deakin University. He was Director of the Australia Myanmar Institute from 2013 to 2017, and previously lectured at the University of Melbourne. His research focus is on international development in conflict-affected situations, and the relationship between everyday peace and community-led local development, particularly in Myanmar. More broadly, his research revolves around 'do no harm' and the impact of sociopolitical factors on participatory development. He has also worked on issues such as sanctions, fragile states, democratic transition, the role of faith and faith-based organisations in development, and development in difficult sociopolitical contexts. He has published over 50 academic papers/chapters, and four books: *Myanmar's 'Rohingya' Conflict* (Oxford University Press, 2018, with Costas Laoutides), *Development Across Faith Boundaries* (Routledge, 2017, edited with Matthew Clarke), *Development in Difficult Sociopolitical Contexts* (ed; Palgrave, 2014) and *Context-Sensitive Development: How International NGOs Operate in Myanmar* (Kumarian, 2012).

Vicki-Ann Ware is Senior Lecturer in International and Community Development at Deakin University, with research interests in community development and peacebuilding approaches that utilise arts and sports-based programming. Her current research explores arts as a pedagogical tool in community development and peacebuilding, primarily in Myanmar and Bangladesh, and mechanisms by which arts can contribute to significant grassroots social change. She is also conducting research utilising asset-based community development to enhance community safety in suburban Melbourne. Vicki has 25 years' experience in arts-based community development in mainland Southeast Asia, particularly in Thailand, Myanmar,

Laos and Cambodia. She has published over two dozen academic papers/chapters. She convenes the Arts/Sports for Community Development Network, an international network of community development practitioners and academics utilising arts/sports-based approaches. She is currently lead editor for the *Routledge Handbook of Arts and Global Development* (forthcoming) and is researching the state of community development practice and theory in contemporary Australia.

Preface

The editors of this book want to thank all those contributors who took the time to write up their experiences of adopting community development approaches in conflict-affected environments. We particularly wish to pay tribute to local practitioners who all too often find it virtually impossible to find the time or space to record their learning. Surviving in circumstances of violent conflict can draw the oxygen out of opportunities to reflect on practice. Priorities can be overtaken by the need to manage difficult and sensitive situations in order to ensure that practice is sustainable.

We have deliberately invited contributions drawn from a range of very diverse conflict-affected environments, but sharing the impact of both state and non-state armed actors. A unique element of the community action recorded is to be able to balance between these countervailing forces and even, at times, mediate between them. This is where community development interfaces with peacebuilding – a subject that is considered in this book but that warrants more detailed examination than we have space to present. However, if there is an overriding message it is that community activism is not only possible, but very necessary, in situations of violent conflict. Similarly, peacebuilding is not merely a post-conflict strategy, it gains its credibility by being applicable both during the violence and in periods of peace negotiations. We are also conscious of the critical role that effective peacebuilding plays in working to prevent a roll-back into either authoritarianism and/or future violent conflict.

Alongside presenting contributions from a range of very different societies and circumstances, the editors welcome the very different perspectives presented by the authors. We do not necessarily agree with each of the analyses put forward, but we feel that it is important that readers are made aware of the various approaches adopted by different agencies and practitioners. For ourselves, we prefer approaches that are locally owned and grounded rather than programmes externally designed and/or adopting a one-sided political perspective. However, we are also acutely aware that in conflict-riven societies, whatever community development strategy is adopted will be seen as 'political', whether a big 'P' or a small 'p', as so often noted by the community-based Women's Sector in Northern Ireland. It is rare for community development to avoid a degree of politicisation in whatever context that it is practised, but it can never escape politics in situations of conflict.

Finally, we welcome those contributions that offer some advice to community activists and workers themselves as to how to survive and avoid burnout in often difficult circumstances. Self-care is not a luxury; it is healthy defiance in the face of what may be seen at times as overwhelming odds. If this collection of stories can be of use to anyone, it is practitioners like you that we have in mind.

1

Introduction

John Eversley, Sinéad Gormally and Avila Kilmurray

Summary

This book is a contribution to understanding the potential role of community development in societies impacted by violent conflict. As an introduction to a number of practitioner case studies, it is important to unpack the key concepts of peacebuilding, conflict and community development. Given this, the chapter will focus on community development and peacebuilding. Much has been written about both these approaches, but in the interests of space and time the authors will concentrate on how peacebuilding and community development can interact in circumstances of organised, severe and often protracted violent conflict.

What is violence?

Clearly there are a multiplicity of communities that are impacted by violent conflict in a wide variety of circumstances and conditions. While 'war' is conventionally seen as being pursued for political purposes and 'organised crime' for economic purposes, the two can often overlap and both invariably entail considerable levels of violence. Political violence is often funded by criminal activity. Criminal violence is often protected by political interests. Who labels a conflict, and how, is a major issue. The designation of 'terrorist' is a labelling likely to be conferred by people holding official power. Terminology is important, as are values, when considering both the understanding and practice of community development and peacebuilding in conditions of persistent violent conflict.

The Uppsala Conflict Data Programme (Uppsala Conflict Data Programme, nd) offers a nuanced definition of conflict, setting 'organised violence' in the context of a combination of state-based armed conflict, non-state armed conflict and one-sided violence. With a baseline of a minimum of 25 fatalities (combatants and civilians) in a calendar year, data is presented in terms of inter-state conflict (which is low); intra-state conflict (which at 54 in 2019 was the highest number in the post-1946 period); intra-state conflict that has been internationalised by external intervention (the

United States being most involved as the secondary warring partner); and non-state conflict (between non-state armed groups, with Syrian fatalities being surpassed by deaths in Mexico in 2019).[1] Fatalities as a result of civil protests are not included in the Uppsala datasets (Pettersson and Öberg, 2020). Many of the conflicts recorded are localised and regional. This has clear implications for locally based peacebuilding and the community-based strategies involved.

The impact and implications of violent conflict were highlighted in the United Nations and World Bank joint report, *Pathways for Peace: Inclusive Approaches to Preventing Violent Conflict* (2018). This recognised that conflicts are often complex and protracted, affecting some two billion people (one-third of the world's population).[2] Emphasising the shift from wars between states to internal and/or intra-state violence, the UN estimated that conflict costs some US$13.6 trillion per annum. It is a threat to the 2030 Sustainable Development Goals agenda. Serious concerns were expressed about the level of fatalities in conflict, levels of military spending, terrorism and increased numbers of Internally Displaced People (IDPs) and refugees, with organised crime being identified as a significant stress factor (United Nations and World Bank, 2018). The importance of strategies that can ameliorate the impact of violent conflict on people and communities has never been more pressing. The contribution of approaches that can highlight and challenge the causal factors of conflict are crucial, and both can benefit from an understanding of community-based activism in sharply contested societies.

Understanding community

An understanding of community underpins any definition of community development. Community has frequently been seen as a nostalgic concept based on the idea of positive interpersonal bonds in contrast to 'society' based on anonymous contractual institutional relationships (Blackshaw, 2010: 4). It has many potential dimensions including physical space with social and psychological connections (Mattessich and Monsey, 2004), as a virtual environment framed by communicative forces within modernity (Delanty, 2003), as the primacy of clusters of identity and as a social practice (Wenger, 1998), as bricolage (Coburn and Gormally, 2017) and relationships in kaleidoscopic combinations (Eversley, 2018: 41).

It has been suggested that the very lack of conceptual clarity of the term contributes to its popularity (Little, 2002: 1). However, the multifaceted, dynamic, overlapping and contradictory nature of community is very important to community development because it allows people with ties to a notion of community, the agency not only to adopt their own understanding but also to adapt it. Table 1.1 demonstrates what makes community and how it impacts on conflict, violence and peacebuilding.

Table 1.1: What makes a community and how it impacts on conflict, violence and peacebuilding

Identifier	Example	Issues which can lead to violence	Peacebuilding and community development activities
Territory	A rural community or a segregated district within or close to a city	A fortress or a prison which some people can't enter or leave: group areas; reservations; informal settlements	Balancing inclusive (common or shared) and exclusive spaces
Interests and conditions	A community based on a particular industry or activity – for example, mining, textile manufacturing	Migrant, nomadic or travelling communities often seen as invaders	Finding common interests
Shared ancestry and identity	Clan, tribe, ethnic group	Contested claims to territory	Identifying advantages of diversity – 'elective affinities'; 'weak ties' are often more important assertions of universal rights and needs
Social capital and networks	Family, friends and neighbours you can rely on	Often defined in terms of opposition to some other kind of community – for example, extracting resources at the expense of the environment or livelihoods of others	Highlighting interdependence
Culture, values and symbols	Speakers of a particular language; practising a specific religion or a lifestyle	Multiple groups	Finding common values while affirming the right to distinctive practices and symbols

Much framing of community emphasises the 'dense overlapping ties' of locale (Taylor, 2003), but even within these terms there is a need to recognise the diversity of those who make up the community. Communities can have a sinister side of both shutting people in or out. Outraged communities can contribute to conflict and division (Brent, 2004). Thus, it is important to be prepared to work within a framework that is both complex and dynamic.

And so to community development

Like community theory and practice, community development is a 'contested and malleable' concept (Meade et al, 2016). It can be viewed as a process of collective action and emancipation or as an outcome resulting in multilevel community improvement (Phillips and Pittman, 2009). In the main, community development is seen as a value-driven movement for co-creating social change (Gilchrist and Taylor, 2011; Beck and Purcell, 2020). Ledwith highlights that while community development claims to begin in the everyday lives of people, too often we have failed to create 'the spaces for critical conversations on the politics of everyday life, and the values that most people care about: those of community, connection, kindness, compassion and caring' (Ledwith, 2020: 1). The aspiration and the challenge of working in a democratic way to question the established norms of everyday life, encouraging collective action to address inequalities or issues of concern is most acute in situations of violent conflict. It is essential that community development has both a strong theoretical underpinning married to transformative and empowering practices. Practice needs to resist actions which Nita Freire (2016) noted 'Assistencialise' others – treating people as passive objects worthy only of benevolent gestures rather than as active subjects capable of transforming their world. Again, a feeling of lack of agency is often central in violent conflicts. Community development and peacebuilding initiatives have to work hard not to reinforce it.

The current International Association of Community Development (IACD) definition of community development reads as follows: 'Community Development is a practice-based profession and an academic discipline that promotes participative democracy, sustainable development, rights, economic opportunity, equality and social justice, through the organisation, education and empowerment of people within their communities, whether these be of locality, identity or interest, in urban and rural settings' (IACD, 2018: 8). This inclusive definition offers some guidance, but also leaves considerable room for potential differences in practice. These were highlighted by Shaw (2008) as, for example, where delivering policies and outputs is seen as more important than the social and democratic purpose of community development. She elaborates on the latter, seeing it as where community development works 'alongside people in communities to assist them in thinking about and articulating their own, often contradictory, experience of policy and taking action around their collective interest and concerns' (Shaw, 2008: 16).

Within this understanding a community development approach connects with people who do not have a voice in policy development or practice. There is an emphasis on the creation of conditions and systems where people can feel that they have greater control over their lives individually and within their community. Community development facilitates people to work collectively to both agree, and bring about, positive social change, with this activism and agency grounded in people's own experience. In practice this entails commitment to a long-term process that supports communities to work collectively to:

- identify their own needs, assets and priorities;
- take collective action using their strengths and resources;
- develop their confidence, skills and knowledge;
- challenge unequal power relationships; and
- promote social justice, equality and inclusion in order to improve the quality of their own lives, the communities in which they live and societies of which they are a part.

This approach is encapsulated in the definition of community development originally adopted by the Community Workers Co-operative, Ireland, in 2006 and then by the All Ireland Endorsement Body for Community Work Education & Training (AIEB): 'A developmental activity composed of both "task" and "process". The task is the achievement of social change linked to equality and social justice. The process is the application of the principles of participation, empowerment and collective decision-making in a structured and coordinated way' (AIEB, 2016: 5). Craig et al (2008) warn, however, that assuming solidarity with the poor and the values of social justice are often not enough to win political gains or policy change.

Nevertheless, value statements remain important. Banks and Westoby (2019: 9) tabulated a number of relevant value statements as seen in Table 1.2. Each one of the concepts and terms used here are highly debatable and bring with them their own complex, contestable field of knowledge. However, while we recognise that this collection of occupational value statements reflects a clear commitment of practitioners to a fairer world, there is a danger of 'empty rhetoric' when it comes to debates over whose rights are prioritised, collective learning from and with who, and what constitutes meaningful participation – issues of intense relevance to peacebuilding.

Table 1.2: Community development values

International Association for Community Development (IACD, 2018)	European Community Development Network (2014)	National Occupational Standards for Community Development Scotland (2015)	All Ireland Endorsement Body for Community Work Ecucation & Training (2016)
• Rights • Solidarity • Democracy • Equality • Environmental and social justice	• Collective learning • Empowerment • Meaningful participation • Collective action for collective outcomes • Equality	• Social justice and equality • Anti-discrimination • Community empowerment • Collective action • Working and learning together	• Collectivity • Community empowerment • Social justice and sustainable development • Human rights, equality and anti-discrimination • Participation

Source: European Community Development Network (2014)

An understanding of peacebuilding

If community development offers a range of definitions, so too does the concept of peacebuilding. At its most simple peacebuilding can be read as building alternatives to war and violent conflict, however it has increasingly been described as being complex and multidimensional in character (Keating and Knight, 2004). An early description by Galtung (1969) of 'positive peace' challenged the neglect of the causes of structural violence (human insecurity caused by political, social and/or economic denial of rights) that so often give rise to violent conflict. A very different understanding was presented in the official discourse of the United Nations, when the then Secretary-General, Boutros Boutros-Ghali introduced 'An Agenda for Peace' in 1992, essentially casting peacebuilding as a post-conflict strategy to avoid a relapse into conflict (Boutros-Ghali, 1992). Figure 1.1 captures the positioning of peacebuilding vis-à-vis conflict and conflict prevention in this scenario.

The scale of the Rwanda crisis in 1994 prompted a shift in emphasis from post-conflict peacebuilding to a recognition of the importance of early warning signals and the ability of peacebuilding to address causal factors of potential violence. By 2016 the UN General Assembly endorsed a view that sustaining peace requires 'activities aimed at preventing the outbreak, escalation, continuation and recurrence of conflict, addressing root causes, assisting parties to conflict to end hostilities, ensuring national reconciliation'

Figure 1.1: Overlapping boundaries between conflict prevention, peacemaking, peacekeeping, peacebuilding and peace enforcement

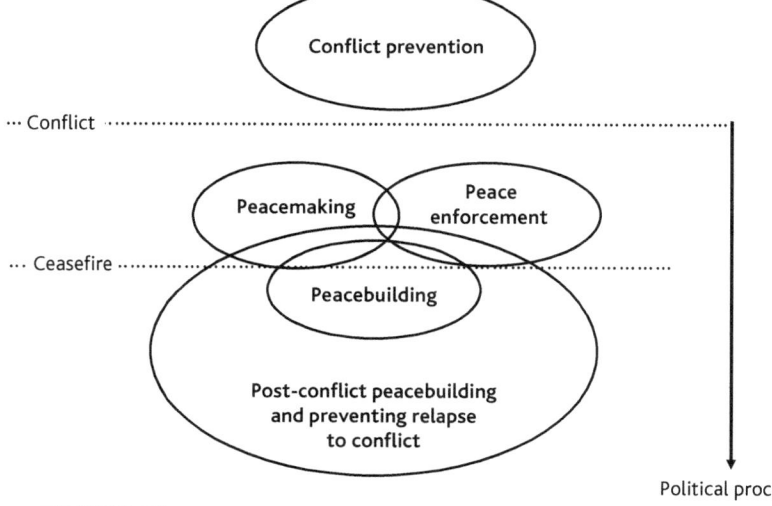

Source: UN (2008: 19)

Table 1.3: Defining key terms in peace activities

Peacemaking	Actions to bring hostile parties to agreement through processes that can involve diplomacy, mediation, negotiation and other confidence-building measures, often undertaken by external parties to the conflict.
Peacekeeping	The deployment of military forces (which can include police) to monitor and oversee peace processes in post-conflict areas by assisting ex-combatants in implementing Peace Agreement commitments.
Peacebuilding	Peacebuilding includes activities that aim to resolve injustice in nonviolent ways and to transform the cultural and structural conditions that generate deadly or destructive conflict. It revolves around developing constructive personal, group and political relationships across ethnic, religious, class, national and racial boundaries. It also includes violence prevention; conflict management, resolution or transformation; and post-conflict reconciliation or trauma healing – that is, before, during and after any given case of violence.

(United Nations, 2016). At the same time the United Nations agreed to undertake a comprehensive review of UN peacebuilding 'architecture' which was published in 2020 (United Nations, 2020).

For many years now, peacebuilding has been distinguished from 'peacekeeping' and 'peacemaking'. Table 1.3 explains the different concepts. As already noted, peacekeeping involves the active intervention of international forces in a situation of warring parties, often focusing on 'truce supervision' duties. The UN and other bodies pay countries to provide peacekeepers. Peacemaking relates to mainly international, and sometimes local, attempts, for example, to broker ceasefires and peace settlements, often working on the interstices between peacekeeping and peacebuilding. Peacemaking terminology can be presented in terms of different 'tracks'. Track One is primarily where official negotiations take place between political and military elites (the representatives of combatant groups with mediators). Track Two operates at the level of non-official mediation, which takes place with civil society and other institutional representatives (such as business, church interests, and so on) but which can include backchannel contacts with combatant groups. Track Three entails interaction with broader humanitarian, development and local community stakeholders that can create an enabling environment for reaching a peace settlement. Variations, such as Track One-and-a half, have been added as demonstrated in Mozambique when St. Egidio, an Italian Catholic non-governmental organisation (NGO) won acceptance to mediate talks between two warring parties.[3]

Peacebuilding is rooted in the understanding that activities are designed to contribute to avoiding or ending armed conflict, and consequently can be appropriate at any stage of violent conflict. Work by John Paul Lederach (1995; 1997) placed an emphasis on the importance of local ownership and

Figure 1.2: Lederach's pyramid

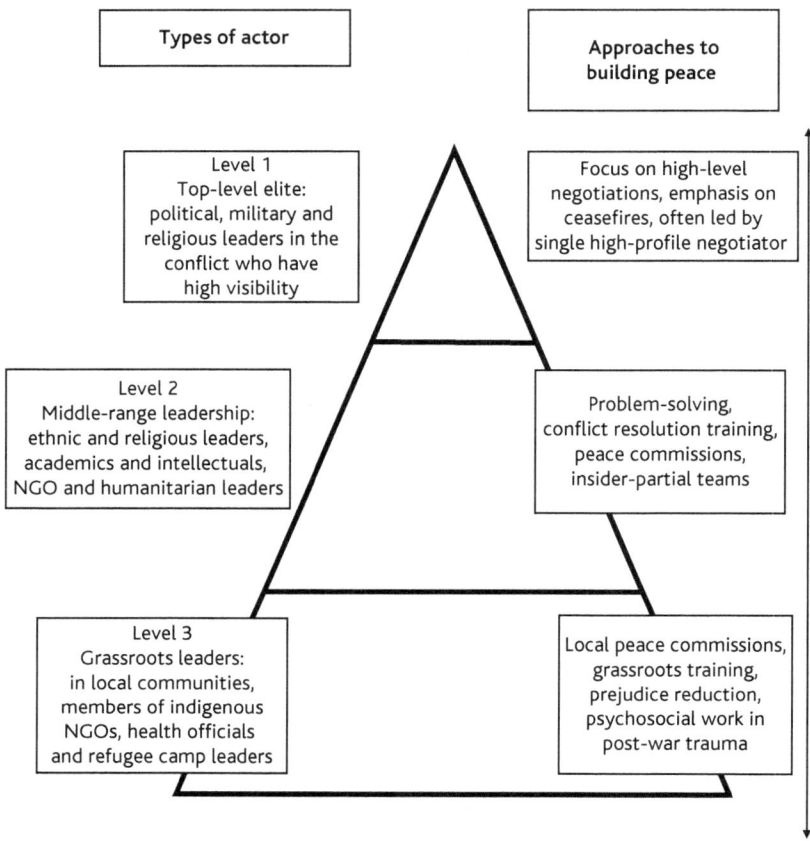

Source: Lederach (1997: 39)

agency in any peacebuilding process. He also argued for a holistic approach to peacebuilding, asserting the importance of participation and coordination between various sectors in contested societies. Figure 1.2 is derived from Lederach's study, highlighting the interconnection between different layers of society, including NGOs and community-based organisations (CBOs).

The nature of conflict is acknowledged as being protracted and non-linear, requiring long-term commitment. Lederach (2003) identifies four change goals – personal, relational, structural and cultural – and warns against over-reliance on state-sponsored peacebuilding processes. Lederach's four goals are very similar to the four I's of oppression – internal, interpersonal, institutional and ideological – which inform emancipation in community development (Colorado Inclusive Funders, nd).

Introduction

In 2004, the Utstein Report presented a palette of potential peacebuilding approaches. It proposed a four-pillar approach (U4). It acknowledged the importance of specific conflict context; the need for sustainable peace processes; and the crucial element of 'local ownership' (Smith, 2004). Collier and colleagues have argued that civil war is 'development in reverse' and Smith says that peacebuilding is 'development going forward in the context of crisis and war' (Smith, 2004: 25). Just as peacebuilding cannot be a path returning to pre-war structures and processes, development cannot be more of the same 'development', which depletes finite resources, perpetuates or reinforces economic or social inequalities or fails to meet basic needs. It needs to be sustainable. Smith refers to the activities of peacebuilding as a palette rather than a toolbox because the activities are best mixed together according to the circumstances (Smith, 2004: 28). The key elements of the palette are socio-economic foundations, security, reconciliation and justice and political frameworks. It offers a holistic approach which is also reflected in community development. Figure 1.3 demonstrates the overlapping boundaries of conflict prevention, peacemaking, peacekeeping, peacebuilding and peace enforcement.

Smith's palette of peacebuilding activities is also reflected in many of the UN's 17 Sustainable Development Goals (SDGs), which were set in 2015. SDG 16 focuses on 'Peace Justice and Strong Institutions' but many of the other goals are relevant to the economic and social framing of peacebuilding. The Utstein palette does not make mention of the SDGs that specifically refer to the environmental pillar of sustainable development, but we would argue the importance of addressing these issues (such as the impact of climate change and management of natural resources) as they are frequent and important contributors to violent conflict. Wars are major impediments to achieving the SDGs. Peacebuilding and community development are essential methods to achieve them. Figure 1.4 defines key terms in peace activities.

From peacebuilding to conflict transformation

The language of conflict transformation offers a more radical edge to peacebuilding and, in community development terms, draws on the analysis of Paulo Freire (1972) who remains an influential thinker in community development. Lederach (1997 quoted in Miall 2004: 4) pointed out: 'We understand the long-term goal of transformation as validating and building on people and resources within the (conflict) setting.' The Berghof Foundation describes conflict transformation as:

> A generic, comprehensive term referring to actions and processes which seek to alter the various characteristics and manifestations of

Figure 1.3: Smith's palette

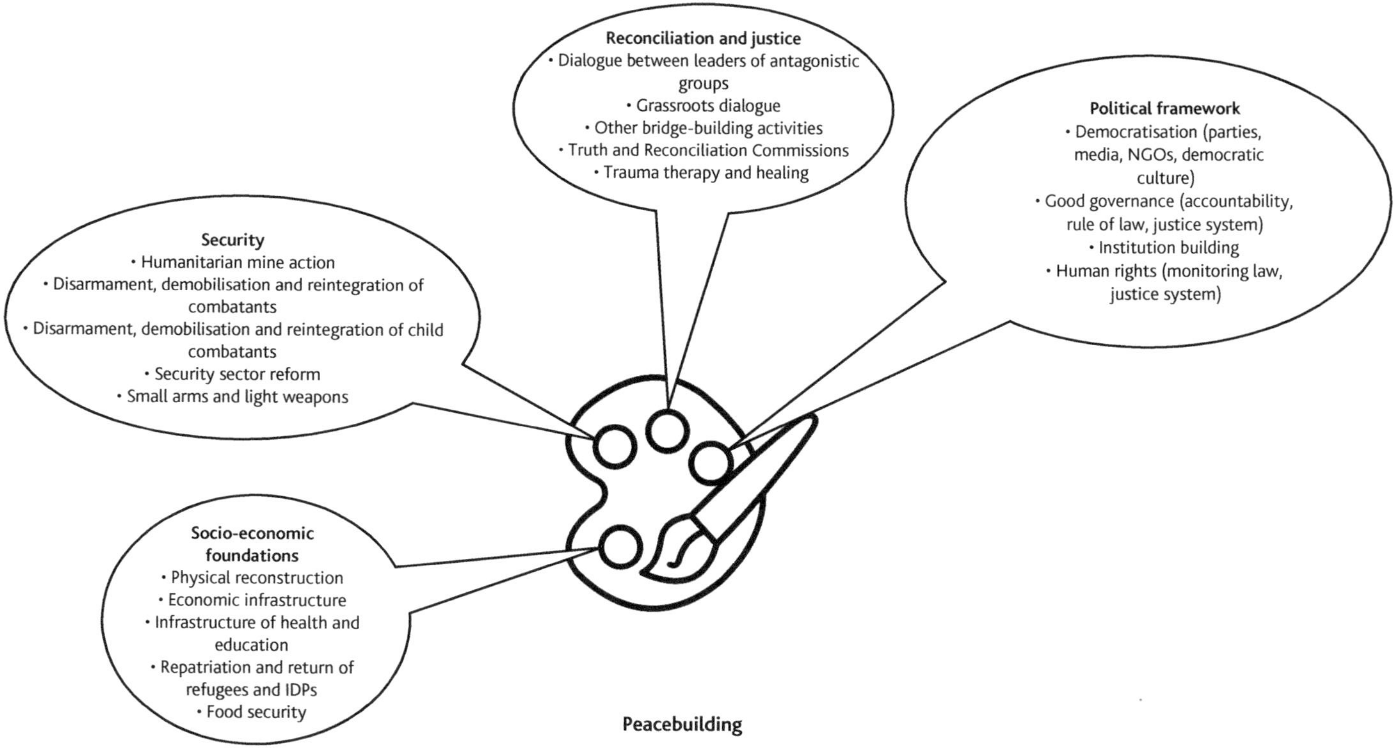

Political framework
- Democratisation (parties, media, NGOs, democratic culture)
- Good governance (accountability, rule of law, justice system)
- Institution building
- Human rights (monitoring law, justice system)

Reconciliation and justice
- Dialogue between leaders of antagonistic groups
- Grassroots dialogue
- Other bridge-building activities
- Truth and Reconciliation Commissions
- Trauma therapy and healing

Security
- Humanitarian mine action
- Disarmament, demobilisation and reintegration of combatants
- Disarmament, demobilisation and reintegration of child combatants
- Security sector reform
- Small arms and light weapons

Socio-economic foundations
- Physical reconstruction
- Economic infrastructure
- Infrastructure of health and education
- Repatriation and return of refugees and IDPs
- Food security

Peacebuilding

Source: Smith (2004: 28)

Figure 1.4: United Nations Sustainable Development Goals for 2030

Note: The use of this image in this publication has not been approved by the United Nations and does not reflect the views of the United Nations or its officials or Member States but is reproduced with the permission of the United Nations Department of Global Communications. https://www.un.org/sustainabledevelopment/

Source: United Nations Sustainable Development Goals for 2030 (United Nations Department of Economic and Social Affairs, 2015)

conflict by addressing the root causes of a particular conflict over the long term. It aims to transform negative destructive conflict into positive constructive conflict and deals with structural, behavioural and attitudinal aspects of conflict. The term refers to both the process and the completion of the process. As such it incorporates the activities of processes such as Conflict Prevention and Conflict Resolution and goes farther than conflict settlement or conflict management. (Austin et al, 2004: 444)

The conflict transformation approach goes beyond merely seeking to contain and manage the violence, working instead to transform the root causes themselves – or the perceptions of the root causes – focusing on structural, behavioural and attitudinal aspects of conflict. Echoing Lederach's (1997) four goals and the four I's of oppression (Colorado Inclusive Funders, nd) mentioned earlier, Väyrynen (1991) noted that practice can encompass:

- actor transformation – changes internally in either the parties involved or the introduction of new parties;
- issue transformation – altering the agenda of conflict issues;
- rule transformation – changes in the norms/rules governing the conflict; and
- structural transformation – transforming the entire structure of relationships and power distribution.

Following the work Paulo Freire, Martha Nussbaum and Amartya Sen, we argue that a radical approach to conflict transformation is not about capacity as an individual attribute with fixed limits, but more about removing the barriers or penalties that obstruct people realising their full capabilities (Robeyns, 2016). This approach of identifying and removing external constraints on agency or action is again central to community development.

The challenges of peacebuilding at community level

The main contextual challenges to peacebuilding at a community level relate to the nature of the conflict and the space for community activism that supports peacebuilding. Drawing on the work of Leatherman et al (1999) on the causes of violent conflict and Ross and Rothman's (1999) work on theory and practice in ethnic conflict management, we synthesise various levels of conflict, the underlying situations, risk factors and potential interventions in Table 1.4.

Local communities are often on the frontline where there is a perceived cluster of grievances drawn from one or more of these causes. The impact of conflict experienced over a protracted period of time invariably gives

Table 1.4: Levels of conflict, risk factors and potential interventions

Level	Underlying situation	'Risk factors' in conflict becoming violent	Community development interventions
Ideology	Differentiation, stratification of social groups/ social hierarchies seen as unjust by some groups and fair by others	Assertion of superiority/ inferiority il/legitimacy of social groups and state. Mobilisation of victim and perpetrator narratives by leaders. Ideology of othering built into socialisation and assertion of duty to act. Violence is the only language other parties understand.	Learning about and from each other together. Finding compatible/ common language and symbols. Reframing narratives. Focus on how conflict is addressed moving from violence to nonviolent methods.
Institutional	Economic, political, social, environmental, legal resources and entitlements unequally distributed	Unmet needs. Contest over who resources belong to. Deterioration in conditions or perception that share in improving situation is unfair. Absence of political and legal channels to redress grievances. States (internal and external) seen as not required to, unwilling or unable to deliver entitlements. Degradation of environment. Alignment of criminal and corrupt groups with political groups. Zero-sum view of change.	Community-led identification of core and common needs and development opportunities. Scrutiny of state. Developing spaces for and skills in negotiation, leading to generating possibilities for 'positive sum' change.
Interpersonal	Social cleavages Polarisation of 'them' and 'us'	Ease of identifying different groups with no-cross-cutting cleavages to attenuate conflict. Segregation, overlapping and contested spaces or forced sharing of spaces. Intolerance of diversity and difference – perceived as existential threat, for example, territorial integrity, way of life.	Building ethical communities; collective action as a result of enhanced sense of agency. Creating or strengthening institutions within communities. Individuals, groups need to feel they have control over their own lives. Confidence-building measures. Identifying/creating neutral and safe spaces for dialogue. Highlighting or forging new identities which cut across traditional cleavages – for example, age and gender.

(Continued)

Table 1.4: Levels of conflict, risk factors and potential interventions (continued)

Level	Underlying situation	'Risk factors' in conflict becoming violent	Community development interventions
Individual/ internal	Diverse social identities. Identities have an instrumental, as well as expressive, value. Lack of agency	Feeling threat to identity is existential. Source of the threat is the 'other'. Collective memories of loss – grievances or golden ages.	Critical consciousness; emancipation starting from internal knowledge and awareness. Transitional and restorative justice. Seek potential for mutual recognition of identities. Developing new sources of pride and identity.

rise to strengthened 'single-identity' narratives that can serve to preclude and stereotype the experience and motivation of other communities. Identifying with a community is seen as essential to survival. Being enclosed within that community accentuates the societal divisions between the 'us' and the 'them', with limited contact narrowing the ability to understand diverse positions and perspectives let alone relate to them. Very often it is difficult to find 'neutral', or pluralist perspectives in these circumstances.

While conflict can enhance strongly 'bonded' communities that adopt a defensive position against 'the other' communities/forces, it can also give rise to less visible fractures within such communities. This does not only apply to groups of minorities caught on the 'wrong side' of the line of conflict, who may be of different identity and/or belief, but it can also result from combatant splits and in-fighting, or to individuals designated as 'legitimate targets' by combatant forces. These intra-communal tensions are often the most difficult to resolve, particularly when they fall outside of the accepted community narrative (for example, people whose occupations result in them being seen as 'collaborators'). These groups can be relegated to the level of lower tier 'victims', often ignored by the main peacebuilding interventions. It can also result in internal tensions within otherwise strongly bonded 'single identity' communities.

A major challenge in community level peacebuilding is getting the space to raise issues – particularly when the latter entail challenges to combatants, whether state or non-state. The stages of the conflict continuum present conflict and peace patterns in a simplified linear but still useful form.

Clearly, peacebuilding interventions and initiatives that might be possible during the conflict emergence or stalemate stages will be different in nature and potential than what might be effected at the conflict escalation or, indeed, dispute settlement stages (Figure 1.5). Similarly, any role for external support/facilitation will depend on the context.

Much is written about the importance of conflict sensitivity analysis (systematic study of the causes, actors and dynamics of a conflict), but this needs to be carried out at the level of local communities, as well as at a macro level (CDA Collaborative Learning Projects, nd). Landim and Thompson (1996), for example, remind us of the role of community-based churches in parts of Latin America under repressive regimes. They emphasise the importance of organisations that have gained recognition and legitimacy within local communities (beyond their formal institutional aspects) because they share a common identity which stresses their commitment to build democracy and civil society, as well as giving a high priority to human rights and advocating for the rights of the marginalised. Given such local hubs community-based peacebuilding can offer a symbol of resistance and act as awareness-raising about alternative, creative ways to achieve a positive peace. They can, in effect, become the heart of webs of relationships that Lederach views as so essential to the building of bottom-up peacebuilding: 'A web of relationships made up of individual people, their networks, organisations and institutions around which social and community life is built' (Lederach, 2001: 842).

A community development approach can help to weave these relationships that allow (space and circumstances permitting) the critical examination of challenging issues, such as intra-community tensions, as well as what the building blocks for peace are in seeking to escape violence and lay the foundations of a sustainable peace. Community development strategies can also serve to enhance local capacities to engage with powerholders, whether state or non-state actors.

Case studies drawn from societies in conflict suggest a range of peacebuilding approaches that can be adopted by community-based and civil society organisations during the various phases of conflict (Table 1.5). Programmes of work to address the various issues illustrated in Table 1.5 (not a comprehensive list) requires activists who are credible and respected, a certain level of resources and access to information and models of practice that draw on both in-country developments and on the experiences of communities in other societies that have emerged from violent conflict.

The Peace Direct/Alliance for Peacebuilding report on Local Peacebuilding (Vernon, 2019) references a range of benefits and opportunities (alongside a number of challenges) provided through local peacebuilding. These include relevance of practice and decision-making; local knowledge; community connections and the ability to build inclusive relationships and trust. It also suggests that locally based peacebuilding work is often cost-effective and sustainable.

Figure 1.5: Conflict escalation and de-escalation model

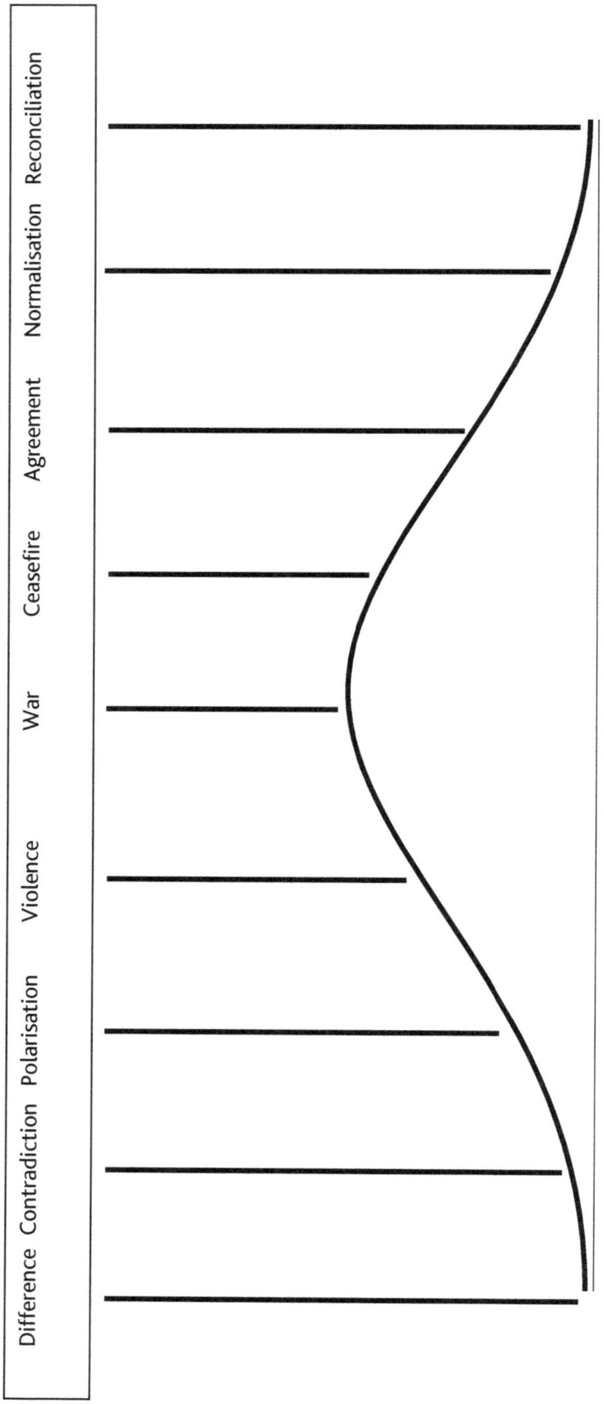

Difference Contradiction Polarisation Violence War Ceasefire Agreement Normalisation Reconciliation

Source: Ramsbotham et al (2011: 13)

Table 1.5: Community development interventions at different stages of conflict

Stages of conflict	Activities	Notes
Accumulated grievances With at least some people feeling they do not have a 'constitutional' opportunity to change the situation	• Documenting discrimination • Giving voice to minority/marginalised groups • Asserting human rights • Models of nonviolence struggle • Being alert to 'early warning' of development of combatant structures	The protection and assertion of human rights continues at all stages of the conflict–peace continuum.
Breakout of violence May begin as spontaneous or unorganised violence	• Documentation of abuses • Programmes to prevent youth engagement in violence • Support work with victims/survivors of violence • Focus on community needs and support services • Support for self-organisation of community • Protection of minorities and women	Effectiveness will largely depend on the nature of community/activist relations with representatives of the combatant parties.
Mutually hurting stalemate No party feels it has won or lost, but all feeling the cost of continuing violence	• Confidence-building within, and between, communities (developing bonding and bridging social capital) • Humanising the impact of the violence on combatants and victims • Preventing the spread of rumour and disinformation • Asserting the priorities and needs of local communities • Defusing potential points of tension (including use/abuse of symbols)	Where non-state actors have been demonised and/or silenced, community initiatives can be useful if giving them political voice. The support work with victims and survivors should continue across the various phases.
Ceasefires/negotiations Maybe tactical in order to refresh support or neutralise internal or external third-party pressure	• Ensuring that the needs of disadvantaged/marginalised communities and groups are reflected in any peace talks • Ensuring that women have a voice in decision-making • Examining new models of participative democracy • Supporting community dialogue to prevent misinformation about the details of peace settlement	Attention to the role of the media is particularly important at this stage to prevent further polarisation at community level. Respected community activists can also act as mediators where necessary.

(Continued)

Table 1.5: Community development interventions at different stages of conflict (continued)

Stages of conflict	Activities	Notes
Implementation of settlements Moving from negative to positive peace	• Translating peace agreements into language(s) understood by local people • Developing participative forums and structures to enhance community voices • Maintaining confidence-building through community engagement • Monitoring the implementation of peace agreement pledges • Reintegration of political ex-prisoners and ex-combatants	Attention needs to be paid to the needs of IDPs and diaspora refugees.
Post-conflict Revisiting the causes of conflict and scars of violence	• Examining approaches to deal with the legacies of the conflict/past • Monitoring the impact (potentially differential) of aid/assistance at community level • Reflect on the impact/legitimacy of violence as a mechanism for change	It is important to consider peacebuilding in dynamic terms in order to be alert to any political roll-back on peace agreements.

Bringing together community development, peacebuilding and conflict transformation

A recurring theme in community-based peacebuilding is that of enhancing the agency of local people during the abnormality and volatility of protracted violent conflict. The best of community-based action asserts the essential added value of envisaging a society that can address the structural causes of conflict, promotes human rights and human dignity and designs and/or implement initiatives that seek to heal the hurts of victims/survivors. For practitioners engaged in areas of conflict, issues of empowerment, participation and the nature of rights are not always straightforward given contested perceptions of the balance of power (and blame), as well as how community members engage with both state and non-state power-holders. As noted already, the conflict context is a crucial determinant in the extent to which community-based organisations and broader civil society can play a constructive role in peacebuilding and conflict transformation. Clearly the state's attitude to community activity/development is also an important factor. If it views community action as illegitimate or a threat, then there will be serious security issues for local activists, as has occurred (and is occurring) in a number of societies.

In a situation where it has been pointed out that community development practice can be contested even in societies that are reasonably politically stable (Ledwith, 2020), challenging power dynamics in the context of violent conflict requires even greater clarity of thought and analysis. Situational peace and conflict analysis (United Nations, 2016) needs to be adapted to frame the potential of community development. This process, however, can be informed by the shared (and often overlapping) values of community development and peacebuilding. These can become the 'checks and balances' to inform the work of activists and development workers, both in terms of what they do and how they do it (Ledwith and Springett, 2009: 4). It must be acknowledged, however, that working with local people to recognise the damaging nature of violence is not an easy process. There is a need for challenging and critical conversations when sufficient trust and relationships have been built. Nonetheless, if grounded in local experience and conscious of acceptable time and pace, sensitive and responsive community development work can enable communities to work together to:

- identify their own needs and actions;
- take collective action using their strengths and resources;
- develop their confidence, skills and knowledge;
- challenge unequal power relationships; and
- promote social justice, equality and inclusion in order to improve the quality of their own lives, the communities in which they live and societies of which they are a part.

The nature of transformational change over the course of this work, as described in the contributions to this volume, is to be found in this practice.

The content of the book

Chapter 2, by Ware, Ware and Kelly, provides a theoretical input on everyday peace as a community development tool. Drawing on, and developing, the recent body of literature focusing on everyday peace, this chapter provides a detailed discussion on the concept, exploring its applicability, the potential limitations and operationalisation of everyday peace into community development practice.

Chapter 3, by Niño Vega, provides insight into the multidimensional aspects of violence experienced in Cúcuta, Colombia. This chapter explores the work of the Youth Analytical Movement for Social Transformation in drawing on their lived realities of violence to work with marginalised young people. It highlights the importance of decolonial peace with an emphasis on peacebuilding from below.

Chapter 4, by Sotieva and Schofield, discusses partnership working in the conflict in the Caucasus. This chapter demonstrates the difficulties yet necessity of collaboration in creating dialogue, relationship building and a shared mission to cooperate for long-term peace. Sotieva and Schofield also pick up on the context of the changing relationship between civil society and states in post-communist societies.

Chapter 5, by Halliru, also focuses on the relationship between civil society and the state in Nigeria. Providing context to the divisions in the country the chapter discusses a range of interventions from those which are bottom-up from communities to those from federal government and international agencies and those originating from powerful leaders. He argues that whatever the origins of peacebuilding processes, for them to be successful in creating a more socially just society, they need to be inclusive and engage the most marginalised in the process.

Chapter 6, by Emmanuel and Gowthaman, focuses on the role of women in community leadership roles in the conflict in Sri Lanka. They draw on their personal activist and practitioner experiences of grassroots community development work. Despite articulating the risks and human costs associated with rights-based community development work, Emmanuel and Gowthaman discuss the long-term commitment to building networks of trust, maintaining solidarity and working towards the slow process of empowerment and institutional strengthening of humanitarian workers.

Chapter 7, by Sousa Silva and Malanquini, is centred on a rights-based approach to community action in Rio de Janeiro, Brazil. The chapter articulates seven key values in which this work is based. It discusses a range of tools used in their practice including the use of creative and arts-based practices to celebrate local identity, conducting participatory community mapping to advocate for adequate public services and activism to defend the rights of local residents.

Chapter 8, by Risal, explores working with community-based women to influence inclusion and peacebuilding in Nepal. Discussing the work of Nagarik Aawaz, a women-led peacebuilding organisation, it highlights the need for local knowledge to put into practice the philosophy that 'peace work is also not only personal, but political as well'. Analysing the role of women in Nepal's peacebuilding process, this chapter advocates for holistic interventions that help women to become change agents, building self-esteem and supporting them in asserting their rights.

Chapter 9, by Sellick, details the process of storytelling in Palestine. Exploring how storytelling can transform power relations, this chapter discusses a project where young Palestinians from the 33 hamlets and villages of the South Hebron Hills recorded the life-stories of their elders. It tells of the need for voice and memory in cultural change and by strengthening inter-generational chains of connectivity can improve a sense of identity.

Chapter 10, by O'Prey, explores community-based action in Northern Ireland. It discusses the impact of differing levels of organised activism and infrastructure and how building small wins can be invaluable in peacebuilding. The chapter argues for long-term commitment and investment in community leadership that meets local needs. It also explores confidence building in relation to bonding, bridging and linking social capital, providing a theoretical take on grassroots community activism.

Chapter 11, by Ware, Ware and Kelly, furthers their discussion on everyday peace in the context of the conflict in Myanmar. Arguing that community development can facilitate an everyday peace framework, this chapter explores the 'intense micropolitical struggle' of everyday frames and applies this to practice in the Rohingya and Rakhine communities in Myanmar/Burma.

Each chapter includes a summary of the conflict and a map to visually locate the area discussed. While we recognise these brief overviews and maps can be debated, they are included to contextualise the area and a sense of the complexity in which the community development practice takes place.

Notes

[1] While non-state armed conflict declining somewhat in 2019 to 67 locations, fatalities caused by fighting between Islamic State affiliated groups and other non-state forces were surpassed by the 11,700 fatalities in Mexico, where 90 per cent were attributed to the Jalisco Cartel New Generation fighting for control with the Sinaloa Cartel.
[2] These figures reflected findings prior to the 2022 war in Ukraine which has again highlighted the use and abuse of terminology in depicting and framing violent conflict.
[3] For further discussion see Diamond and McDonald (1996).

References

All Ireland Endorsement Body for Community Work Education & Training (2016) *All Ireland Standards for Community Work*, Galway: Community Work Ireland. Available at http://www.communityworkireland.ie/wp-content/uploads/2016/03/All-Ireland-Standards-for-Community-Work.pdf

Austin, A., Fischer, M. and Ropers, N. (eds) (2004) *Transforming Ethnopolitical Conflict: The Berghof Handbook*, Wiesbaden: VS Verlag. Available at https://berghof-foundation.org/files/publications/handbook_glossary.pdf

Banks, S. and Westoby, P. (eds) (2019) *Ethics, Equity and Community Development*, Bristol: Policy Press.

Beck, D. and Purcell, R. (2020) *Community Development for Social Change*, London: Routledge.

Blackshaw, T. (2010) *Key Concepts in Community Studies*, London: SAGE.

Boutros-Ghali, B. (1992) *An Agenda for Peace*, New York: United Nations. Available at https://www.un.org/peacebuilding/content/2020-review-un-peacebuilding-architecture

Brent, J. (2004) 'The desire for community: Illusion, confusion and paradox', *Community Development Journal*, 39(3): 213–23.

CDA Collaborative Learning Projects (nd) *Practical Learning for International Action*. Available at https://www.cdacollaborative.org/

CLD Standards Council (2015) *Community Development National Occupational Standards*, Scotland: CLD Council. Available at https://cldstandardscouncil.org.uk/wpcontent/uploads/SummaryCDNOStandards2015.pdf

Coburn, A. and Gormally, S. (2017) *Communities for Social Change: Practicing Equality and Social Justice in Youth and Community Work*, New York: Peter Lang.

Colorado Inclusive Funders (nd) *The Four I's of Oppression*. Available at http://www.coloradoinclusivefunders.org/uploads/1/1/5/0/11506731/the_four_is_of_oppression.pdf

Craig, G., Burchardt, T. and Gordon, D. (2008) *Social Justice and Public Policy, Seeking Fairness in Diverse Societies*, Bristol: Policy Press.

Delanty, G. (2003) *Community*, London: Routledge.

Department of Peace and Conflict Research (nd) *UCDP Definitions*, Uppsala: Uppsala University. Available at www.pcr.uu.se/research/ucdp/definitions/#tocjump_5828039264603797_9

Diamond, L. and McDonald, J.W. (1996) *Multi-track Diplomacy: A Systems Approach to Peace*, West Hartford, CT: Kumarian Press.

European Community Development Network (2014) *Community Development in Europe Towards a Common Framework and Understanding*. Available at http://eucdn.net/wp-content/uploads/2014/10/2014-24-09-EuCDN-Publication-FINAL.pdf

Eversley, J. (2018) *Social and Community Development: An Introduction*, London: Macmillan.

Freire, P. (1972) *Pedagogy of the Oppressed*, Harmondsworth: Penguin.

Galtung, J. (1969) 'Violence, peace and peace research', *Journal of Peace Research*, 6(3): 167–92.

Gilchrist, A. and Taylor, M. (2011) *The Short Guide to Community Development*, Bristol: Policy Press.

IACD (2018) *Towards Shared International Standards for Community Development Practice*. Available at http://www.iacdglobal.org/wp-content/uploads/2018/06/IACD-Standards-Guidance-May-2018_Web.pdf

Keating, T. and Knight, W.A. (2004) 'Introduction: Recent developments in postconflict studies – peacebuilding and governance', in T. Keating and W.A. Knight (eds) *Building Sustainable Peace*, Tokyo: United Nations University Press and University of Alberta Press, pp xxxi–lxii.

Landim, L. and Thompson, A. (1996) *Non-Governmental Organisations and Philanthropy in Latin America: An Overview*. Available at https://www.academia.edu/7298589/Non_governmental_organisations_and_philanthropy_in_Latin_America_An_overview

Leatherman, J., DeMars, W., Gaffney, P. and Väyrynen, R. (1999) *Breaking Cycles of Violence: Conflict Prevention in Intrastate Crises*, West Hartford, CT: Kumarian Press.

Lederach, J.P. (1995) *Preparing for Peace: Conflict Transformation across Cultures*, New York: Syracuse University Press.

Lederach, J.P. (1997) *Building Peace: Sustainable Reconciliation in Divided Societies*, Washington, DC: US Institute of Peace.

Lederach, J.P. (2001) 'Civil society and reconciliation', in C.A. Crocker, F. Hampson and P. Anall (eds) *Turbulent Peace: The Challenges of Managing International Conflict*, Washington, DC: US Institute of Peace, pp 841–855.

Lederach, J.P. (2003) *The Little Book of Conflict Transformation*, Intercourse, PA: Good Books.

Ledwith, M. (2020) *Community Development: A Critical and Radical Approach*, Bristol: Policy Press.

Ledwith, M. and Springett, J. (2009) *Participatory Practice: Community-based Action for Transformative Change*, Bristol: Policy Press.

Little, A. (2002) *The Politics of Community Theory and Practice*, Edinburgh: Edinburgh University Press.

Mattessich, P. and Monsey, M. (2004) *Community Building: What Makes it Work*, St. Paul, MN: Wilder Foundation.

Meade, R., Shaw, M. and Banks, S. (2016) *Politics, Power and Community Development*, Bristol: Policy Press.

Miall, H. (2004) 'Conflict transformation: A multi-dimensional task', in *The Berghof Handbook*. Wiesbaden: VS Verlag.

Paffenholz, T. (2015) 'Unpacking the local turn in peace', *Third World Quarterly*, 36(5): 857–74.

Pettersson, T. and Öberg, M. (2020) 'Organized violence 1989–2019', *Journal of Peace Research*, 57(4): 597–613.

Phillips, R. and Pittman, R.H. (eds) (2009) *An Introduction to Community Development*, Abingdon: Routledge.

Ramsbotham, O., Miall, H. and Woodhouse, T. (2011) *Contemporary Conflict Resolution*, Cambridge: Polity Press.

Robeyns, I. (2016) 'The capability approach', *The Stanford Encyclopedia of Philosophy*. Available at https://plato.stanford.edu/archives/win2016/entries/capability-approach/

Ross, M.H. and Rothman, J. (eds) (1999) *Theory and Practice in Ethnic Conflict Management: Conceptualizing Success and Failure*, Basingstoke: Macmillan.

Shaw, M. (2008) 'Community development and the politics of community', *Community Development Journal*, 43(1): 24–36.

Smith, D. (2004) *Overview Report of the Joint Utstein Study of Peacebuilding – Evaluation 1/2004*, Oslo: PRIO, International Peace Research Institute, Oslo & Royal Norwegian Dept. of Foreign Affairs. Available at https://www.regjeringen.no/globalassets/upload/kilde/ud/rap/2004/0044/ddd/pdfv/210673-rapp104.pdf

Taylor, M. (2003) *Public Policy in the Community*, Basingstoke: Palgrave Macmillan.

United Nations (2016) 'Review of the United Nations peacebuilding architecture', Resolution adopted by the General Assembly on 27 April. Available at https://documents-dds-ny.un.org/doc/UNDOC/GEN/N16/119/39/PDF/N1611939.pdf?OpenElement

United Nations (2020) 'Peacebuilding and sustaining peace', Report of the Secretary-General. Available at https://documents-dds-ny.un.org/doc/UNDOC/GEN/N20/203/77/PDF/N2020377.pdf?OpenElement

United Nations and World Bank (2018) *Pathways to Peace: Inclusive Approaches to Preventing Violent Conflict*, Washington, DC: World Bank. Available at https://openknowledge.worldbank.org/handle/10986/28337

United Nations Department of Economic and Social Affairs (nd) *Sustainable Development: The 17 Goals*. Available at https://sdgs.un.org/goals; https://www.un.org/sustainabledevelopment/

United Nations Development Group (2016) *Conducting a Conflict and Development Analysis*. New York: UN DG.

United Nations General Assembly (2016) *Review of the United Nations Peacebuilding Architecture Resolution 70/262*, New York: United Nations. Available at https://www.un.org/en/development/desa/population/migration/generalassembly/docs/globalcompact/A_RES_70_262.pdf

United Nations Secretary General (2020) *Peacebuilding and Sustaining Peace*, New York: United Nations. Available at http://www.un.org/en/peacebuilding/pbso/pdf/SG%20report%20on%20peacebuilding%20and%20sustaining%20peace.As%20issued.A-72-707-S-2018-43.E.pdf

Uppsala Conflict Data Programme (nd) *UCDP Definitions*. Available at www.pcr.uu.se/research/ucdp/definitions/#tocjump_5828039264603797_9

Väyrynen, R. (1991) 'To settle or to transform? Perspectives on the resolution of national and international conflicts', in R. Väyrynen (ed) *New Directions in Conflict Theory: Conflict Resolution and Conflict Transformation*, London: SAGE, pp 1–25.

Vernon, P. (2019) 'Local peacebuilding: What works and why?', Peace Direct/Alliance for Peacebuilding. Available at www.peaceinsight.org/reports/whatworks

Wenger, E. (1998) *Communities of Practice: Learning, Meaning and Identity*, Cambridge: Cambridge University Press.

2

Everyday peace as a community development approach

Anthony Ware, Vicki-Ann Ware and Leanne Kelly

Introduction

The dominant approach to peacebuilding at a community level, as opposed to elite-level peace processes, revolves around ideas of building or strengthening social cohesion between individuals, groups and authorities. In this context, social cohesion is conceived of in terms of overcoming horizontal social cleavages within society, and vertical cleavages between the state and the people. A social cohesion approach to peacebuilding thus fundamentally commences with the idea of bringing people together, physically, socially and emotionally, to search for common ground or shared needs/mutual benefit. It relies on rehumanising the Other, developing empathy and rebuilding relationships, including between state authorities and the people.

The issue is that violence leaves a pervasive fear of further violence, and the more frequent or severe the violence, the deeper that fear. Given this, most work seeking to strengthen social cohesion after violence is usually agonistic, cautious and sensitive. Nonetheless, the principal threat to social cohesion after violence at the everyday level, apart from more actual violence, is that the slightest confrontation may trigger further fear, and that the ongoing suspicion drives social practices that maintain or expand these cleavages. The more extreme the past violence, and frequent the triggering of fear, therefore, the more likely that bringing people together, seeking to rebuild empathy, and searching for common ground or mutual benefit, may be premature. Even a deep sense of awkwardness encountering the Other may, potentially, trigger fear more than advance social cohesion. There are situations in which the social cleavages are so great, and fears so acute, that engagement and (social) cohesion may be premature, unsafe or even inflammatory. Such is the situation in the case study we explore in Chapter 11 in this book, regarding Myanmar's Rohingya conflict after the horrific ethnic cleansing of 2017. In such cases, and perhaps far more widely, we propose an alternative community development peacebuilding approach, built around the idea of 'everyday peace'.

This chapter explores the concepts of 'the everyday' and of 'everyday peace' in detail, highlighting its relevance to community development practice, particularly that which adopts appreciative inquiry and awareness-raising approaches. Everyday peace is presented in the literature as the means by which ordinary individuals and groups navigate everyday life in deeply divided societies, in ways that first avoid or minimise both awkward situations and conflict triggers, and (only) then consider active steps to engage with the other. At the minimalist end of the spectrum, everyday peace may be simply eking out safe space in which a façade of normality prevails, despite the conflict, allowing people to get on with life (Mac Ginty, 2014: 555). At this level, as Mac Ginty argues, everyday peace may be the first peace, the first inter-group contact after violence, or the last peace in the sense of being the last remaining bridging social capital before total rupture. However, everyday peace can grow from this, to evolve into wider peace formation, and become a foundation upon which social cohesion may be (re)built. We argue that everyday peace, because its focus is on the routine practices of ordinary people as they get on with their everyday lives, is highly relevant to community development theory and practice.

The remainder of this chapter is divided into five sections. The first explores the concept of the everyday in social theory in some depth, noting that despite long being in the literature, until recently it was largely lost in referential obscurity, presented as the opposite of the extraordinary people and events that shape history. More recently, however, it has been recognised as a site of considerable agency, in which ordinary people exercise creative resistance to dominant structures and narratives and reclaim a degree of autonomy from otherwise all-pervasive cultural forces. The second section explores the concept of everyday peace derived from this new understanding, and the principles and typologies of everyday peace identified and debated in the literature in some depth. This culminates in a presentation of our own typology of everyday peace social practices. A third section then explores the innovations of everyday peace that make it particularly applicable to community development theory and practice. Notably, these include its focus on the agency of ordinary people and routine practices within everyday life, its exploration of the potential significance of pooling the small acts of a large number of people with limited agency, and the way in which it recognises the potentially positive intent and impact of practices more easily perceived as being negative. This recognises the peace behaviour of the vast majority of people in even the most conflict-affected context, allowing an appreciative inquiry or strengths-based approach in almost any context. A fourth section explores how this agency can be manipulated by dominant structures and elite actors, raising some cautions about this approach. The final section explores operationalisation of an everyday peace approach into community development practice, laying out some principles we document in our later case study in Chapter 11 exploring this approach in Myanmar's Rohingya conflict.

The everyday

Everyday life has long been a central idea in anthropology and sociology yet has only emerged as an explicit focus in recent decades. As Kalekin-Fishman (2013: 714) puts it, until quite recently, 'everyday life' was the elephant in the room, so to speak, an idea relied upon by sociologists in much of their work yet ignored as a theme in its own right. As she writes:

> Thus Rousseau (2007 [1762]) based his conceptualization of the social contract and his vision of the good society on a perception that the family, embedded in everyday life, was the 'natural' form of social organization. Adam Smith (1937 [1776]) analyzed the social division of labor which served individuals' 'everyday' needs. Similarly, throughout his writings, Durkheim explains the division of labor (1984 [1893]), the forms of religious life (1965 [1912]), and the effects of anomie (1951 [1897]) in terms of everyday life with examples from relations in families and in communities. Central to Marx's (1975 [1844]; Marx and Engels, 1975 [1848]) concern with the evils of the capitalist system was the perception that because of the work conditions it demanded, there is a 'loss of self' which destroys ties of family and friends. People are left with concerns (eating, drinking, procreating), aspects of everyday life which are not fully human. (Kalekin-Fishman, 2013: 714)

As Lefebvre notes, the everyday is usually defined negatively, as the residue left over after specialised activities are abstracted (Felski, 2000: 80).

Weber's work is a clear case in point. Weber (1976: 140; also 1922 [1978]: 241, 1111, 1115) explained his charismatic ideal as '*spezfisch außertäglich*', meaning, 'outside the everyday'. His ideas about agency and social change posit charisma and charismatic individuals as the major revolutionary forces in history, and he used references to everyday, ordinary individuals to illustrate a direct contrast. While he never said so directly, by referential juxtaposition Weber implied ordinary, everyday events and actions have minimal impact; change is driven by the extraordinary.

As a result, despite the prevalence of the concept of the everyday in sociology, anthropology, philosophy, economics and politics for centuries, everyday life was predominately 'denigrated as a kind of passive enactment, lacking in creative, productive or emancipatory force' (Ring, 2006: 178). 'Everyday life is typically distinguished from the exceptional. ... The distinctiveness of the everyday lies in its lack of distinction and differentiation' (Felski, 2000: 80). It is the place of the routine, the ordinary and the mundane, of the practices and discourses that come to be taken for granted, and the ongoing labour that goes into (re)producing these. Felski sees philosophers such as Lukács and Heidegger making the everyday synonymous with an inauthentic, grey, aesthetically impoverished existence. Yet, as a term, the everyday remains strangely amorphous. More marginalised groups, particularly women, the poor working class, and so on are more closely identified with the everyday, although in reality, even privileged, elite, charismatic individuals (in the Weberian sense) also have everyday lives – it is just that they can also transcend the everyday, at least on occasion, to have extraordinary agency or engage in extraordinary events. It is thus, nonetheless, largely seen as a private, feminine, apolitical space maintaining the status quo, distant from the forces driving change or innovation (Ring, 2006: 2).

More recent studies have, however, recognised everyday life as a site of intense micropolitical action, a field of struggle contributing to and altering narratives and practices around closely related macro issues – a place of resistance to cultural norms and innovation in social practice. De Certeau (1984) was perhaps the first to offer this significantly different understanding of the everyday. Drawing heavily on Foucault and Bourdieu, he explores everyday life as a place in which ordinary, 'common' people adopt 'tactics' to reclaim autonomy from all-pervasive cultural forces, reappropriating traditions, language, symbols, art and exchange within their everyday situations. In so doing, ordinary people subvert the meanings, symbols and representations which the elite and powerful seek to impose. Ordinary people are thus not mere 'consumers' of 'culture' – and institutions, structures and elite leaders its 'producers' – but ordinary people constantly, actively, ingeniously modify and then defend their own, new meanings. Everyday life is thus a highly creative space, in which ordinary people, despite being largely subjugated by institutions, structures and narratives, exercise continuous creativity, poaching, adapting and reimagining the rules, narratives and meanings pushed upon them by society and the elite. By their very nature, these acts are defensive and opportunistic, used in more limited ways and seized momentarily within spaces, both physical and psychological, otherwise produced and governed by more powerful strategic relations. Nonetheless, to de Certeau, the everyday is a space of considerable agency, in which ordinary people exercise creative resistance, continually reclaiming as much autonomy and agency as they can, and using that to adapt, reimagine and recreate.

The concept of 'everyday peace'

In discussing 'everyday peace', we therefore adopt Roger Mac Ginty's (2014: 500) broad, simple definition of 'the everyday' as 'the normal habitus for individuals and groups, even if what passed as "normal" in a conflict-affected society would be abnormal elsewhere'. This includes both the mundane and routine, but also the micropolitical, creative and agentic everyday resistance to the dominant rules, narratives and meanings. Focus on the everyday brings to the fore practices and narratives that appear routine and are otherwise taken for granted, seeking to revisit their agency and impact.

Reflecting this growing recognition of the significance of everyday practices in conflict situations, international relations and conflict–peace studies have been giving it growing attention over the past decade or two (for example, Davies and Niemann, 2004; Montsion, 2010; Kessler and Guillaume, 2012; Autesserre, 2014). New terms have entered the academic literature, including 'everyday politics' (for example, Hilhorst, 2013; Autesserre, 2014), 'everyday conflict' (for example, O'Driscoll, 2021), 'everyday nationalism' (for example, Fredman, 2020) and 'everyday diplomacy' (for example, Cheuk, 2016; Henig, 2016; Marsden et al, 2016; Morris, 2016). Kleinman (2000) talks of the 'violences of everyday life', referring to the way collective and individual experiences of violence are so thoroughly interwoven. Study of the everyday is thus becoming increasingly mainstream across the social and political sciences, and conflict–peace studies in particular.

Within this, perhaps the greatest academic attention has been given to the notion and study of 'everyday peace'. Mac Ginty's (2014: 549) definition is probably the most oft cited and representative. He frames everyday peace as 'the routinized practices used by individuals and collectives as they navigate their way through life in a deeply divided society that may suffer from ethnic or religious cleavages and be prone to episodic direct violence in addition to chronic or structural violence'. A growing academic literature has researched and analysed the social practices adopted by ordinary people, as they seek to get on with their lives in ways that avoid or de-escalate awkward or risky encounters, or sometimes even deliberately seek to deepen their engagement with other conflict parties (see, for example, Ring, 2006; Richmond, 2009; Mac Ginty, 2013, 2014, 2017, 2021; Williams, 2013, 2015; Berents, 2015, 2018; Berents and McEvoy-Levy, 2015; Dutta et al, 2016; Mac Ginty and Firchow, 2016; Randazzo, 2016; Marijan, 2017; Firchow, 2018; Lundqvist, 2019; Visoka, 2020; Yoshizawa and Kusaka, 2020; O'Driscoll, 2021; Ware and Ware, 2021; Ware et al, 2021). This literature refutes earlier ideas of everyday actions lacking agency to bring major change and explores the importance of ordinary individuals and groups on peace–conflict dynamics, and the potentially significant agency they enact through everyday life and social behaviour, towards peace formation and maintenance. This emphasis on the agency of ordinary people and everyday life contexts makes this approach extremely relevant to community development.

Questions of peace, agency and micropolitics in everyday life are still not well addressed, despite the burgeoning recent literature (Williams, 2015: 5). Nonviolent and peaceful societies not only exist but are actually the norm throughout human prehistory and history (Kurlansky, 2006; Sponsel, 2017).

As Williams (2015: 9) puts it: 'The dominance of academic inquiry seeking to explain violence masks the fact that much of everyday life in conflict settings is not characterised by perpetual inter-community [physical] violence.' The problem is that 'war and violence have proven to be far more seductive foci for academic analysis whilst issues of peace have been typically relegated to a position of referential obscurity' (Williams, 2015: 4). Everyday peace proliferates yet goes largely unremarked (Ring, 2006: 65). Perhaps central to this is that everyday nonviolence coexists with inequitable power relations, which while stopping short of open conflict, widely manifest as domination, repression, coercion, exclusion, marginalisation, and so on.

Laura Ring (2006) was the first academic to use the term 'everyday peace'. An anthropologist doing ethnographic research while living in Karachi, Pakistan, she looked at the everyday peace practices adopted by people from diverse ethnic backgrounds thrown together as neighbours in the same urban apartment complex. She noted just how much hard work many people put into maintaining nonviolence, often even cordial relations, when the context was full of deep ethnic tensions, hate speech and narratives promoting conflict. She documented how this localised everyday peace played out and was maintained even when serious communal violence erupted around them from time to time. Philippa Williams (2015), a geographer, expanded this idea in the context of ethnographic research observing Hindu–Muslim violence in the religious city of Varanasi, Uttar Pradesh, northern India. Both described a range of everyday social practices contributing to peace and violence. Combatting the notion of the everyday being apolitical, Williams, notes how highly political peace is, at any level, and that peace narratives, while appearing benign and a universal good, may accept yet conceal and perpetuate uneven power relations and marginality, contributing to a 'violence of peace'. Rather than peace and violence being opposites, or peace being an absence of conflict or violence, peace – including everyday peace – is always intertwined with conflict and (in)justice in complex ways.

Perhaps the most prolific researcher exploring everyday peace, Roger Mac Ginty (2013, 2014, 2017, 2021), then took the idea and looked at it globally, seeking to conceptualise and define it more clearly, publishing a 'rudimentary' typology of social practices believed to constitute everyday peace (Mac Ginty, 2014), followed up by a detailed monograph exploring the concept in depth (Mac Ginty, 2021). Meanwhile Pamina Firchow and Mac Ginty, separately and together, have developed and expanded the idea of everyday peace indicators, and launched their everyday peace indicators project (Mac Ginty, 2013; Mac Ginty and Firchow, 2016; Firchow, 2018).

According to Mac Ginty, everyday peace focuses on the everyday actions adopted by ordinary community members seeking to get on with their lives without precipitating violence and aims at least at nonviolent coexistence with at least occasional engagement. At its most minimal level, everyday peace may be simply 'eking out safe space in a conflict context and allowing a façade of normality to prevail' (Mac Ginty, 2014: 555). For Mac Ginty, avoidance is the principal everyday peace social practice. Our reading of the diverse literature, as elaborated in what follows, and Mac Ginty's (2021) later work, however, suggests it can deepen into much more engaged and substantial relationships, and contribute significantly to wider peace formation (see Ware et al, 2021).

Everyday peace does not presuppose altruistic motivations. It recognises that a diversity of motives and ambitions coexist, which for some may be a loathing of the Other but simply not wanting to participate in violence, all the way through to a strong desire to build peace and harmony. People opt for nonviolence, non-escalation or peaceful coexistence with neighbours for a diversity of reasons, ranging from pure self-preservation through to a deep commitment to shared humanity (Mac Ginty, 2014; Brewer et al, 2018). Many who act for everyday peace share at least some of the fears, grievances and prejudices of those urging violence and harm. Yet, to resist powerful forces in quiet, subtle, routinised ways requires deliberate, thoughtful effort to minimise risk, de-escalate situations and establish amicable coexistence.

Everyday peace social practices

Putting the work of these scholars together, and drawing on a decade of empirical practice in Myanmar, we have elsewhere detailed a typology of eight of social practices constituting everyday peace (Ware and Ware, 2021), in Table 2.1.

Innovations of everyday peace and applicability to community development

This framework offers a number of innovations for peacebuilding, which are particularly applicable to community development theory and practice. The first, as Mac Ginty (2013) argues, is that that everyday peace offers great scope for crowd-sourced participatory input, giving the approach an ability to listen to 'hidden transcripts' found in deeply divided societies. Importantly, he argues the process of communities thinking about what peace might look like and how it could be realised has the potential to contribute to conflict transformation and peace.

A second important innovation of everyday peace is that, rather than seeing behaviours usually perceived as negative, such as avoidance, ambiguity or blame-shifting, as being inherently negative, everyday peace reconceptualises them as potentially positive actions towards peace. Certainly, practices normalising things like avoidance can entrench discrimination, and may strengthen the same forces that institutionalise rigid identities and the sort of

Table 2.1: Types of social practice that constitute everyday practice

Avoidance	Contentious or sensitive topics, talk of historic issues High-risk people, places, situations, offensive displays Escapism into other activities Not drawing attention to oneself
Reading	Ethnically informed identification and social ordering Sensitised alertness, hypervigilance, to avoid/engage without provocation Constantly judging motives, morals, attitudes and feelings of others
Ambiguity	Discarding or concealing signifiers of identity Non-observance, 'not seeing' Dissembling in speech and actions
Shielding	Keeping more volatile and aggressive people away from confrontations More peaceful dealing with confrontations themselves Using overt displays of anger and hostility to highlight to members of one's own group that the matter is dealt with
Civility	Interactions in shared public spaces, especially transactional economic engagements Ritualised politeness, attention to the etiquette of status Acts of tolerance Shifting blame to outsiders, a minority within own group, or the system
Reciprocity	Neighbourliness and sociality based on exchange of gifts, assistance Expectation of delayed reciprocity, mutual indebtedness Active maintenance, non-resolution of exchange tension Type of exchange normally reserved for kin
Solidarity	Intercommunal networking around everyday issues Groups engaged in cooperation and accommodation 'Imagined community', even if rhetorical or discursive, narratives of communal harmony
Compromise	Sustained dialogue, negotiation and conflict resolution Submission, surrender, renunciation as acts of agency Justice conceded or suspended for status quo Peace contingent on concealing patterns of inequality and uneven power

sectarian cultures driving conflict. However, often the first steps to defusing conflict – anywhere, even with loved ones within a family – is to avoid contentious or sensitive topics, carefully read the situation, choose not to say some of the things you feel at the time, and so on. Mac Ginty (2014) frames these as potentially acts of agency by those who seek coexistence or nonviolence but feel largely powerless to effect the macro conflict. Notably, if adopted out of a desire to defuse the situation, such practices contain elements of resistance or subversion towards the conflict narratives and extremist discourses, challenging the social divisions underlying the conflict by avoiding the sensitivities and triggers. Avoidance-type behaviours of some topics, people or places may also be acts to protect and regulate other neutral spaces, within which it is possible to engage safely. As such, everyday peace challenges the false binary between negative and positive peace, transcending such distinction (Williams, 2015), and encourages intra-communal work in preparation for a time intercommunal social cohesion-oriented work may commence.

A third innovation of everyday peace is the recognition that, even in the most violent conflict situations, a majority of ordinary people resist acting on the more extreme conflict narratives, which call for violence and destruction, and refuse to participate in harming others. By adopting practices that avoid sensitivities and triggers, by avoiding certain people or topics or places, and so on, a majority of people caught up in even the most extreme conflict situations have already acted to resist conflict narratives. While this may be motivated more by self-preservation than cosmopolitan values or attempts to make peace, such nonviolent responses to violence and extreme narratives remain an act of resistance. A majority have already made a choice to refuse violence, even if they share the fears, grievances and concerns upon which the narratives play. Therefore, in almost any conflict, a vast majority of people reject personal participation in violence and adopt at a minimum a conflict-avoiding stance in defiance of conflict narratives and the cajoling of many elites.

Everyday peace thus directly facilitates an appreciative inquiry approach. Appreciative Inquiry is a strengths-based approach 'designed to help local people identify their achievements. This process can be very empowering for people who have always considered themselves poor and disadvantaged. When they look for their strengths, they are often amazed to discover how resilient, adaptive and innovative they are' (Neil Ford in Elliott, 1999: vi). It creates the opportunity for the community development worker to start peacebuilding work not just with a few, very progressive individuals, but with the majority of people on both sides. This recognises that people's everyday peace actions already rupture totalising ideas of conflict and division, and the social practices they already engage in hold potential to contribute to wider peace formation, if strengthened and pooled. It recognises that most people have already displayed a range of social practices preferencing coexistence over violence. Their resistance of the violence exhorted by conflict narratives and social forces already demonstrates significant agency in the face of overwhelming power. It recognises that such acts often involve a high degree of bravery, and considerable innovation, creativity and improvisation, even if the actions appear minimalistic to outsiders, or as negative acts. That is a very solid community development foundation for peacebuilding work.

Limitations: the dark side

That said, everyday peace is not a panacea. It does not necessarily confront conflict behaviours or narratives, nor the attitudes or systems that sustain them. Indeed, if it institutionalises avoidance-type behaviours and normalises injustice, everyday peace could help maintain the moral distance (Singer, 1972; Chatterjee, 2003) that conflict entrepreneurs rely on to 'other' individuals and groups, drive conflict narratives and perpetuate sectarian culture. Unless injustices and grievances are dealt with, somehow, at some point, a perpetuation of everyday peace without ongoing progress is likely to entrench discrimination and strengthen the same forces that institutionalise rigid identities and sectarianism.

For example, Williams (2015), in her ethnographic monograph on everyday peace in India, questions the justice and sustainability of everyday peace. She vividly illustrates ways in which everyday peace and nonviolence are inherently and highly political and can be 'played with' by those with power to manipulate responses and perpetuate inequalities and injustices. Noting that everyday peace resides in local capacity to create real and imagined spaces of connection, tolerance and civility, Williams highlights that maintaining such peace usually requires glossing over rather than addressing the underlying injustices, disparities and inequalities. In this sense, everyday peace is less than just, and can fail to deal with the major underlying conflict drivers.

Peace, at any level, always involves some sort of compromise or surrender. These can be very positive acts when offered freely as an act of agency, but they are often extracted from the less powerful by the more powerful. What is called compromise is more commonly really domination and coercion, more than free agency motivated by an ideal of peaceful relations. Everyday peace may thus be contingent on concealing patterns of inequality and uneven power, indefinitely deferring the quest for justice (Williams, 2015). It is open to the potential of significant abuse by the powerful and may entrench or deepen inequalities and social divisions. When everyday conflict does occur, it is usually perpetrated by those with the most power or 'symbolic capital' (O'Driscoll, 2021), and even the threat of conflict is thus an act of power on another. Those with more power may threaten to destabilise a situation, knowing the less powerful are more likely to compromise or surrender, and relying on the majority of people to engage in everyday peace social practices even more actively, to de-escalate tensions and risk (Williams, 2015).

Optimism about the potential of everyday peace to contribute to wider peace formation must therefore be tempered with realistic understanding of power, including the potential, if not likelihood, for everyday peace practices to be manipulated. We would argue, however, that this need not be the case, and that the stability of everyday peace is a necessary foundation for longer-term nonviolent processes to address justice and reform. Everyday peace does reflect agency, albeit limited by constraints such as these, and thus does offer a framework for potentially supporting and strengthening bottom-up peacebuilding agency. Where it reinforces conflict-calming measures, protects or expands neutral spaces, evokes a set of ground rules or parameters for mutual, respectful, nonviolent coexistence, and brings peace entrepreneurs together, it becomes a foundation for potential wider peace formation. To that extent, it is a potentially useful framework to augment bottom-up, community-led development programming in conflict-affected settings.

Operationalisation of everyday peace into community development practice

Operationalising an approach aiming to strengthen everyday peace formation through community development is not without its problems. By definition, everyday peace typologies catalogue the types of agency people have been observed exerting in conflict settings, on their own. Hence, the idea of turning this into an external intervention could perhaps be seen as oxymoronic. Nonetheless, we argue that within a Freirean community development context, there is potential to support conscious awareness-raising about the situation people face, the extent of the agency they have, and the range of actions they might take based on global observations of social practices. Such an approach is based on Paulo Freire's (1972) idea of 'conscientisation', whereby empowering people to act with agency starts by them learning to perceive the social, political and economic contradictions causing their 'oppression' (his term) and discovering for themselves how to take action against the oppressive elements of that reality.

By-stepping groups of people committed to peace through an analysis of their actions and situation, using an appreciative inquiry approach to highlight the positive practices and acts they have adopted intuitively, and presenting other options for advancing nonviolent coexistence from the typology of social practices, community development can adopt everyday peace as a framework for practice. With awareness-raising and reflection on actions contributing to peace at an everyday level and allowing people space to deliberate on how they may want to take these ideas forward, we believe it is possible to create opportunities for them to strengthen their own sense of agency and make more informed choices. In this, we would argue strongly against any notion of 'everyday peacebuilding' – everyday peace is what people themselves do, and the most we can bring are frameworks to help them reflect on that. The most we can offer is help in possibly 'strengthening everyday peace formation'. We also note that the operationalisation of everyday peace occurs best within the context of strengths-based or asset-based community development (Kretzmann and McKnight, 1993; Mathie and Cunningham, 2003), building on appreciative inquiry and allowing peace to emerge largely as a by-product of another activity.

As mentioned earlier, the theoretical framework of everyday peace is agnostic to motives – that is, people may still hate the Other, yet practice everyday peace out of self-preservation, simply because they do not want violence. Rather than seeing this as negative, interventions aimed at strengthening the emergence of everyday peace can view this as a positive and realistic first step, upon which peacebuilding can grow.

Conclusion

Everyday peace offers a robust framework with a range of innovations that fit very well with community development practice. Everyday peace can only be enacted from the bottom up, so community development's focus on locally led initiatives, active participation and subsidiarity provide theory and tools that support the furtherance of everyday peace practices. Layering everyday peace with community development offers deeply divided societies a realistic 'real-world' approach that addresses issues of conflict and attempts to ameliorate them gently, in a way that does not cause further harm. Everyday peace strengthens people's agency and celebrates the small, everyday peaceful actions that people take to promote peace. Over time, these small, micro-solidarities may accrue into a situation where deeply divided societies can coexist nonviolently side-by-side, if not as friends, at least as functioning neighbours. A key advantage of this approach is that it builds on the pre-existing social practices of a majority of people, and through consciousness-raising, allows ordinary people to potentially act for peace with greater agency via everyday activities.

Chapter 11 in this volume offers a practical, in-depth case study of how everyday peace has been successfully layered within a specific community development programme, in the extreme case of Myanmar's Rohingya conflict after the 2017 ethnic cleansing event.

References

Autesserre, S. (2014) *Peaceland: Conflict Resolution and the Everyday Politics of International Intervention*, Cambridge: Cambridge University Press.

Berents, H. (2015) 'An embodied everyday peace in the midst of violence', *Peacebuilding*, 3(2): 1–14.

Berents, H. (2018) *Young People and Everyday Peace: Exclusion, Insecurity and Peacebuilding in Colombia*, Milton Keynes: Taylor & Francis.

Berents, H. and McEvoy-Levy, S. (2015) 'Theorising youth and everyday peace(building)', *Peacebuilding*, 3(2): 115–25.

Brewer, J., Hayes, B., Teeney, F., Dudgeon, K., Mueller-Hirth, N. and Wijesinghe, S. (2018) *The Sociology of Everyday Life Peacebuilding*, New York: Springer.

Bushe, G.R. (2011) 'Appreciative inquiry: Theory and critique', in D. Boje, B. Burnes and J. Hassard (eds) *The Routledge Companion to Organizational Change*, Oxford: Routledge, pp 87–103.

Chatterjee, D. (2003) 'Moral distance: Introduction', *The Monist*, 86(3): 327–32.

Cheuk, K. (2016) 'Everyday diplomacy among Indian traders in a Chinese fabric market', *Cambridge Journal of Anthropology*, 34(2): 42–58.

Davies, M. and Niemann, M. (2004) *International Relations and Everyday Life*, London: Routledge.

de Certeau, M. (1984) *The Practice of Everyday Life*, Berkeley: University of California Press.

Dutta, U., Kashimana Andzenge, A. and Walkling, K. (2016) 'The everyday peace project: An innovative approach to peace pedagogy', *Journal of Peace Education*, 13(1): 79–104.

Elliott, C. (1999) *Locating the Energy for Change: An Introduction to Appreciative Inquiry*, Winnipeg: International Institute for Sustainable Development. Available at https://www.imaginationclub.org/documents/Locating_energy_for_change-intro_to_AI.pdf

Felski, R. (2000) *Doing Time: Feminist Theory and Postmodern Culture*, New York: New York University Press.

Firchow, P. (2018) *Reclaiming Everyday Peace: Local Voices in Measurement and Evaluation after War*, Cambridge: Cambridge University Press.

Fredman, O. (2020) 'Peace formation from below: The "mirëdita, dobar dan!" festival as an alternative to everyday nationalism', *Nations and Nationalism*, 26(2): 447–60.

Freire, P. (1972) *Pedagogy of the Oppressed*, Harmondsworth: Penguin.

Henig, D. (2016) 'Hospitality as diplomacy in post-cosmopolitan urban spaces: Dervish lodges and sofra-diplomacy in post-war Bosnia-Herzegovina', *Cambridge Journal of Anthropology*, 34(2): 76–92.

Hilhorst, D. (2013) *Disaster, Conflict and Society in Crises: Everyday Politics of Crisis Response*, London: Routledge.

Kalekin-Fishman, D. (2013) 'Sociology of everyday life', *Current Sociology Review*, 61(5–6): 714–32.

Kessler, O. and Guillaume, X. (2012) 'Everyday practices of international relations: People in organizations', *Journal of International Relations and Development*, 15(1): 110–20.

Kleinman, A. (2000) 'The violences of everyday life: The multiple forms and dynamics of social violence', in V. Das, A. Kleinman, M. Ramphele and P. Reynolds (eds) *Violence and Subjectivity*, Berkeley, CA: University of California Press, pp 226–41.

Kretzmann, J. and McKnight, J. (1993) *Building Communities from the Inside Out: A Path toward Finding and Mobilizing a Community's Assets*, Evanston: Assets-Based Community Development Institute, Institute for Policy Research, Northwestern University.

Kurlansky, M. (2006) *Nonviolence: The History of a Dangerous Idea*, New York: Random House.

Lundqvist, M. (2019) 'Post-war memorialisation as everyday peace? Exploring everyday (dis-) engagements with the Maoist martyrs' gate of Beni Bazaar in Nepal', *Conflict, Security & Development*, 19(5): 475–96.

Mac Ginty, R. (2013) 'Indicators +: A proposal for everyday peace indicators', *Evaluation and Program Planning*, 36(1): 56–63.

Mac Ginty, R. (2014) 'Everyday peace: Bottom-up and local agency in conflict-affected societies', *Security Dialogue*, 45(6): 548–64.

Mac Ginty, R. (2015) 'Where is the local? Critical localism and peacebuilding', *Third World Quarterly*, 36(5): 840–56.

Mac Ginty, R. (2017) 'Everyday social practices and boundary-making in deeply divided societies', *Civil Wars*, 19(1): 4–25.

Mac Ginty, R. (2021) *Everyday Peace: How So-called Ordinary People Can Disrupt Violent Conflict*, Oxford: Oxford University Press.

Mac Ginty, R. and Firchow, P. (2016) 'Top-down and bottom-up narratives of peace and conflict', *Politics*, 36(3): 308–23.

Marijan, B. (2017) 'The politics of everyday peace in Bosnia and Herzegovina and Northern Ireland', *Peacebuilding*, 5(1): 67–81.

Marsden, M., Ibañez-Tirado, D. and Henig, D. (2016) 'Everyday diplomacy', *Cambridge Journal of Anthropology*, 34(2): 1–126.

Mathie, A. and Cunningham, G. (2003) 'From clients to citizens: Asset-based community development as a strategy for community-driven development', *Development in Practice*, 13(5): 474–86.

Montsion, J.-M. (2010) 'Research (im)possibilities: Reflections from everyday international relations', *Altérités*, 7(2): 79–94.

Morris, J. (2016) 'Not soft power, but speaking softly: "Everyday diplomacy" in field relations during the Russia-Ukraine conflict', *Cambridge Journal of Anthropology*, 34(2): 110–126.

O'Driscoll, D. (2021) 'Everyday peace and conflict: (Un)privileged interactions in Kirkuk, Iraq', *Third World Quarterly*, 42(10): 2227–46.

Randazzo, E. (2016) 'The paradoxes of the "everyday": Scrutinising the local turn in peace building', *Third World Quarterly*, 37(8): 1–20.

Richmond, O. (2009) 'A post-liberal peace: Eirenism and the everyday', *Review of International Studies*, 35(3): 557–80.

Ring, L. (2006) *Zenana: Everyday Peace in a Karachi Apartment Building*, Bloomington: Indiana University Press.

Singer, P. (1972) 'Famine, affluence, and morality', *Philosophy & Public Affairs*, 1(3): 229–43.

Sponsel, L. (2017) 'The anthropology of peace and nonviolence', *Diogenes*, 61(3/4): 30–45.

Visoka, G. (2020) 'Everyday peace capture: Nationalism and the dynamics of peace after violent conflict', *Nations and Nationalism*, 26(2): 431–46.

Ware, A. and Ware, V.-A. (2021) 'Everyday peace: Rethinking typologies of social practice and local agency', *Peacebuilding*, https://doi.org/10.1080/21647259.2021.1997387.

Ware, A., Ware, V.-A. and Kelly, L. (2021) 'Strengthening everyday peace formation after ethnic cleansing: Operationalisation of a framework in Myanmar's Rohingya conflict', *Third World Quarterly*, 43(2): 289–308. https://doi.org/10.1080/01436597.2021.2022469.

Weber, M. (1922 [1978]) *Economy and Society*, 2 vols, Berkeley, CA: University of California Press.

Weber, M. (1976) *Wirtschaft und Gesellschaft*, 5th edn, edited by J. Winckelmann, Tübingen: J.C.B. Mohr (P. Siebeck).

Williams, P. (2013) 'Reproducing everyday peace in North India: Process, politics, and power', *Annals of the Association of American Geographers*, 103(1): 230–50.

Williams, P. (2015) *Everyday Peace? Politics, Citizenship and Muslim Lives in India*, Chichester: Wiley Blackwell.

Yoshizawa, A. and Kusaka, W. (2020) 'The arts of everyday peacebuilding: Cohabitation, conversion, and intermarriage of Muslims and Christians in the southern Philippines', *Southeast Asian Studies*, 9(1): 67–97.

3

Peacebuilding with youth: experience in Cúcuta, Colombia

Nohora Constanza Niño Vega

Summary

In Colombia, in the wake of a long-term armed conflict that resulted in multiple acts of violence with many victims, peacebuilding has become the daily work of various social and governmental actors. Successive governments adopted peacebuilding strategies in relation to non-state armed actors in the 1980s and 1990s. Then again in 2005 with regard to the paramilitary groups, with an emphasis on mitigating the violence, achieving their demobilisation and their reintegration into civilian life. More recently, the Havana peace agreement with the Revolutionary Armed Forces of Colombia–People's Army (FARC-EP), has become a milestone, leading to a post-conflict scenario.

The process of demobilisation[1] of paramilitary groups started in 2005 under the government of Alvaro Uribe Vélez. This was a highly critiqued process due to the difficulties in gaining truth, justice and reparation. The Havana process (2016) has also had to overcome a series of stumbling blocks such as a change of government and the staggering level of continuing violence that has resulted in the deaths of nearly a thousand social leaders and ex-combatants. This clearly demonstrates that the post-conflict path so regularly discussed by the state government and international agencies is not being experienced on the ground.

In the light of this still violent context, talking about peacebuilding, particularly a peace built from below, means talking about day-by-day processes which have the potential to form different relationships and deliver on the actual protection of life rather than it being spoken about as meaningless rhetoric.

This chapter shares reflections on the peacebuilding actions carried out by a youth social organisation in the border town of Cúcuta. It demonstrates the ways in which peacebuilding processes in conflict areas such as Colombia have the greatest impact on community cohesion when they are defined and implemented from below. Everyday peace arises by and for local communities, who are the main promoters and connectors, not only of their lived reality but also of the possibilities of local transformation.

This process also helps us to understand the political role that young people play in the city of Cúcuta; a role that lays the foundations of social transformation from their own experience and analyses how it interacts with communities living in violent and conflictive environments. It demonstrates how young people, who are so often seriously criminalised by society and governments, can be crucial players in enabling scenarios of positive change in their environments.

To present this analysis, the chapter is divided into three parts. Firstly, we will set the scene, with particular reference to the border town of Cúcuta, which allows the reader to understand the context and lived realities arising out of the different types of violence in this area. Secondly, we will address the theoretical position, reflecting the discussion on peacebuilding, as understood from a decolonial perspective, that contributes to the conceptualisation of peace from below. Finally, we will look at the case of the Youth Analytical Movement for Social Transformation (MATS), an initiative of local young people who have organised and developed work with violence-affected peripheral and marginalised communities in the city, who wish to move to less hostile settings despite the continuing presence of armed actors there.

Setting the scene
The violent dynamics in Cúcuta, the confluence of different violences

Like much of Colombia itself, the border town of Cúcuta has suffered from the impact of various types of violence that have been perpetrated in the country. From the political violence resulting from the uprising in armed guerrilla groups, to the violence of the state, often perpetrated in collusion with paramilitary groups, and the criminal violence associated with drug trafficking and other illicit activities.

In this confluence of different streams of violence, it is recognised that the perpetrators may overlap in terms of violent activity, requiring consideration of a spectrum of diffuse violence in which those who took up arms against the state, as in the case of guerrillas, might also engage in the drug trafficking business to generate income for their armed activities. Similarly, paramilitarism, and its subsequent reorganisation into post-demobilisation armed groups, has also shifted into criminality with the capacity to effect destabilisation in the spaces where they operate (National Center for Historical Memory, 2016). In addition, the city's historical crime gangs have linked their micro-trafficking with the illegal businesses run by other criminal groups that have greater territorial control in the city.

In recent years, there has been the additional element caused by the Venezuelan exodus, where individuals associated with the so-called 'Tren

Figure 3.1: Map of Colombia showing Cúcuta

Source: https://d-maps.com/carte.php?num_car=15143&lang=en

de Aragua', a criminal group from the interior of Aragua state in Venezuela, have crossed the border to participate in the criminal activities that take place in the territory around Cúcuta (Venezuela Investigative Unit, 2020).

Due to its border status Cúcuta, the capital of the north of Santander, has been seen as a geostrategic space for different armed actors who are both based in, and have passed through, the area. In the 1970s and 1980s members of the National Liberation Army (ELN), FARC-EP and the People's Liberation Army (EPL) all had a presence in the city of Cúcuta.

These guerrillas, according to the non-governmental organisation (NGO) Progresar (www.funprogresar.org/), saw the border department of the North Santander as a strategic site for their military mobilisation. Equally during that period, the guerrillas established binding ties with those people and communities that were living in poverty, experiencing precariousness and abandonment by the state in rural areas. The ELN guerrilla organisation developed the largest presence in the north-east of Santander territory with several fronts, among them the Carlos Velasco Villamizar Urban Front, in the city of Cúcuta itself.

The EPL also had an important presence in the region, especially in the Catatumbo area and along the Venezuelan border. By the 1990s, a process was put in place that allowed the decommissioning of weapons and the reintegration of combatants into civilian life. While this was taken up by some combatants, there were others that formed a dissident grouping that currently still operates in the territory. In the 1980s, the FARC-EP consolidated its presence, making Catatumbo one of its main operating territories with its 33rd Front located there. Later, the arrival of the Arturo Ruiz Mobile column led to its entry into Cúcuta and the metropolitan area. Despite the operation of the three different guerrilla groups in the territory, it was only the ELN that achieved a strong position in the city of Cúcuta.

As the government organisation Consultoría para los Derechos Humanos y el Desplazamiento (International Displacement Monitoring Centre, 2014) points out, the ELN faced the challenge of shaping the so-called 'base communities' in the peripheral and marginalised spaces of the city of Cúcuta, becoming in the process a dominant force for social regulation and control. Its dominance is recognised in communes 6, 7, 8 and 9 in Cúcuta. As the International Displacement Monitoring Centre (2014) notes, the city was a political stronghold for the ELN due to their engagement with communities and social movements (including student and trade union movements) while it strengthened its military position by maximising the supply of weapons and ammunition from across the border. Economically, in order to finance its operation, this guerrilla group made use of extortion, kidnapping and various activities in both the legal and illegal commercial sector of the city.

By the end of the 1990s, paramilitaries used the discourse of 'self-defence' to counter the presence of the guerillas. The violence associated with these developments, as experienced in the Catatumbo Block under the command of Salvatore Mancusor, generated terror in the city of Cúcuta. The strategy was operationalised through a structure attached to the Campesinas De Córdoba and Urabá Self-Defenses (ACCU) and sought to exercise territorial control in four strategic areas of the north of Santander: the province of Ocaña; the Catatumbo region, mainly the municipalities of Tibu and El Tarra; Cúcuta and its metropolitan area: Villa del Rosario, Los Patios, El Zulia and Puerto Santander; and the Sarare subregion, especially the municipalities of Labateca and Toledo.

Despite this discourse of 'self-defence' and the focus on combatting the guerillas, the paramilitaries sought to cement their economic, political and military dominance in the area, including prioritising 'the control of the exploitation of natural resources, the management of illicit crops and drug trafficking routes that were fed by their access to the Venezuelan border and the Caribbean Sea' (Niño, 2019: 314). In fact, the bloc became an important source of funding for the United Self-Defence Forces of Colombia due to its control over illegal border activities such as drug trafficking and smuggling.

The paramilitary presence in the city and surrounding areas has had a significant impact on the understanding of violence by both its citizens and the authorities. What we call the 'aesthetics of violence' used by these so-called 'self-defence groups' – paramilitaries – was strongly associated with carrying out massacres and enforced disappearances. In the city of Cúcuta, the Border Block is recorded as perpetrating more than 10,000 murders, causing 100,000 victims of displacement and the enforced disappearance of thousands of people (Ascanio et al, 2012). Paramilitaries adopted various forms of public coercive control of territory such as the use of threatening pamphlets, daylight killings and the compilation and circulation of death lists. The victims were mostly social leaders, members of community action boards – local organisational forums – grassroots social organisations, trade unions, displaced populations and local members of left-wing parties.

The paramilitary enforcement was not only related to their military strength but also to their control over what was considered good and evil. This imposed binary code gave rise to a sense of mistrust of 'the other' in local communities, encouraging suspicion of neighbours and led to the fragmentation of community ties (Niño, 2019). This resulted in a situation whereby the violence of these paramilitary groups had a long-term impact on community organisation and trust, shattering the potential for solidarity and cohesion for many years. Likewise, during the paramilitary presence, the narratives that they used to validate actions such as 'social cleansing' became commonplace and provided a rationale for the elimination of 'people seen as unwanted' from local communities.

Subsequently, under the Justice and Peace process carried out by the Alvaro Uribe government, during 2005, the paramilitaries demobilised and legal proceedings were initiated. In the case of the north of Santander and Cúcuta, this led to the identification of the intrinsic relationship between the paramilitaries and the police, military, members of the Administrative Department of Security–Presidential Security Corps and the Municipal Prosecutor's Office. The highlighting of these links fuelled the lack of trust by citizens not only in their neighbours but also in the democratic institutions responsible for ensuring their security.

Despite this demobilisation process, post-demobilisation groups (CNMH, 2016) were formed that operated and currently operate in the context of paramilitarism, making use of similar strategies to maintain social and territorial control. In 2016, the regional Ombudsman's Office noted that the city had been impacted by feuding between post-demobilisation armed groups called the Gaitanist Self-Defence of Colombia/Urabeños and Los Rastrojos, who have contested the border corridor between north Santander and Táchira state in Venezuela. This dispute led to selective killings, enforced disappearance, threats, restrictions on mobility, recruitment of children and adolescents, extortion and forced displacement (Attorney General's Office, 2016).

As already noted, the recent Venezuelan exodus has resulted in powerful crime gangs from Venezuela becoming a presence in the area. Consequently, the city and its metropolitan area has experienced permanent conflict with armed actors who have settled, resulting in increased insecurity among the residents. Layered on top of the paramilitary narrative which justified murder, communities are currently haunted by the increase in micro-trafficking and drug use locally. This has resulted in heavy-handed actions by both legal and illegal authorities. The overall violent context, actions and narratives result in a distinction between those lives that are seen as meaningful and others that are regarded as disposable. It is in this very difficult context that communities and social organisations have to work, bringing with them a commitment to peacebuilding.

Peace, inequality and justice: building peace from below

Within this context an important element of peacebuilding processes is community development and recognising the potential of empowered communities to transform their environments and challenge the expressions of violence exercised within them. This section discusses peacebuilding processes from a decolonial perspective. Much of the literature related to peacebuilding and conflict transformation still comes from the global North, which sometimes ignores the efforts that locally based communities in the global South have made to develop their own knowledge, practices and tactics of resistance in the face of violent environments.

Critical perspectives on peacebuilding theories and what is called liberal peace is drawn upon (Richmond, 2009, 2011a; Chandler, 2010; Mac Ginty, 2017). These authors indicate that the concept of liberal peace has been a model of thought that seeks to shape the scenarios for peace in territories that are immersed in dynamics of violent conflict. The concept, much used by agencies such as the United Nations (UN) incorporates the reform of the security field and the processes of disarmament, demobilisation and reintegration (DDR), institutional development, as well as an emphasis on governance and the human rights framework.

For Richmond (2009), an understanding of liberal peace contains four lines of thought: victor's peace, institutional peace, constitutional peace and civil peace, each targeting different areas of governance, with an emphasis on high level governmental power and structural functionalism. He also notes that while liberal democratic peace focuses on national political institutions and their international implications, it is also cognisant of the social and civil spheres.

Within this perspective, civil peace can identify emancipatory processes and local agency, usually being framed within international liberal norms. But while it can encompass direct actions and the mobilisation of citizens seeking the defence and promotion of human rights, it tends to place greater emphasis on individual mobilisation within NGOs, often international NGOs (INGOs), rather than maximising collective community agency, which can be portrayed as involving potentially problematic cultural history.

Although the first element of liberal peace is what Richmond (2009) calls a conservative peace that focuses on ensuring basic security, it does not necessarily create the conditions for social transformation, being primarily seen as a guarantee of social welfare and justice. The second element of liberal peace may address needs and rights, which are often championed by NGOs, trade unions and social movements, but the strategies adopted can privilege care from an organisational perspective as opposed to adopting a more participative approach with grassroots communities.

There is a real danger that liberal peace, which is primarily focused on security and institutionality rather than community solidarity and social justice, offers little effective challenge to the established political and business elites. Indeed, there has been criticism of this approach to peacebuilding given that it tends to maintain normative and political hierarchies rather than taking account of everyday community experience and priorities which are a fundamental aspect of building and sustaining peace.

Mac Ginty (2014) also points out how thinking from the perspective of liberal peace has been framed and bolstered by a level of standardisation and technification represented by descriptions of 'best practices' and 'lessons learned'. This reinforces the sense that the ownership of peacebuilding practices and experiences is external to the knowledge and capabilities of the communities themselves, who are usually seen as having limited agency. Concerns have been expressed that case studies used often focus on interventionist policies and practices that can minimise understanding of the key role of local people in peacebuilding processes.

The liberal peace perspective has not escaped a critical and decolonial review, which allows us to understand the limitations of a perspective that has been developed in the global North, imbuing it with aspects of Eurocentrism in its discourse and practice (Fontan, 2012; Sabaratnam, 2013; Cruz, 2018, 2020, 2021; Sandoval and Capera, 2020). In contrast, the decolonial perspective of peace promotes the notion of peacebuilding that develops from below, that is a decolonising peace (Fontan, 2012). This encourages attention to be given to the importance of local and community processes. It means that counter-narratives to official institutional ways of understanding and exercising peacebuilding processes not only exist but are recognised. In this context, a peace that is centred on justice and care, as well as the building of relationships with 'the other', can be seen as having the potential to deliver the necessary social transformation, challenging the deep inequalities that so often motivate violent conflicts. Richmond (2011b) argues that peace from this perspective allows us to take account of local conditions, including identifying and highlighting those existing political and economic structures and policies that are indifferent to local community interests or to people's pain and suffering.

What has become known as 'the local turn' provides for a deeper understanding of indigenous culture and traditions as well as the dynamics that can fuel or transform conflict. It also offers greater focus on daily life experiences, human security (in place of militarised security) and a new social contract whereby state institutions are concerned with the care and wellbeing of all citizens. Furthermore, using the local as a starting point and recognising the individuals and communities as owners of the peacebuilding process, places an emphasis on participative decision-making and co-design of political economic and social processes and norms, unlike in the liberal peacebuilding experience where the roles of elites and agencies are predominant.

Mac Ginty (2014) accepts the importance of grounded agency – where people plan actions and respond to their experience of violence as it affects their lives. This response will be clearly influenced by the intensity and nature of the violence at any particular point in time. It also often includes incidences where local people and communities negotiate space and understandings with armed actors, as Perea (2016) analysed in his study of relations between communities and violent actors in Latin America. A decolonial and peacebuilding commitment requires starting from the micropolitical conditions of communities, recognising their forms of day-to-day agency of peace practice.

It is then relevant to ask what worldviews are played out in territories where ethnically diverse communities converge? What practices and tactics have communities developed to address these environments of violence and what relationship have they fostered with the various armed actors and other stakeholders?

This decolonial conception of peace draws on theoretical developments from decolonial feminism to account for the intersectionality in conflicts. It also shifts the dominance of the state and institutions in the peacebuilding process, even in scenarios where a type of state presence can be characterised by its absence in practice. In such situations other forms of social regulation usually develop. Indeed, it is not unusual to find situations where communities develop rules of coexistence that allow the regulation of the different areas of life and relationships. These understandings, as Peña points out (2019), often encompass peace within specific territories rooted in a moral and geographical imagination that includes not only a reconstruction of social relations and the promotion of development, but also encompasses deep relationships with nature, a sense of place and a reassertion of territorialities affected and made invisible by war.

Peña (2019) argues that even the notion of territorial peace promoted by the agreements in Havana has been reconstructed by community organisations to align with their experiences. The peasant organisations of the Cimitarra Valley in the Middle Magdalena and the Nasa Indians through the Association of Indigenous Cabildos of north Cauca, as well as the Black Communities Process, have demonstrated local experiences of territorial peace in what Richmond (2011a) articulates as 'everyday peace' approaches. They recognise solidarity, love, trust, natural wealth and identity as indigenous, Afro or peasant. It is these important dimensions that are seen as fundamental elements of this everyday practice; a practice committed to agency, creativity and forms of social organisation that both strengthen, and are strengthened, by roots in local territories, identities and visions of justice and sovereignty.

This is not territorial peace designed from above as a process of integration into the state, but a peace that is understood as harmonisation – respecting the mandates of human life with the mandates of nature. The territory, it is suggested, consists in the reappropriation of a geographical space for the realisation of a decent community life. In this way, territorial peace understood from below is one that is able to transform 'the spatiality of war and violence, in its material and symbolic appropriation so that it makes sense again and fulfills its functions of which it was stripped – the territory– because of armed conflict' (Peña, 2019: 14). Peña's model distinguishes between a geographical imagination and a moral imagination. Peacebuilding has to address both the direct relationships with territory which might include what it is used for, its economic value, its natural features and how it is defined (and named) as well as the relationships with other people which may include the perception of 'us' as a community living in harmony, heroic or as victims deserving reparation, and 'them' as an enemy and thus what they do or don't deserve (Peña, 2019).

For their part, Jaramillo et al (2018: 28) also adopt a decolonial perspective, highlighting what they call the Community Institutions for Peace, as forms of territorial action that have been able to establish themselves as 'daily networks of social practices, power strategies that become over time, mobilisers of local organisational memory'. In this sense, they have become community organisational forms that help manage citizen coexistence and the management of relationships and everyday practice.

With regard to the Colombian case, Castro (2020) points out that peacebuilding has found it difficult to be able to move beyond the more established liberal notions of peace to a collective political project capable of rethinking the social order. With peace framed as being achieved through agreements between the state and the armed actors, the process has in effect marginalised any participation by the affected communities and the Colombian society as a whole. Despite the Havana agreement enabling the disarmament and demobilisation of the continent's oldest guerrilla movement, the FARC-EP, and adopting a discourse that touches on territorial peace, the agreement is still largely framed within a logic of institutional and top-down negotiation. Any translation to the local requires recognition of the economic, social and cultural characteristics of the various communities involved. The question remains – how do these framework agreements effectively speak to, and take account of, the daily exercise of peace at various community levels?

As we will discuss in what follows, there are concrete experiences in the country where peace has materialised from below. It calls on the community organisation: its knowledge, its aspirations, projects and discourses that work to manage and respond to conflict and violence on an everyday basis. Although the classic and critical elements of peacebuilding have been helpful in strengthening these dynamics, the real value lies in our own ancestral knowledge and ability to see and understand the self-care of both ourselves and of the other; all aspects that have shaped these local peacebuilding experiences.

The political subject of peace from the perspective of youth: from criminalised youth to taking action for peace

Young people have long been subjects of suspicion due to the sense of insecurity often experienced in Latin America, and the increasing participation of young people in illegal and criminal activities (Reguillo, 2008; Niño, 2016; Valenzuela, 2019; Urteaga and Moreno, 2020). However, young people are not only perpetrators but also victims of violence. In the period from 2003 to 2014, 90 per cent of homicides were in the 15–29-year-old category in Latin America (Villalta et al, 2016, cited in Muggah et al, 2018: 1).

As the Conflict Analysis Resource Centre (Schob, 2014) points out, the violence perpetrated by young people in Colombia is not necessarily linked to the dynamics of internal armed conflict or organised criminal violence, although the increasing use of young people and minors for these purposes is clearly recognised. However, young people have been socialised in a context of long-term violent conflict and deep-rooted organised crime resulting in a heterogeneity in their forms of involvement and participation in violence. It is for this reason that society often views young people as criminals and stigmatises them as figures of terror. Consequently, the response to young men, specifically, is characterised by heavy-handed policies and practices to 'contain' their threat. In this sense, they are usually not perceived as potential agents of change and peacebuilding but as objects of authoritarian containment. Of course, in real terms this approach is mainly brought to bear on certain racial groups and those from lower social classes.

Even within this framework of criminalisation, young people have offered significant resistance to such stereotyping. In Colombia, student movements and social organisations have resisted the drive by the recent incoming government that sought to undermine the agreements reached with FARC.[2] As Zapata Cancelado (2016) notes, young people have rarely been visible within either the theoretical or practical frameworks of global peace scenarios, although in Colombia it is increasingly possible to identify organised action by young people looking to contribute in the peacebuilding process.[3]

Young people living in the city of Cúcuta experience different aspects of violence and therefore have to adopt strategies that allow them to live amidst such daily violence. In doing so, not only do they challenge the negative perceptions of what society expects of them (Berents and McEvoy-Levy, 2015) but they also counter the expectations of various violent actors operating in areas of territorial control. However, just as the criminalisation of young people is not homogeneous, neither is the response of those young people whose diverse experience of race, gender and social class impacts on the day-to-day processes of peacebuilding.

MATS, which works in the city of Cúcuta, is a youth organisation that was established out of meetings of young men and women who gained social connections from within both the university and from youth activities and spaces within Cúcuta.

The experience of the MATS in Cúcuta: a view from below

MATS was developed when a group of young students decided to organise themselves and to leave their academic environment to work in the community, in which they had personal and professional connections. Essential trust and confidence was built from close personal relationships, influencing the youth social organisation that was created.

Many of today's members joined the organisation due to their personal experiences and struggles, but particularly due to the struggles they experienced as students and their life journeys.

In the words of its founder:

'MATS is closely linked to my personal life story, I am a young survivor of the conflict, I was in La Gabarra just on the night of the massacre of '99, also for multiple reasons I was emancipated from the age of 14 and I participated in dance groups, I volunteered to travel around the country. Then I returned to the Catatumbo, being in Tibu and saw the confusion of the Catatumbo organisation there. I spent three years in Tibu developing processes in collaboration with the victims' unit. Then I went to Pamplona to train in a diploma of human rights and sexual diversity. In order to graduate I have to do a replica of the exercise and so then I developed an organisational process in Tibu with the diverse population and the constitution of the first LGBT [lesbian, gay, bisexual and trasngender] collective was achieved. As a consequence we received threats a month later and had to leave the municipality. The nice thing about this is that the community are the ones who hid me for three days, the sicarios were looking for me in certain parts but the people denied I was there. I couldn't take the pressure anymore and talked to the representative and they pulled me out of Tibu. Then, I arrived in Cúcuta and then of course a "Chinese man who grew up"[4] volunteering and knowing processes of the communities, I arrived in Cúcuta and found that the scenarios were very academic. I look back at my process to be recognised as a victim and I started looking for participation scenarios, but all these scenarios were in auditoriums either on the hotels or the university and I identified that there were many officials and professionals with many proposals for solutions and they were very good at reports. But for a person like me who was trained in community work in which decisions were made about what had to be done, having to attend meetings focused on theoretical or contextual discussions, with a lot of people who relied on academics, research, who were unaware of the real context it was very difficult. So I decided if there was no space for collective ideas then you have to create it and that is why the idea was born. The first members were my closest friends. Over time, the volunteering process began, which came to have more than 23 people involved in the work. However, not having the necessary funding, there was no way to sustain the processes and colleagues had to make decisions to leave to take care of their needs.' (Joseph, personal communication, 10 October 2020)

The development of this type of organisation highlights the need for a commitment to transformation from below. For young people participating in MATS, it was essential to move from lecture halls into communities to establish the real needs and challenge previously held assumptions. Those involved are clear that as an organisation they are not sole developers of projects but facilitate community processes that enable and guide actions that are always focused on the community and what local people deem necessary for their transformation.

The work developed in the neighbourhoods Las Delicias and Manuela Beltran, on the outskirts of the town, show how the youthful experience of community work is connected to community development practices, that have been discussed in the introduction of the book. Communities need to identify their own needs and priorities; take collective action drawing on their strengths and resources; develop confidence, skills and knowledge; challenge power relations and promote social justice.

These elements can be seen in the experience of Young Peace Leaders (JOLIPAZ) and the Concienciación and Formación Canabica (Cannabis Awareness Training), aimed at children and young people as well as cannabis users in the area. The development of this programme came from dialogue with local communities who identified cannabis use as an issue in their area. Work with the community also found that the neighbourhoods were being affected by the presence of illegal armed groups, organised criminal gangs, the sexual and labour exploitation of children, school dropout and illicit substance use by children and adolescents. Faced with this reality, the local people suggested that a place was required where children and young people could spend their leisure time. From this, arts and sports schools were born.

Although resources were limited, many of us cycled to the neighbourhoods, went without eating and, though we faced difficulties, we developed 'skin-to-skin processes with communities'. One of the main challenges as a resource-starved organisation was building initial connections and relationships when things like refreshments could not be offered as a condition for participation. These communities, given that they contain many families that are victims of armed conflict, have developed an expectation of the project interventions offered by larger organisations that provide certain rewards for cooperation and development work. Resources are usually allocated for the provision of refreshments given the need among the target population for access to food. However, this was difficult for organisations such as the youth initiative given lack of resources:

> 'Having snacks became a norm in the community and many people from our processes left at first when they saw no refreshments. However, when they saw that we did not mind staying working with those five or six young people they returned and understood that the snack could not be the sole purpose of the process. We have been very honest with the community in saying that we have no resources, that many of us get there with money out of our own pocket, it comes from us because we believe that the community should be accompanied and

that processes should be generated by other workers.' (Joseph, personal communication, 9 October 2020)

It took years of activity and cooperation in the community to overcome this barrier of local expectations. Another issue to be dealt with was security, given that these areas on the edge of the city are controlled by illegal armed actors. At first, the neighbourhoods seemed at ease with the presence of the activists, as if nothing happened there. However, the constant suggestion of not arriving alone and not leaving alone did raise suspicion that something was going on but that people were not yet willing to talk about it.

> 'As we searched, we found that the community identified certain neighbourhood kids as those who stole, raped, killed, and extorted and they weren't interested in them. This had originated because the same community had begun a trajectory of rejecting these young people. One of the leaders of the community action board had a son who was involved in drug consumption and in gang behaviour and the concerned president tells me we have to do something. We managed to find a common course of action.
>
> Firstly, we started working clandestinely in the backyard of a house because the community's rejection of working with them was strong. We then began training with them, we connected them with the cannabis community in Norte de Santander and began to hold workshops for self-cultivation so they knew all the derivatives and the possible development of a company there. In a staggered way we began to show the work in the neighbourhood.' (Joseph, personal communication, 10 October 2020)

Based on the experiences of cannabis use of the young people who are a part of MATS youth, they identified this as a major problem in these neighbourhoods. The same situation had already been observed in work carried out in areas surrounding the neighbourhoods worked by the youth organisation (Niño and Calderón, 2020). Consumers of illicit substances are seen by locals as the 'subjects of evil' that haunt them, even though there are organised armed structures that could be identified as a bigger problem. This view is due to the fact that an official narrative has been constructed in which violent acts are understood between certain illegal armed actors and not others. In this sense, as long as you are not involved with the 'unacceptable' actors there can be a certain 'security' amid the uncertainty of living in the context of violence.

Meanwhile, consumers of drugs are viewed as a direct evil both for their drug consumption and that they access the resources they need by robbing their own neighbours. For this reason, they become a direct threat to people in neighbourhoods. The young people of the organisation gradually understood that the consumption is not the problem but rather both the violence and their own marginalisation. They had direct experience of how societal marginalisation stripped them of their own worth and dignity, effectively distancing these young people within the community. The MATS exercise recognised how marginalisation could be countered by fostering a process of recognition of the young people as part of the community – son of one's neighbour, of the chairman of the communal action board, of the lady of the corner.

Working at this peace process, daily and from below, the youth organisation understood that drug consumption is also linked to drug dealing networks that operate in the area and that are engaged in violence that the organisation could not manage. However, working with the young consumers on positive actions was a way to reinstate them as part of the community. Projects included involving the young people in maintaining the only public recreation space, the neighbourhood sports court, in good condition. They also formed security brigades, maintaining the security of the environment and supporting people to transport goods to markets, actions that had a positive economic impact for the locals.

In the context of this process, the *jíbaro* (the person in charge of issuing marijuana) of the neighbourhood, saw that the youth organisation had no intention of involving the police, but instead emphasised the worth of the young people and their contribution to the community, notwithstanding the young people's consumption of drugs.

Alongside this process MATS developed work with JOLIPAZ. Focusing on a number of young people that had previously been involved in a United Nations High Commissioner for Refugees (UNHCR) programme, invitations were issued to participate in a number of workshops. Given the age of these young people, however, already over 15 years, it was found that their economic obligations meant that they were unable to participate. However, connection was made with this group of youth when MATS followed up on the community suggestions that children and young people needed spaces for arts and sports. The organisational strategy was then to set up a school with different activities such as dance, rap, graffiti and football as an instrument, a 'tool project', through which they introduced other priority themes such as assertive communication, conflict resolution and human rights.

Within the organisation's narrative about its accompanying processes, it is important to highlight how the joint work with the residents, and with the neighbourhood structure of the community action boards, allowed not only the identification of the most pressing problems, but also suggested possible routes of action. This solution-focused approach was rooted in the deeper understanding that in the face of internal community violence and distrust of state institutions, it was important not to argue for institutional approaches that ran counter to community interests and preferences.

Of course, these decisions are not easy. They can become dilemmas when at odds with the rights of individuals and the complicated relationships of the community vis-à-vis the state. However, according to the members of the youth organisation, training and information has been put in place at the community level so that there can be greater knowledge and understanding of state policies and approaches. Raising such issues would not be possible without a real commitment to fully understand the experience and reservations of the community and the priority given to respecting local resources, skills and knowledge that is the basis of consensual action strategies.

Conclusion

This chapter draws on the particular experience of a youth organisation that is committed to building peace in the border town of Cúcuta to enable us to highlight the importance of recognising a perspective of peacebuilding from below. Such a perspective is important to critique the concept of liberal peace, which is so often exclusionary of the lived experiences of diverse communities, and particularly those communities that are most impacted by violence. This is not to distract from, or deny, the important contribution peacebuilding and conflict transformation has made more generally at a global level, but the Cúcuta example speaks to the so-called decolonial peace which emphasises bottom-up perspectives. This recognises the crucial importance of the experiences and knowledge of local communities and the ways in which they construct their own ideas of what peace is and how the peacebuilding process is conducted within their communities.

Equally, peacebuilding from below acknowledges the daily work done by communities and social organisations to introduce transformation processes in situations where conflicts have become violent. It is an everyday peace, which is able to recognise the multidimensional nature of the violence and builds on learning from how people survive and take action within this difficult environment. This includes knowing how to react to an escalation of violence and accepting where and when it is not possible to consider collective, public actions due to the situation being too dangerous and complex. But at the same time being prepared to engage in peacebuilding initiatives when it is possible.

This is an essential part of the knowledge that local communities develop based on the grounded experience of living and working in a violent environment. Assessing what is possible and what approaches might work, and when, is informed by the relationships that local people amass as well as their calculation of risk and benefit. Importantly, communities have learned to understand and interact with the different rhythms of violence that constitutes their day-to-day construction of peace.

Notes

1. A process in which many victims still await compensation and reparation for their suffering.
2. The recent incoming government refers to the administration of President Duque which was in place when this chapter was written. The Duque administration was critical of the Havana Agreement concluded in 2016. Summer 2022 saw the election of a new pro-Agreement president – President Gustavo Petro.
3. It is also important to recognise the fundamental role that young people, who are not necessarily organised, play as compared to those who have been rejected by society and stripped of their dignity (Niño, 2017). It is these young people who are at a liminal point of being considered by others – teachers and family – as about to 'get lost' to the world of illegality, who also have dreams, desires, affections. It is these young people who often manage to return to a place of respect for the lives of those who, for some reason, actively participate in violent groups ending up being despised socially and politically.
4. Colombian colloquial form to describe a young man.

References

Ascanio, E., León, E. and Cañizares, W. (2012) 'Frontera Norte de Santander-Táchira', in A. Ávila (ed) *La frontera caliente entre Colombia y Venezuela*, Bogota: Corporación Nuevo Arco Iris, pp 203–344.

Attorney General's Office (2016) 'Colombia 2016 human rights report'. Available at https://www.state.gov/wp-content/uploads/2019/01/Colombia-2.pdf

Berents, H. and McEvoy-Levy, S. (2015) 'Theorising youth and everyday peace(building)', *Peacebuilding*, 3(2): 115–25, https://doi.org/10.1080/21647259.2015.1052627

Castro, F. (2020) 'Ficciones coloniales de la paz', in CINEP, *Estudios Críticos de Paz. Perspectivas decoloniales*. Available at https://www.cinep.org.co/

Chandler, D. (2010) 'The uncritical critique of "liberal peace"', *Review of International Studies*, 36: 137–55.

CNMH (Centro Nacional de Memoria Histórica) (2016) Grupos Armados Posdesmovilización (2006–2015): Trayectorias, rupturas y continuidades. Available at https://centrodememoriahistorica.gov.co/wp-content/uploads/2020/01/grupos-armados-posdesmovilizacion-2006-2015.pdf

Cruz, J. (2018) 'Los Estudios de Paz latinoamericanos en la Encrucijada Producir o Reproducir, Una Mirada Desde las Epistemologías del Sur', *Revista CoPaLa*, 3(5): 9–21. Available at http://www.revistacopala.com/

Cruz, J. (2020) 'Estudios Críticos de Paz y Conflictos: Una Perspectiva Decolonial', in CINEP, *Estudios Críticos de Paz. Perspectivas decoloniales*. Available at https://www.cinep.org.co/

Cruz, J. (2021) 'Colonial power and decolonial peace', *Peacebuilding*, 9(3): 274–88.

Fontan, V. (2012) 'Replanteando la Epistemología de la Paz; el Caso de la Descolonización de Paz', *Perspectivas Internacionales*, 8(1): 41–7.

González, F., Castañeda, D. and Barrera, V. (eds) (2016) 'Potencialidades para la Paz de las Organizaciones Sociales en Tres Municipios Afectados por el Conflicto Armado', Bogota: CINEP (Centro de Investigación y Educación Popular). Available at https://www.cinep.org.co/

International Displacement Monitoring Centre (2014) 'Colombia displacement continues despite hopes for peace'. Available at https://www.internal-displacement.org/sites/default/files/publications/documents/201 401-am-colombia-overview-en.pdf

Jaramillo, J., Castro, F. and Ortiz, D (2018). *Instituciones Comunitarias para la paz. esbozos teóricos, experiencias locales y desafíos sociales*, Bogota: Universidad Nacional de Colombia. Facultad de Derecho, Ciencias Políticas y Sociales. Instituto Unidad de Investigaciones Jurídico Sociales Gerardo Molina.

Mac Ginty, R. (2014) 'Everyday peace: Bottom-up and local agency in conflict-affected societies', *Security Dialogue*, 45(6): 548–64.

Mac Ginty, R. (2017) 'Everyday social practices and boundary-making in deeply divided societies', *Civil Wars*, 19(1): 4–25, https://doi.org/10.1080/13698249.2017.1343410

Muggah, R., Garzón, J. and Suarez, M. (2018) '"Hard-handed L": The costs of repression and the benefits of prevention for young people in Latin America', Strategic Article, Igarapé Institute. Available at https://igarape.org.br/.

Niño, N. (2016) 'Niños, Niñas, jóvenes y Grupos Armados Ilegales: Experiencias de Exclusión e Inclusión Social en América Latina', *Argumentos: Revista de Crítica social*, 18: 177–206. Available at http://publicaciones.sociales.uba.ar/index.php/argumentos/article/view/2029/1724

Niño, N. (2017) 'Las Tramas de la Violencia: Construcción de Subjetividad Política en Contexto de Violencia Armada', Doctoral Thesis, Facultad Latinoamericana de ciencias Sociales México. Available at https://www.flacso.edu.mx/

Niño, N. (2019) 'La Narrativa de la Violencia Paramilitar en Cúcuta: Dificultades en la Construcción del Trauma Cultural', in N.A. Botello and C. Tognato (eds) *Sociedad, Cultura y Esfera civil. Una agenda de Sociología Cultural*, Mexico City: Flacso, pp 313–36.

Niño, N. and Calderón, O. (2020) 'Los Jóvenes y su Aceptación de los Actores Armados de la Violencia Armada', in J. Treviño Rangel and L.H. Atuesta Becerra (eds) *La Muerte es un Negocio: Miradas Cercanas a la Violencia Criminal en América Latina*, Mexico City: Centro de Investigación y Docencia Económica, pp 137–60.

Peña, L. (2019) 'Paz Territorial: Conectando Imaginación Moral e Imaginación Geográfica', Documento de trabajo 5-2019, Bogota: Instituto Colombo-alemán para la Paz. Available at https://www.instituto-capaz.org/wp-content/uploads/2019/11/Documento-de-Trabajo-N6-V3-2.pdf

Perea, C.M. (2016a) *Glimpsing Peace: Power and Conflict in the Latin American City*. Bogota: Random House Mondadori.

Reguillo, R. (2008) 'Las múltiples Fronteras de la Violencia Jóvenes Latinoamericanos entre la Precarización y el Desencanto', *Pensamiento Iberoamericano*, 3: 205–25.

Richmond, O. (2009) 'A post-liberal peace: Eirenism and the everyday', *Review of International Studies*, 35(3): 557–80.

Richmond, O. (2011a) 'Critical agency, resistance and a post-colonial civil society', *Cooperation and Conflict*, 46(4): 419–40.

Richmond, O. (2011b) 'Resistance and post-liberal peace', *International Relations*, 16: 13–46.

Sabaratnam, M. (2013) 'Avatars of Eurocentrism in the critique of the liberal peace', *Security Dialogue*, 44(3): 259–78.

Sandoval, E. and Capera, J. (2020) 'Una mirada Anti-hegemónica y Descolonizadora de los Estudios de Paz en Nuestra América', in A. Ballardo Márquez- Fernández (ed) *Epistemologías decoloniales para la paz en el Sur-Global Homenaje al filósofo del pensamiento antihegemónico*, Bogota: Universidad de los Andes, pp 19–50.

Schob, M. (2014) 'Demobilizing and reintegrating whom? Accounting for diversity in DDR processes: An analysis of the Colombian case', Conflict Analysis Resource Centre. Available at https://www.cerac.org.co/assets/pdf/Other%20publications/WP21_Mia%20Sch%C3%B6b.pdf

Torres, D. (2020) 'Otras paces posibles. Apuestas para el buen vivir', *Estudios Críticos de Paz. Perspectivas Decoloniales*, 73–7. Available at https://www.cinep.org.co/

Urteaga, M. and Moreno, H (2020) 'Jóvenes mexicanos: violencias estructurales y criminalización', *Revista de Estudios Sociales*, 73: 44–57.

Valenzuela, J. (2019) *Trazos de sangre y fuego:Bionecropolítica y Juvenicidio en América Latina*, Bielefeld: Bielefeld University Press. Available at http://www.calas.lat/sites/default/files/valenzuela_trazos_de_sangre_y_fuego_0.pdf

Venezuela Investigative Unit (2020) 'Gamechangers 2020: Tren de Aragua and the exportation of Venezuelan organized crime'. Available at https://insightcrime.org/news/analysis/criminal-winner-tren-de-aragua/

Zapata Cancelado, M.L. (2016) 'Jóvenes y construcción de paz en Colombia', in M. Gutiérrez and J. Tatis Amaya (eds) *¿Herederos de la guerra? Jóvenes, conflicto armado y paz*. Bogota: Editorial Pontificia Universidad Javeriana, pp 17–28.

4

Dialogues to develop civil movements in the Caucasus

Larissa Sotieva and Juliet Schofield

Summary

The chaotic process of disintegration of the Soviet Union provoked conflicts across the region. In the Southern Caucasus, the competing claims for sovereignty between the national elites of the constituent soviet republics (Georgia, Armenia and Azerbaijan) and the autonomous regions (South Ossetia, Abkhazia and Nagorny Karabakh) descended into armed violence in the early 1990s, ending inconclusively with ceasefires but no peace deals, resulting in a situation of no peace, no war, leaving three 'de facto' unrecognised states. Meanwhile the North Caucasus region was also in upheaval, with first the Ossetian–Ingush conflict, the two Chechen wars, and latent conflicts brewing across the five North Caucasus republics. Significant escalations of war in Georgia in August 2008 and Nagorny Karabakh in the autumn of 2020 testify to the volatility in the region.

The role of community leaders has been pivotal in rebuilding these shattered communities across the region. Emerging from the soviet system, which oversaw a weakening of independent civil action by treating it as dissidence, it was the national intelligentsias or the elites that took it upon themselves to try to prevent further resumption of hostilities and build peace. They were well placed to do so, having strong social capital. Indeed at times there has been a blurring between what we might now call 'civil society' and the 'ruling class', as elites moved between the two.

This chapter examines how local intelligentsia drove community development in the conflict-affected regions, reaching out across the conflict divides and beyond to find allies in their mission. Much of it was spontaneous, a response to the emergency situation they found themselves in and a response to the needs of the conflict-affected societies. While the civil elites sought support from international organisations, they had their own clear agenda and were not passive beneficiaries, having no desire for dependency. One particularly bright illustration of NGOs is that which between 1998 and 2005 brought together active civil society from across the north and south of the region in a shared mission and mutual exchange. The format was an adaptation for the new and emerging 'civil society' of a traditional Caucasian method of dispute resolution, wherein neighbours are invited to play the role of mediator and facilitator. Despite the many divisions and conflicts within the region, and thus potential differences between members of the forum, their common motivation to transform their societies and strong sense of Caucasian identity – possibly greater than during the Soviet period even – led to this being a dynamic and solidaristic network which also initiated many community projects with practical outcomes. While facilitated by an international NGO, the management structure put ownership in local hands, and the Forum to some extent took on the role of international NGO, facilitating cross-regional capacity building, in particular reaching those areas neglected by the international community.

The chapter provides examples of how through various initiatives the network operated as mediator, dialogue facilitator, civil society capacity builder, early warning and conflict prevention mechanism and an engine for community development. It reflects that the distinctions between national elite and local community development are false distinctions in this context – or where there are 'local leaders' who are not part of the 'elite', their work is almost completely dependent on them. The Soviet intelligentsia became the new 'civil society', and in the early years there was not always a clear division between 'authorities' and 'civil society' – indeed, the authorities relied on this elite to mobilise for their society's rehabilitation, and actively encouraged their participation in various international fora and dialogues across the conflict divide. However, as the years have progressed, the space for civil society has been squeezed, and they have once again become the new dissidents. Having been the ones who sought to prevent resumption of conflict and build peace – and made significant achievements in this respect – as civil society actors they have been caught up in the new hybrid dynamic of the conflicts themselves. As recipients of foreign funding they are designated a 'side' in the anti-Western culture wars that stem from the geopolitical stand-off between Russia and the West. Seventeen years on from the last Forum meetings, its members look back on this experience as highly formative and significant in terms of 'changing the environment', with multiple spin-offs that owe their origins to Forum participants. Unfortunately, it proved impossible to maintain funding for the network, and it ceased to exist as a formal structure in 2005, but the contacts and relationships it fostered, and its vision, remain.

Setting the scene

Governance in the Soviet era

There were several layers of governance in the Soviet system. At the top of the hierarchy was the Communist Party and Union-wide organs in Moscow

Figure 4.1: Map of the Caucasus

Note: We are grateful to Armenica.org for permission to use the map for which they hold the original copyright.
Source: https://www.dreamstime.com/caucasus-central-asia-countries-political-map-national-borders-english-labeling-illustration-caucasus-central-asia-image105224968

who developed ideology which then the regions should follow. At the local (regional) levels, this Soviet ideology was then 'adapted' – becoming infused with local characteristics and elements of the specific region's culture, customs and general way of life.

The centrally conceived Soviet ideology could have easily been imposed in the form in which Moscow intended and it would have been faithfully implemented by the local Communist Party nomenclature were it not for the 'subclass' or the Soviet 'intelligentsia', being the third link in the Soviet social hierarchy after the working class and the peasantry. The Soviet intelligentsia in each region did everything in their power to preserve their national culture and identity, resisting the ideological manipulation of individual and public identity in order to avoid dissolving into the image of 'Soviet man', despite enormous pressure.

The different nationalities of the Soviet Union understood that they were being deprived of their traditional and cultural identity which was replaced with a new one – possibly even better, as some then thought. However, many resisted this imposition and remained committed to preserving their traditional beliefs and way of life, and the intelligentsia was an influential authority within such circles, superior even to the Communist Party.[1]

The breakup of Soviet Union

During and after the chaotic disintegration of the Soviet Union in the early 1990s a number of latent conflicts turned into active violence. Freedom-hungry representatives of the Soviet intelligentsia and the elites of the constituent republics of the Soviet Union sought to create their own independent states based on nationalist principles, while ignoring the needs and interests of other national minorities living within their Soviet borders.

Specific conflicts

South Caucasus

The South Caucasus region consists of the former Soviet republics of Armenia, Azerbaijan and Georgia, and the disputed territories of Abkhazia, South Ossetia and Nagorny Karabakh.

The Armenians of Nagorny Karabakh, an autonomous region within the borders of Azerbaijan, had petitioned Moscow for its unification with Armenia already back in August 1987. There was a full-scale war between Armenia and Azerbaijan between 1992 and 1994, ending with a ceasefire, but no peace agreement. The most recent Karabakh war of the autumn of 2020 saw Azerbaijan regain the vast majority of the territory, an overwhelming defeat for Karabakh Armenians.

Claims for greater self-determination of the previously autonomous regions of South Ossetia and Abkhazia were resisted by the newly independent Georgian state, with the political stand-offs descending into full-scale violence in South Ossetia from December 1990 to June 1992 and Abkhazia between August 1992 and September 1993.

North Caucasus

The most notable conflicts of the North Caucasus region were the Chechen war of independence from Russia (December 1994 to August 1996, and again in 1999–2000), and between Ossetians and Ingush in the Prigorodny District of North Ossetia – but there were also many latent conflicts across the unstable region, and spillovers of the effects of the Chechen conflicts in particular in Dagestan and Ingushetia.

Not homogeneous but some commonalities within the Caucasus

Broadly speaking, majority communities asserted their right to be independent states based on their identities, while ignoring the needs and interests of minorities living within the borders which had been established during the Soviet era. However, there were also minorities which had also long aspired towards independence and made similar moves in the same direction. Majority and minority communities both felt encouraged by the Russian leader Boris Yeltsin's statement in 1990 that each nation should 'take as much sovereignty as they could swallow' (Yeltsin Centre, 2015). The minorities were differentiated variously by ethnicity, religion, language. Sometimes the different communities were interspersed but other communities were geographically separate within the formal state boundaries.

Before the descent into armed violence

Prior to the outbreaks of armed conflict the region was characterised by often inoperative, ineffective and weak governance. This power vacuum was filled by informal leaders from within the ranks of the intelligentsia, some of whom later came to actual power filling formal leadership positions. At this point, there was still a chance that the opposing groups could find options for peaceful coexistence.

On the one hand there were leaders who fomented the violence by asserting:

- a belief in the distinctiveness and superiority of their group (and therefore inferiority of an 'Other');
- the absolute and exclusive right to territory with the illegitimacy of any other claims;
- the absence of alternative dispute mechanisms or institutions through which to pursue their aspirations.

In the Caucasus, historians played a particularly significant role in this process, doing their utmost to present the past in a way that supported the nationalists' claims in the present – inflaming the conflicts, and even the outbreak of military hostilities in the process.

On the other hand, there was another segment of national intelligentsias, which understood the dangers of nationalism and who took it on themselves to do everything possible to prevent a military escalation. They sought out opportunities to smooth relations between the conflicting parties within their own societies. They organised dialogues between the intelligentsias of the opposing parties, sought out meetings with the nationalist leaders and tried to convince them that confrontation was the road to defeat for all.

During the armed violence

Even prior to the outbreak of hostilities, national minorities were subject to systemic persecution, driven out of their workplaces, their homes occupied and appropriated by the majority population, endorsed and abetted by the state. When violence erupted into armed conflict it led to further deaths, injuries and large displacements of people. Former neighbours and friends became enemies.

During hostilities, the national (that is ethno-national) intelligentsias were close to the authorities. Their agendas coincided. Against what was seen as an existential threat, cohesion was seen as essential. However, while many members of national elites, the Soviet era intelligentsia and community leaders incited conflict or sought peace while war raged, some were active in other ways. Many took up arms in defence of their people, their homes, freedom and the right to live in dignity; some were engaged in humanitarian activities; while others provided information support (as journalists or as part of the information services of the respective parties), seeking external support, getting their message out to the world.

Some broke the boundaries of internal consolidation and solidarity and reached out to the warring parties on humanitarian issues such as prisoner exchange and the search for missing persons. In this way, channels were created during wartime, through which people from across the conflict divide were in contact and dialogue with each other, doing an enormous job of alleviating human suffering. People who had close family ties on the other side of the conflict divide played an important role in this respect – in particular the families of the national elites. But not all could claim affinity to the 'elite' class, and it is this category of people that could be classified as 'community leaders' in the common understanding of the term. At a time when all communications between the warring parties were cut, it was these mixed families, or families with members living on both sides of the divide, who were able to bridge the divide, as a way of meeting their own practical needs and responding to the urgent humanitarian needs of their families. After the end of hostilities, they found ways to get around the closed borders, and many of them were engaged in small businesses and informal trade across the divide.

Post-violence

Military victories and defeats have generally not resolved the conflicts. The absence of political solutions resulted in protracted insecurity for the populations in question, in particular those who found themselves living close to the former frontlines. De-facto, unrecognised borders, weak governance and destruction of economic infrastructure produced conditions rife for the flourishing of criminality. Insecurity, displacement, unemployment – all forms of horizontal and structural violence experienced by the populations, contributed to the trauma and often found their physical expression through gender-based violence.

Official peace talks have made little progress, there are no political settlements on the table, and a combination of time, isolation, propaganda and periodic escalations of violence have contributed to the deepening entrenchment of positions and alienation between the conflicting sides.

After the ceasefires, the cohesion and internal group solidarity which characterised the violent phase was less of an imperative. The Soviet intelligentsia began to form a new 'civil society', one with great leadership potential and huge resources of informal authority. For the first time in the post-Soviet space, Western-style NGOs began to appear. Later external or international organisations supported the institutionalisation of civil society, and the civil movement itself sprung up as an active and spontaneous public response to the needs of the conflict-affected societies.

Community development and peacebuilding
Local to local

In the immediate post-Soviet era, when we talk about 'local' or 'community leaders', we are essentially talking about the 'national elite' of each society. There is no strong distinction between 'national' and 'local' in this respect, and neither is there always a clear distinction between 'elite' as 'ruling class', that is holding formal positions of power – or seeking power through political parties – and the informal power and influence of the 'elite' from within what is now called 'civil society'. The origins of this are to be found in the specifics of the Soviet system, in the weakening of social/civic processes during that period. It is a common trait in the various conflicts across this region, in terms of the influence national elites had both in stoking the conflicts and in attempting to resolve and transform them.

Outsiders to the region often use the term 'community leader' to refer to both 'local' and 'national' level leaders. Thus, the distinction between what can be expected of one or other kind of leadership becomes blurred – though unequivocally, what the 'national elite' can do is beyond the scope of local 'community leaders' and vice versa. Such important nuances are of paramount importance in understanding conflict dynamics, the role of leadership in conflict and how to make use of leadership and community potential for peace.

Immediate post-violence problem-solving through new partnerships to meet immediate needs

Civic activists and leaders began to register their NGOs. For some this was an institutionalisation of long-standing civic activity. They began to seek out like-minded people and resources from Western partners and donors but also from within the region. It was clear that all post-conflict societies in the post-Soviet region had similar problems, and some had already gained experience of dealing with them. For example, Armenia had an effective system of physical and psychological rehabilitation for war victims which they offered to Abkhazians and Georgians. Others sought to learn from the humanitarian experience of international organisations and an active search for partnerships and access to international resources began. This created a system of strategic cooperation, a space for both internal civil dialogue and dialogue with the outside world at the level of civil society and international institutions.

Despite the fact that many leaders of the civil movement had contacts with representatives of the other side of the conflict, such contacts were quite sporadic and, as a rule, in relation to specific humanitarian cases. There was no systematic or strategic approach to this type of activity or understanding of what was to become known as 'peacebuilding' or 'public diplomacy'.

There were no dialogue processes as such at that point in the Caucasus, and peacebuilding was not on any of the public agendas after the end of hostilities. It was simply not relevant in the territories torn by war. Civil society was more concerned with rehabilitation, formation and development of their societies. Basic needs were a priority. The societies could not think about long-term plans for conflict resolution. Besides, the wounds were still fresh, the pain was too acute to think about any cooperation. To be sated with peace, to rest, to recover, to get back on your feet – these were both people's personal and societal goals.

A new role for leaders

Just as in the Soviet times, after its breakup, it was the Soviet intelligentsia that held a long-term strategic vision for the societies, having already gained some experience of civil activity during the war. They took the lead in seeking ways to transform the conflicts. They had earned their social capital in practice, not just by association. They understood the need to create conditions for dialogue primarily as a mechanism to prevent a resumption of hostilities, but also to seek resolution and transformation to ensure long-term human security and development, the recovery of social, economic and other spheres of life. They understood that there could be no return to the past, the path to renewal lay through international cooperation and that included with their opponent, too.

The role of external assistance

External organisations brought financial resources, experience from elsewhere, specific skills and knowledge and the ability to act as independent or neutral mediators. They also brought theory and an ideological framework, for which initially there was enthusiasm, though later it became clear that there were no blueprints. Most Western assistance to the region was framed within a 'Liberal Peace' paradigm – that is, the belief that the conflicts could eventually be resolved through democratic institutions. More specialised peacebuilding interventions were influenced by inter-group contact theory – that is, bringing people from across conflict divides together to build mutual understanding, and eventually to find mutually agreeable solutions. This was especially pertinent in a region which after the breakup of the Soviet Union was more divided than at any time in its history, with multiple closed borders keeping societies in conflict physically apart.[2]

In the immediate post-conflict period of the early 1990s, Western peacebuilding organisations and mediators began to offer their services – seminars and training on 'Conflictology' – sharing their experience from other parts of the world to equip the conflicting parties with skills to work with the conflicts. Civil leaders willingly joined such events, understanding that a neutral mediator was needed to facilitate dialogue with representatives from the other side of the conflict divide. These skills were also useful for working within their societies, where mediators and facilitators were also needed to raise the pressing problems faced by the post-conflict societies and to facilitate the transition from the Soviet to a democratic model of society.

International peacebuilding NGOs gathered people for training from all over the Caucasus and Russia, bringing together people from the different conflict-affected regions. There was an understanding of the commonalities of the post-Soviet conflicts, in particular in the Caucasus region. In focus too was Russia's role and interests in the South Caucasus, and hence, anticipation of how scenarios might develop.

At that time, Georgia and Chechnya were of particular interest to Western facilitators and international organisations. In Georgia's case this is possibly because of Georgian President Shevardnadze's invitation to the international community to assist them in post-war rehabilitation and reconciliation. In the case of Chechnya, Russian Prime Minister Chernomyrdin signed an agreement with the United Nations High Commissioner for Refugees (UNHCR) to help displaced people and people left homeless during the first Chechen conflict. The Georgian–Abkhaz and Chechen conflicts found themselves the focus of attention of the international community, with funds allocated for civil society organisations, while the Georgian–Ossetian and Karabakh conflicts, and other North Caucasian conflicts, remained outside the scope of special interest, which gave those societies a strong impression of Western priorities in the region.

After the 1993 ceasefire, establishing a Georgian–Abkhaz dialogue became a priority for the Georgians. However, the Abkhazians, where almost every family had lost someone, were so traumatised by this devastating war that it was impossible to imagine a bilateral meeting of the two societies. However, attempts to establish a civil dialogue process began to yield results thanks to the high level of professionalism and social capital of a few key individual mediators at the time. The first dialogues were on humanitarian issues, on the search for missing persons towards the end of 1995, and a number of what were to become major dialogue formats were in their inception stages during 1996 and 1997. Groups of Georgians and Abkhazians formed, between whom professional trust developed, and a shared understanding of their common problems and desire to work on them. Most of these individuals had experience of joint humanitarian cooperation during the hostilities and it was this foundation that enabled the creation of this dialogue process.

The international facilitators of dialogue came from various sources: the main dialogue processes were those of the University of California, Irvine (first meeting 1997); and the 'Schlaining' process initiated by the Berghof Foundation and Conciliation Resources, which didn't begin until 2000, but evolved from a Caucasus-wide meeting organised in cooperation with United Nations Volunteers (UNV) in 1996, and a bilateral, Georgian–Abkhaz meeting in January 1997 (Kobakhia et al, 2012).

These dialogue processes that developed in the first few years had a broad resonance in both societies. Dialogue participants came under great public attention, with the transcripts of dialogues published, everything talked about in dialogue meetings was further discussed within the societies. The respective authorities made use of their intellectual and social capital, responding to them depending on how they perceived their message communicated to the other side and the outside world – whether they considered it right or wrong.

From censorship to self-censorship to free expression

During the Soviet era censorship was clear and complied with by almost everyone. In the post-Soviet, post-conflict context, the mechanism of Soviet censorship evolved somewhat. In the immediate post-war period, self-censorship within the societies exceeded any Soviet-era censorship. Self-censorship worked in a similar way to the Soviet period, in that people knew what you can say in public – that is what the authorities expect of you, according to the prevailing ideology – and in your kitchen with family and friends you can say what you really think. Often these opinions were diametrically opposed, but they somehow could be comfortably reconciled in a person's head. Yet this talent to hold both public and personal opinions simultaneously tended to hinder the formation of definitive positions on social or political issues or clarity around one's relationship and responsibility to society.

The expression of personal opinion in public became more welcome and valued, being considered a novelty, a sign of democracy, which all Soviet societies aspired to after the collapse of the USSR. However, criticising one's own society outside its confines was still not acceptable, and considered to be unpatriotic and accordingly condemned, and often even persecuted.

What distinguished the first generation of post-Soviet, post-war civil activists was that they did not accept the Soviet model of information manipulation. Instead, they developed their own communication etiquette based on values of openness, transparency, freedom of speech, the right to express their opinion regardless of the audience, location, and so on.

Looking beyond immediate needs: the Caucasian Forum of NGOs

People were initially sympathetic and supportive of political and civil dialogue in the first few years, in the hope of rapid change. Then as time elapsed, this support subsided. Inflated expectations of dialogue gave way to frustration and irritation. After all, the war was over, they had persevered, endured and now, according to their military-patriotic propaganda, they should be enjoying a decent life, but it was not the case.

In the Georgian–Abkhaz context, it became increasingly difficult for international facilitators to maintain a bilateral dialogue, which the Abkhazians felt was not yielding any practical benefits to their community. After all, the societies' expectations of dialogue were to convey their point of view, to argue in favour of their position, to succeed, to win, and subsequently to bring practical and tangible results.

On the Georgian side, although it was easier for them to participate in bilateral dialogue, and this was welcomed by the authorities, they also faced questions from the public that no one could provide answers to. For example, Georgians displaced from Abkhazia wanted to know when they might expect to be able to return to their homes; and more generally, people wanted to know when would reintegration of Abkhazia finally take place – when would the Abkhazians get tired of isolation and economic blockade?

The driving force and conviction behind the dialogue efforts of civil society leaders was – and remains – that the conflicts could only be resolved through peaceful means. In contrast to their societies, they did not expect quick and visible results, but they also understood that the absence of such processes would mean a high probability of a resumption of hostilities.

Increasingly during the preparatory phase of bilateral dialogue meetings, Abkhaz participants started to raise with facilitators the sense of wariness that had appeared in society in relation to such meetings, as well as the limitations of such a format. It was clear that the process was in crisis, and it required a sensitive and creative approach to preserve it.

The Abkhaz concerns were discussed with all, Abkhaz and Georgians alike, and solutions sought. One suggestion by dialogue participants was to employ a variation of the traditional Caucasian method of dispute resolution, wherein neighbours are invited to play the role of mediator and facilitator. This led to the decision to invite representatives of other Caucasus regions, North and South, to join the bilateral Georgian–Abkhaz meetings – resulting in July 1998 in a large gathering of civil activists from across the wider region, discussing over several days regional conflict trends and the problems of post-conflict recovery faced by their societies.

The discussion was so intense and fruitful that they were worried that it might never be possible to repeat the experience. Thus, in order to strengthen such needed cooperation, the group decided to formalise its relationship and signed the Elbrus declaration, named after the place where the meeting took place and including an articulation of the new network's mission and shared values.

The Caucasus Forum of NGOs was born, with a mission of peacebuilding, conflict prevention and recovery. The dynamism of its formation was not only down to common motivation of its members to transform their societies and conflicts, nor the expert facilitation, but also due to a strongly expressed feeling of a shared Caucasian identity, despite their many conflict lines. The Forum also invited civil society representatives from other parts of the former Soviet Union, in a recognition of shared identity and historical context.

It turned out to be a unique process of mutually beneficial exchange. Representatives of those regions that had suffered armed conflict were able to share their lessons of failed attempts of prevention with those from other parts of the region where conflict had not yet broken out, but where potential was high. They also conveyed the message in the strongest possible terms that armed conflict was not the way to achieve their goals of a free and democratic society. They could see for themselves the destruction wreaked in neighbouring conflict-ravaged regions, and the enormous difficulties subsequently faced by those societies, to meet even basic human needs, while their original goals, for which they fought and gave their lives, were pushed much further down the line.

The path to practical change in the Caucasus

Cooperation began not only in terms of exchange of expertise and experience, but also on a practical level. Representatives from the North Caucasus, the Southern Russian regions and six regions of the South Caucasus (three recognised and three unrecognised) were united. While some parts of the region got more support from international organisations, the Caucasus Forum devised the 'Forgotten Regions' programme as one of the network's first practical initiatives to support civil society in those parts of the region less well served by international donors, in particular, but not limited to South Ossetia and Nagorny Karabakh.

The Forum provided both educational and technical assistance, including computers and access to the internet. Training was delivered by members of the Caucasus Forum from other parts of the region, where there was more experience. This capacity building helped to establish several multilevel civil dialogues across the Caucasus, including:

- bilateral Georgian–Abkhaz dialogue;
- dialogue between Armenians and Azerbaijanis on Nagorny Karabakh;
- Georgian–Ossetian dialogue;
- all-Caucasian dialogue;
- dialogue between the capitals and peripheries;
- dialogue between civil society and authorities in the respective regions;
- dialogue with Russian civil society organisations; and
- dialogue with Western institutions.

As the network grew in strength, various social and professional groups, academics and practitioners from different regions, and conflicting parties started to express interest in cooperation.

Facilitation of the peacebuilding network

However strong the demand for change among the active part of civil society, without structural support they would not be able to achieve it.

The expert facilitation of the network by International Alert's programme manager, Gevorg Ter Gabrielyan, and deputy executive director Martin Honeywell, was instrumental in bringing the network to life. They supported the concept of a regional format, which required considerable adjustments to the original bilateral project plan. They also understood that the successful outcome of the first meetings would mean further changes to the plan. International Alert understood its mission, role and responsibility. It was responsive to the ideas of the participants and their plans, helping them to build a strategic approach according to opportunities identified, and taking into account all obstacles, within limited resources. International Alert assisted in facilitation, in providing new skills, such as conflict analysis, conflict sensitivity, advocacy skills, and so on, providing opportunities to study and learn from peace processes around the world.

One significant practical assistance through the Forum was to help many members connect to the internet for the first time, to facilitate communication and access to information. This was at a time when the internet was just taking off in this part of the world, but the conflict-affected regions were particularly cut off from such technological innovations. This in itself was a major leap forward for civil society, for example in Abkhazia, as up until then they had to rely on the UN mission to send and receive letters, as phone/fax lines were highly unreliable. Once NGOs had the internet, they became popular hubs where people of all generations, especially youth, came to connect to the world.

The Forum was not, of course, always an idyllic vision of peace and harmony. It would be difficult to be so considering it comprised of multiple parties in either overt or covert conflict with each other. Establishing the network was a complex process, requiring a high level of facilitation skills, and a strategic approach to turn it into a functioning mechanism. Sensitivity to both the expressed and concealed opinions, feelings, interests, fears and concerns of network members determined the viability or fate of this project. And along with active engagement, initiative and a high level of expertise on conflict, Gevorg also showed extraordinary wisdom, patience and empathy towards all. He believed in people, and this was reciprocated. This belief in the individual reflected positively also on the organisation that he represented.

This is a crucial dynamic of the partnership between 'international' and 'local' in the Caucasus region. As a rule, trust building with external facilitators takes place with individuals – only then being extended to the organisation or institution – and this trend persists to this day. While an organisation may gain a good reputation and track record, the success of an externally facilitated project depends on the quality of the individuals involved, their personal values, behaviour and verbal and non-verbal communication skills.

At the same time, local facilitation of the Caucasus Forum alongside international actors was embedded from the start, with a local network coordinator selected on an annual basis by the network's coordinating council. The local coordinator facilitated both the network and the network's cooperation with International Alert. As fundraiser, and the source of all funds for the network's activities, the INGO grant manager was accountable to donors. There was plenty of scope for a power imbalance in this relationship between 'international' and 'local'. International Alert's professionalism was in providing a safe space for dialogue, while observing strict neutrality as an organisation and supporting each member regardless of what conflict party they represented and their political views. And over time, International Alert handed more and more ownership of the network's practical activities to the participants, essentially becoming an equal participant itself, while retaining the strategic management functions.

The dynamics of internal relations between the participants: mirroring conflicts in the Caucasus

It was an incredible journey through disputes, discussions, recriminations, attempts to prove to each other the facts of tragic events during armed hostilities, to establish trust among the members of the Caucasus Forum, and an understanding of a shared mission – to work for a long-term peace through cooperation with each other, to find ways to rehabilitate and develop their societies.

The network was a microcosm or model of the Caucasus open and latent conflicts. The members – among whom were both NGOs and individual experts – articulated in words and behaviour all the nuances of the roots of conflicts, which for the most part remain internalised, but which are key to escalating conflict potential into open warfare. Analytical discussions sometimes took an emotional turn.

The dynamics of relations within the network highlighted the main contradictions between the parties, how these contradictions are perceived by the different parties, how they see each other through the prism of conflict and how they see themselves through the eyes of their neighbours observing their conflict. Furthermore, the network provided an example of how relations between the societies could develop in reality, and what needs to be done to bring the parties closer to understanding the conflict, and how to transform it. Everyone learnt from one another, perspectives changed, new insights gained and understanding evolved to a new level.

The basic ground rule was an understanding that the members did not participate as representatives of their societies, but only as themselves as individuals, which removed some obstacles to participation, making it easier for participants to speak more freely and be open to others. Not being expected to carry public responsibility was especially relevant for individuals participating in dialogue in the presence of individuals from the opposing, 'enemy' party, allowing more room for manoeuvring group dynamics.

Just as network members influenced each other through their interactions, so did they influence their home communities. Network members' reputation and social capital was an important factor in ensuring this style of communication and the filtering of pan-Caucasian cooperation into the internal public discourse in the individual members' respective societies. Again, we can observe a replication of the Soviet model of public leadership – if the first civil leaders came from within the national elites of the respective societies, they also gathered motivated and talented people around them, forming a new 'national elite' – active civil society and the NGO sector.

Achieving practical results: pan-Caucasus associations

The move to discuss broader issues raised public expectations. Participants in dialogues recognised the need to achieve some practical results, to meet the immediate needs of the societies. To this purpose, the Caucasus Forum started to establish spin-off networks of people with common professional interests or common experiences of war.

Various Caucasus-wide associations were established, such as the Caucasus Business and Development Network, the Caucasian Women's League, and networks of ex-combatants, people with disabilities, cultural figures and young journalists. These networks became platforms for different initiatives aimed at bringing practical changes for their respective target groups, in terms of their social, economic opportunities or professional capacities. Such practical, tangible benefits arising from a dialogue process helped to popularise and build support for the Caucasus Forum across the Caucasus and the Commonwealth of Independent States more widely.

Ex-combatants' network

Ex-combatants were one particularly influential social class, enjoying considerable authority, rights and reputation among the population – essentially an informal second power after the government. Civil society leaders determined to transform social and political life took a strategic step in engaging them in dialogue in search of peaceful coexistence. The ex-combatants' network worked to create an accessible environment for disabled veterans and to create employment opportunities, enabling them to reintegrate fully into their communities. Their initiatives reached out also to others facing similar barriers, including people with disabilities who were not war veterans.

This approach, supporting ex-combatants' reintegration into peacetime society, even while the societies remained psychologically in war-mode, pursued several goals. Primarily it was physical, psychological and social rehabilitation for war victims. Through the positive example of disabled people's rehabilitation, they sent a message to the rest of society that they can change a lot through their own efforts. Furthermore, ex-combatants' high standing in society meant they had a platform to promote the idea that the conflicts could only be resolved through peaceful means. They could endorse dialogue processes and the idea of cooperation with the 'enemy', whom they themselves had recently fought on the battlefield, and in doing so shatter the militaristic mood of the societies. In turn, this created space for bilateral dialogues, such as the Georgian–Abkhazian and Armenian–Azerbaijani dialogues. The public message was that if ex-combatants who sacrificed their health on the battlefield for the nation were engaging in dialogue with the 'enemy', then it must be patriotic – giving some immunity to bilateral dialogue participants, shielding them somewhat from coming under pressure from both their authorities and their societies.

Caucasian Women's League

Another example is that of the Caucasian Women's League, which brought together some Caucasus Forum members with new participants identified through the network's activities in the region. The Women's League raised issues faced by women in conflict and post-conflict societies. For example, in the Georgian–Abkhazian context, Women's League members raised humanitarian issues and established mechanisms to respond to the infringement of minority rights. Under the auspices of the League, they organised bilateral meetings of Georgian and Abkhazian women, including one significant meeting with the participation of the two foreign ministers from both sides which took place in the UK in July 2003. This meeting discussed minority rights, on the basis of which they developed approaches at both the official and civil levels to protect the rights of national minorities, to cooperate with women's organisations in relieving tension in the Gal/i district of Abkhazia.

The network raised the issue of the role of women in post-Soviet Caucasus. The diversity of cultures and religions in the Caucasus even in Soviet times determined attitudes towards women in its different parts. Gender equality was declared, but the reality was far from it. With the traumatic collapse of the USSR and the subsequent conflicts, a search for a new identity redefined attitudes towards gender often quite radically. The societies viewed themselves as moving back towards the traditions lost during the Soviet period. However, their notion of 'tradition' was interpreted very freely, without serious academic support, and often depended on what goals were pursued by those who were imposing their ideas of 'tradition'.

The conflicts – both latent and violent – have been particularly harsh in dictating social norms and gender roles. The stereotypical role of the Caucasian man was reduced to that of protector and warrior, while the role of woman was to support her husband, bear children and look after the home. Women's active social role, which was nominally given to her by the Soviet authorities, was taken away, and male dominance further strengthened. This trend has minimised woman's influence on conflict dynamics, while her role in supporting conflict, to be its rear guard, fulfilling its social obligations, has increased.

However, women make up the larger part of active civil society. They have provided a role model for how it should be. Through their personal example women civil society leaders have been able to make an influence on some radical trends in relation to gender social roles.

Joint monitoring missions: conflict prevention

Another successful area of the Caucasus Forum's work was combining efforts to influence de-escalation of conflicts within the region when they arose. This required analytical and advocacy skills, to persuade different stakeholders to take preventive action – the respective authorities, civil society and international actors. Caucasus Forum members included academics and analysts who took on the role of monitoring escalations and through this the Caucasus Forum were able to carry out early response and prevention initiatives which had a huge public political and public resonance.

One such monitoring mission was in response to events in the disputed Kodor/i Gorge in October 2001 when a gang of paramilitaries led by Chechen warlord, Ruslan Gelayev, invaded, causing great alarm in Abkhazia and around the Georgian–Abkhaz conflict – an event which could have provoked a renewed armed escalation of the conflict. The Caucasus Forum had already carried out several monitoring missions: to Karachay-Cherkessia in 1999 and the Pankisi Gorge in 2000, but this was the first such monitoring that was carried out immediately during a deterioration of the armed conflict.

This event was interpreted very differently by the media in Abkhazia, Georgia, Russia and the West, giving the situation even more manipulative overtones, increasing the risks, and those parties in favour of war tried to use it to their advantage.

Understanding that it is often misunderstanding of a situation and the lack of objective third-party analysis that can lead to an armed escalation, the Caucasus Forum Coordination Council sent two of its experts to the region, to interview local people and investigate what took place. The two experts (one Armenian and the other Ossetian) had no political or ethnic affiliation to the Georgian or Abkhaz context and were both approved by Georgian and Abkhazian network members. This ensured trust in the objectivity of their findings. The report they published on their return was one of the most objective analytical sources on the events and its conclusions were not challenged by either party. This played a significant role in de-escalation of the situation and raised the reputation of Caucasus Forum in particular, but more generally, of the role civil society community leaders can play in conflict prevention.

Conclusion

This chapter has examined how local intelligentsia drove the search for peace and community development in the conflict-affected regions, reaching out across the conflict divides and beyond to find allies in their mission. It focuses in particular on the phenomenon of the Caucasus Forum of NGOs, an adaptation of a traditional Caucasian method of dispute resolution for the new and emerging civil society, bringing in neighbours to mediate and facilitate each other's conflicts which became a dynamic and solidaristic pan-Caucasian network. The Forum ceased to exist as a formal structure in 2005. Although it was not planned, it had done its job. It built capacity and relationships that remain to this day, with the processes it set in place meaning that, even now, the Forum's vision is still alive.

We have shown how through various initiatives the network operated as mediator, dialogue facilitator, civil society capacity builder, early warning and conflict prevention mechanism and an engine for community development.

Our account demonstrates that the distinctions between national elite and local community leaders are false distinctions in this context. Even where there are local leaders who are not part of the elite, the national elite depend on local leaders and vice versa. The Soviet intelligentsia became the new 'civil society', and in the early years there was not always a clear division between 'authorities' and 'civil society'. As the years have progressed, the space for civil society has been squeezed, and they have once again become the new dissidents. Having been the ones who sought to prevent resumption of violence and build peace – and made significant achievements in this respect – as civil society actors they have been caught up in the new hybrid dynamic of the conflicts themselves. As recipients of foreign funding, they are designated a 'side' in the anti-Western culture wars that stem from the geopolitical stand-off between Russia and the West.

Civil actors are coming under increasing professional, political and personal pressure. Putting themselves at risk for the greater good, speaking up when others are silent, they are finding that they increasingly have to defend themselves from political and sometimes even physical attacks, and have resumed practising self-censorship as during the Soviet years. At the same time, the professionalisation of the sector, and increasing demands to produce evidence of impact, even as it becomes harder to achieve, competition for funds and low salaries are a turn-off for new people entering the sector. Civil society actors need to be able to put mechanisms in place to prevent burnout (both on a professional and personal level) and support their mental and physical wellbeing, but currently this is little recognised by donors and large institutions.

Fifteen years on from the last Forum meetings, its members look back on this experience as highly formative personally but also significant in terms of 'changing the environment', with multiple community level spin-offs that owe their origins to Forum participants. Multiple factors played a role in the demise of the Caucasus Forum. An obvious one was failure to secure funding to continue the network, both its institutionalisation and activities – but that was partly a symptom of other dynamics both within the network, between the network and International Alert in its hybrid donor/facilitator/participant role and in the political context.

The Forum came into being as a result of unique confluence of interpersonal and professional skills and expert co-facilitation which enabled individuals to develop trust in each other and International Alert, even when mistakes were made, and inevitable disagreements arose. However, as trust accumulates on an individual basis, rather than an institutional one, any change in composition of the network and personnel at International Alert was bound to influence dynamics. The network floundered as it matured. It sought to institutionalise itself (registering as a legal entity in the Netherlands), at the same time as personnel changes at International Alert and a shift in donor priorities occurred. Gevorg, in his own essay on the Forum (Ter-Gabrielyan, 2012), references one of the factors in its demise as the decline in leadership in its original form – by which he refers both to the changing motivations of the original Forum members as the context changed, as well as reflecting on his own personal influence as both 'insider' and 'outsider' facilitator, being an Armenian living outside the region representing an international NGO. He describes his success in fundraising as a result of his ability to translate post-Soviet and Caucasus problems into the language of Western concepts, and vice versa. This, we would conclude, is a problem still evident in the international/local dynamics in the region.

Notes

[1] For a comprehensive analysis of how the national elites in the Soviet republics adapted to Soviet rule, how Soviet rule strengthened national identities and facilitated the evolution of the type of nationalism that led to violent conflicts on the breakup of the Soviet Union, see Suny (1994).

[2] For an overview of the ideological framework and theories underpinning Western peacebuilding see Steinberg (2013).

References

Kobakhia, B., Javakhishvili, J., Sotieva, L. and Schofield, J. (2012) *Mediation and Dialogue in the South Caucasus: A Reflection on 15 Years of Conflict Transformation Initiatives*, London: International Alert.

Steinberg, G.M. (2013) 'The limits of peacebuilding theory', in Mac Ginty, R. (ed) *Routledge Handbook of Peacebuilding*, Abingdon: Routledge, pp 36–53.

Suny, R. (1994) *The Revenge of the Past: Nationalism, Revolution and the Collapse of the Soviet Union*, Stanford: Stanford University Press.

Ter-Gabrielyan, G. (2012) 'The experience of the Caucasus forum: An experiment in holistic peacebuilding', in B. Kobakhia, J. Javakhishvili, L. Sotieva and J. Schofield (eds) *Mediation and Dialogue in the South Caucasus: A Reflection on 15 Years of Conflict Transformation Initiatives*, London: International Alert, pp 148–94.

Yeltsin Centre (2015) Boris Yeltsin speech in Kazan as the head of the Supreme Soviet of the RSFSR, 6 August 1990, 'Boris Yeltsin: "Take as much sovereignty as you can swallow"'. Available at https://yeltsin.ru/news/boris-elcin-berite-stolko-suverineteta-skolko-smozhete-proglotit/

5

Working for social justice through community development in Nigeria

Samir Halliru

Summary

Conflicts and violent crisis are often the aftermath of poverty and other forms of social injustice prevailing within human communities. This analysis of Nigeria demonstrates that social injustice alone does not fully explain violent conflict.

The chapter critically discusses the Nigerian context, the nature of violent conflicts and their impact on communities. It also explores the ways which have been tried to mitigate the eruption or escalation of violent conflicts in Nigeria. It looks at centre-outward initiatives and suggests that where they have not worked or have had limited effect, the limited role given to community development has been a factor in their failures. Then it goes on to look at initiatives which have had a community development dimension.

It is argued that community development to promote social justice for the victims of poverty, displacement and violent conflict in Nigeria can reduce these threats to wellbeing. Freire (1993) maintained that any person who proclaims commitment to the liberation of individuals and communities from the shackles of poverty, displacement and violent crisis but is unable to enter into communion with the people, is self-deceiving. This chapter maintains that a peacebuilding process to create social justice and liberation for the victims of poverty, displacement and violent conflict needs to get closer to the poor and marginalised by engaging them in the process.

Setting the scene

The causes of violent conflicts in Nigeria

Very often the causes of conflict are contested. This is particularly true in Nigeria. It is very important to understand that violent conflict in Nigeria

Figure 5.1: Map of Nigeria

Source: https://d-maps.com/carte.php?num_car=4867&lang=en

is not all of one form or one kind of location. The conflicts have multiple and different causes.

Structural causes

There are historical and contemporary structural reasons why the potential for conflict is deeply rooted in Nigeria.

It is important to understand how Nigeria was created in the first place. The name was coined by Flora Shaw, a *Times* of London journalist in 1897. She later married Lord Lugard who was the governor of the two entities which became Nigeria in 1914. Lord Lugard described it as a forced marriage between the north and south of what became Nigeria. He was also the author of the famous Dual Mandate which essentially justified the imposition of a paternalist and authoritarian model of social development on the people of Britain's colonies and the economic exploitation of their resources. Lugard also set out (though he did not invent) the principle of 'indirect rule' in which local administration would largely be in the hands of people he called local 'chiefs'. Where chiefs could not be identified, lacked any kind of authority or were not acceptable to the colonial authorities, 'warrant' or proxy chiefs were installed (Lugard, 1926; McCaslin, 2018; Cheeseman et al, 2019). These concepts were fundamental to later colonial development, even if they were not always implemented (Ikime, 1968). One example of the impact of British colonial policy is that it encouraged a sense of division between the north and the south, with southerners more educated than the northerners, which has been the basis of subsequent 'conflictual identity formation and discriminatory practices'. European missionaries settled first in the south. In northern Nigeria Islamic education was already well-established. Originally, the northerners resisted Western education but later it become accepted with missionary schools all over the north (Osaghae and Suberu, 2005). In the first place the northerners resisted Western education because it was brought by Christian missionaries. Fafunwa (2019) observed that this antipathy towards education was based on the view that Western education was solely the Christianisation of the locals. When the government took over schools run by the missionaries, the issues of non-acceptance of Western education were mitigated. Although they are not representative of many Muslims who do accept Western education, given this context, it is perhaps not surprising that a minority of Muslims have made resistance to Western education central to their violent campaigns in northern Nigeria in the 21st century.

The historical legacy is reflected in the contemporary institutional structure of Nigeria. The boundaries of the geopolitical zones (regions) and states are largely those defined in the colonial era but the balance between the centre and the states has changed over time. For example, both periods of centralisation under military rule and attempts to strengthen states might have exacerbated or even caused conflicts (Ahmed and Dantata, 2016). Although federal structures are often designed or said to be a mechanism for promoting the inclusion of minorities, they can have the opposite effect by allowing states to discriminate against minorities within their areas (Tarr et al, 2004). An example is the settler–indigene feud between Indigenes and Hausa settlers, in Plateau State. There are people on both sides who use violence to address their conflicting interests. Who 'started it' and whether both or neither sides have legitimacy in using violence and the forms of violence, is contested.

As is also the case in many other conflicts in this book, majoritarian or plurality based (first-past-the-post) electoral systems which do not protect the interests of minorities can amplify disadvantage and discrimination (Reynolds, 2006). In Nigeria public revenue is overwhelmingly collected federally and distributed to the states (Osaghae and Suberu, 2005). The difficulties with this are explored in the section on 'Interventions by the federal government in Nigeria'.

Inequality, poverty, economic and environmental competition

Felix (2016) argues that violent conflicts in Nigeria are mainly based on the conditions of human insecurity such as poverty, unemployment, hunger and environmental challenges.

Nigeria's wealth is very unequally distributed but this is not necessarily reflected in official and international data. Poverty rates remain high in Nigeria, with over 40 per cent of the population being poor. This shows a considerable drop from the 64 per cent poverty profile that was recorded in the Nigeria Living Standards Survey (NLSS) in 2003–4 but is still high in global terms and in relation to many other African countries. In 2018 it had a Gini coefficient of 35.1 (where 0 is a completely equal society and 100 is extreme inequality). Compared to the rest of sub-Saharan Africa this is not highly unequal. However, the measure does not reflect young people or differences between males and females, north and south, urban and rural. The causes, manifestations and measures necessary to stop violence against women and young people are often different to those in relation to adult men. Issues like the international trafficking of women and children (more common from the south of Nigeria), often for sexual exploitation, widespread female genital mutilation and structural violence such as the absence of legal rights or education opportunities for girls and women are not measured by gross domestic product and other monetary measures (World Bank nd; Felix, 2016; Ojelabi, 2020).

The Niger Delta conflict is the most obviously resource-related conflict – fighting over who wins and who loses from the extraction of oil. This is discussed further in the section on religious linguistic and ethnic divisions. Even the most widespread violent conflicts are only partly related to inequality and poverty: most obviously, conflicts between nomads/pastoralists and farmers, or indigene–settler conflicts reflect environmental challenges too. However, environmental conflicts are rarely independent of other issues. There may be environmental degradation, a scarcity or an abundance of natural resources to fight over, but the issues of whose land or water it is reflect social identities too. Obioha (2008) has analysed a number of 'environmental' conflicts in northeast Nigeria, noting the differences in what they are about and who they are between.

Farmers and herders have long-standing conflicts with each other, claiming lives and property with cattle rustling and kidnappings. The conflicts between herders (pastoralists) and farmers are mostly caused by resources (mines, farms and reserves) and eco-zonal conflict over water, grazing and hunting rights as well as environmental degradation, resource scarcity, demographic and climate change (Blench, 2004, 2010; Shettima and Tar, 2008; Gwary et al, 2017). Conflict often relates to Fadama lands[1] which were left uncultivated, especially for use as dry season grazing reserves by herders. Over the years, these reserves and cattle routes were either encroached by, or sold to, farmers. These situations built up tensions and serious conflicts between farmers and herders which have, over the years, led to police and court cases. Unable to get justice as they saw it through those mechanisms, the herders have resorted to banditry (discussed later in the chapter) and kidnapping for ransom. The northern western states covering Zamfara, Sokoto, Kaduna, Niger and Katsina are the epicentre of kidnapping and killings. Olaniyi and Terzungwe (2020) report that 344 students were kidnapped in Kankara secondary school in Katsina State by armed bandits. The state's ineffectiveness, reluctance to uphold law and complicity in law-breaking, also demonstrate the blurring of boundaries between state, non-state and anti-state violence.

Religious, linguistic and ethnic divisions

As Mamdani (1999) says, indirect rule was based on two political identities, one based on 'race' homogenised and unified people as 'natives', the other fragmented, or divided people by ethnicity. Ranger (1993) highlights that it was central to imperial control (hegemony) to invent categories such as 'African' and to differentiate people by religion, ethnicity and language. Nonetheless there is real diversity in social identities: at least 250 identifiable ethnic groups and 500-plus languages. However, Yoruba, Hausa, Igbo and Fulani people account for over half the population and English is an official language. It is important to recognise that ethnicity, language and religion are all dynamic social constructions, often defined mainly by their relationship to an 'other', so identities may fuse or separate. Crude characterisations of which groups people belong to and who they are in conflict with do not always endure (Osaghae and Suberu, 2005).

Homogenising religious groups in Nigeria illustrates this. According to the World Fact Book, the population of Nigeria in 2018 was 53.5 per cent Muslim, 10.6 per cent Roman Catholic, 35.3 per cent other Christians, and 0.6 per cent were other religions (Central Intelligence Agency, nd). Neither Muslim nor Christian communities are homogeneous. There are conflicts within each broad faith as well as between them. There are strong geographical patterns of location of different communities but in some places their location is contested. The conflict with Boko Haram, originally in the northeast of Nigeria, is the most obviously religion-based conflict but it is not the only one. The overlap between religious, ethnic and socioeconomic identities in Nigeria is illustrated by, for example, the composite identity of 'Muslim Hausa settlers' on the one hand and 'Christian Plateau indigenes' on the other (Felix, 2016).

Bagaji et al (2011) argued that the triggering events for violence in the Niger Delta region are two key cleavages between ethnic and religious identity groups. The first is cleavage at the national level, the difference between the north and south, and sometimes religious differences between the Muslim Hausa-Fulani north and the Christian south. The second type of cleavage, which is triggering violence in the Niger Delta, are local feuds, which create interethnic and inter-community conflicts. Brunner (2002) noted that the central dimension of the conflicts in the Niger Delta region is the struggle between the major ethnic groups, the Ijaw, Itsekiri, Urhobo and Andoni, who are regarded as landowners and holders of the local power.

The nature of violence

Nigeria reflects Galtung's categorisations of 'Personal, Structural and Cultural' violence (Galtung, 1969; Felix, 2016). Over the years, the country has experienced various types of violence. The nature of the violent conflicts experienced varies between regions, states and communities within Nigeria. Felix also notes that different kinds of violence are closely knitted together, similar to the idea of confluence in Chapter 3 in this volume, on Colombia. Nigeria also reflects Galtung's analysis of conflict being at times latent and at times breaking out into open violence.

Examples of this include:

- The indigene–settler conflict in Plateau State and Niger Delta region conflicts: Plateau indigenes see the Hausa people settling as a threat to their economic security. However, some of the people regarded as 'settlers' might have lived/settled in the area in question for more than 200 years.

Historically their ancestors had migrated and settled in the area, and they have no home other than their current settlement.
- Direct or open violence is expressed in the form of verbal and physical attacks and land disputes. Farmer–herder clashes spill over into electoral-cum-political violence (Segun, 2013; Theophilus et al, 2013; Felix, 2016).
- Recently, during the EndSARs protests (against police brutality in Lagos State), particular ethnic groups were attacked. This has often led to the escalation of violent conflicts across the country with the aggrieved parties carrying out reprisal attacks, killings and vandalising properties. Cultural violence involves deconstructed religious sentiments, customs, traditions and cultural beliefs that lead to escalation of violent conflicts (Felix, 2016).
- As Osaghae and Suberu (2005) point out, different identities become salient, are mobilised and politicised at different times. A conflict may morph from an ethnicity-based identity to a religious or geographical one and may move in and out of being violent.

The term 'banditry' is widely used in Nigeria, going back to the beginning of the 20th century though its scale has escalated in recent years. It refers to actions such as armed kidnapping, cattle rustling, and village or market raids. It involves the threat of, or actual, force. It may involve rape or killings. Very importantly it covers both politically and economically motivated actions and may or may not be associated with identity-based conflicts. It can be urban or rural (Okoli and Ugwu, 2019).

As Akpan and colleagues point out, there is a strong gender dimension to violence and peacebuilding in Nigeria:

- how violence and peace are defined – often with violence against women being ignored;
- formal peacebuilding efforts generally being male-dominated;
- sometimes the wellbeing and liberty of women are sacrificed in the interests of peace – as in Chinua Achebe's famous novel *Things Fall Apart* published in 1957 (Akpan et al, 2014).

Local and regional patterns

The Plateau conflict is replicated in other states. Similar situations were also seen in Kaduna and Osun States. The conflict between the people of the towns of Ife and Modakeke in Osun State in Southwestern Nigeria is an example of a conflict which has ethnic and indigene–settler dimensions to it, where the conflicts have not gone away entirely, but where the violence has subsided in the last 20 years (IDEA, 2001; Kabir, 2020).

In the northeastern region, the major issue affecting the area is Boko Haram. In the northwest it is farmer–herder conflicts and more recently banditry and kidnappings (Azad et al, 2018). These issues are unleashing serious violence, conflict and displacement to many communities in the north. Boko Haram violent conflicts left both Muslims and Christians alike as victims of insurgency through killings and displacement. For example, on 30 November 2020, 43 rice farmers were killed while harvesting their crops at rice fields in the Garin Kwashebe area of the Borno State. Boko Haram said they had done it because, they claimed, the farmers had no right to be there (Lere, 2020).

Global attention was paid to the kidnapping of the Chibok girls in 2014 and subsequent school and college kidnappings, some clearly not by Boko Haram but by economically motivated bandits. Evidence shows that women and girls who were displaced by Boko Haram conflict were sexually abused, including rape and exploitation (Human Rights Watch, 2016). The impact of such insurgencies has been noted by Hegre and colleagues (2012). Family and community systems are mostly destroyed through targeting women, the recruitment of children into rebel groups, massive displacements, and losses of life and properties. It can be argued that when children are separated from their families and communities, it raises the potential of people becoming more exposed to poverty and violence. Conflict disrupts social networks thereby leading to social dislocation, and a decline in interpersonal and communal group trust (Hegre et al, 2012).

The violence in northeast Nigeria is part of a bigger crisis. According to UNHCR (2020), the Lake Chad Basin region is struggling with humanitarian crisis with over 3.4 million people being displaced, including over 2.7 million internally displaced persons (IDPs) in northeastern Nigeria, over 684,000 IDPs in Cameroon, Chad and Niger, and 294,000 refugees in the four countries. Although part of the northeast had been captured by the insurgents, the Nigerian military has regained control in some parts. Civilians in Nigeria, Chad, Cameroon and Niger continue to be affected by poverty, displacement, violation of human rights and forced recruitment into the activities of Boko Haram (UNHCR, 2020).

Interventions

Interventions by the federal government

The federal government in Nigeria has initiated various programmes to try to promote economic and social development and address political tensions within the country. These programmes provide evidence on whether it is possible and effective to reduce violence by improving economic and social conditions.

The Niger Delta Development Commission (NDDC) was established in 2000 on the basis of a law which guaranteed a special allocation of 13 per cent of the federal budget to the southern oil-producing states. This was meant to address a long-standing grievance which is that the states generate a disproportionate share of government revenue. People there feel that not only do they not get a fair share back, but they suffer disproportionately from the oil industry, including the impact of pollution on the environment and human health. The south, often supported by the government, has perceived the north as parasites. The crisis within the Delta region has continued to claim lives and properties with the significant impact that threatens the stability of the Nigerian economy (Bagaji et al, 2011; Adedayo, 2018). The conflict has led to kidnappings and killings (of expatriates and settlers) as well as the damage and destruction of major government structures. The conflict around the region started as a struggle to save the region from environmental challenges, including gas flaring, caused by the crude oil exploration in the Delta region. Adedayo (2018) observes that unrelenting agitations within the Delta region has turned the region into a trouble spot of pipeline sabotage, kidnapping and armed struggles for more than three decades. In 2015–16, the activities of Niger Delta Avengers (a militant group) reduced crude oil production from 2.2 million barrels per day to about 800,000. This has had a negative impact on the Nigerian economy, which is highly dependent on oil as a source of revenue generation. Unfortunately, the NDDC has not resolved the tensions. It is seen as corrupt and incompetent by many observers, but some attribute its failures specifically to lack of local engagement (Isidiho and Sabran, 2015).

The government has also implemented World Bank funded projects such as the Local Empowerment and Environmental Management Project (LEEMP) and the Community and Social Development Programme. The design for both was led by the International Development Association.

LEEMP was not intended to contribute to conflict resolution but to address economic and social development needs by strengthening the participation of local people. It was designed to promote action at federal, state and, particularly, local government levels to support environmentally sustainable and socially inclusive development, and promote state beneficiaries' participation in the planning, co-financing and implementation of multi-sectoral micro-projects. The end-of-project evaluation by the World Bank was sceptical about its outcomes (Independent Evaluation Group, 2011). There are a series of evaluations of specific state or local LEEMP projects, most of which focus on the poverty reduction outcomes where there were some successes. Data on the extent of local participation has tended to focus on the numbers of participants rather than on the quality or depth of participation.

The initial programme of the Community and Social Development Project (CSDP) was intended to sustainably increase the access of poor people to social and natural resource infrastructure services across 26 states. The World Bank favourably evaluated the programme. A second element of the programme was added in 2015 to help finance the costs to scale up activities in the six northeast states of Nigeria, which have been ravaged by the Boko Haram insurgency. Overall, it is addressing the consequences of violent conflict by social protection measures. For example, funds are to be used to provide trauma and psychosocial support to returnee households and internally displaced groups and individuals. It is described as Community Driven Development (CDD) and claims to be promoting 'participatory decision making at the local level (the participatory community planning process)', empowering 'communities to allocate scarce resources across sectors and strengthening the ability of the communities to control valuable resources' (International Development Association, 2016: 14). In fact the strategy of the programme and the rules for what money can be spent on were devised in Washington and the federal government controls overall spending. Analysts of participation have long been concerned that participation initiated by powerful state or non-state actors can be manipulative, coercive or fake – what are actually top-down projects masquerade as grassroots or 'local' projects – masking centralisation or playing off local interests against each other (Cooke and Kothari, 2002; Tarr et al, 2004; McNutt and Boland, 2007).

One interpretation of the experience of these programmes is that economic and social development programmes cannot bypass the political problems which are both cause and effect of the socioeconomic situation. Specifically, top-down programmes without real local engagement may not even succeed in their economic and social reconstruction, after violence and destruction, let alone contribute to wider notions of peacebuilding.

Interventions by leaders within established power structures

A second strategy for bringing about peace and stability within areas affected by conflict is work led by established civic, religious or ethnic leaders.

There have been dialogues between the three major religions: Islam, Christianity and Traditional Indigenous, in an effort to promote cooperation, harmony and tolerance without which there might be continued violence. Ahmad (2011) maintained that interfaith dialogue is one of the best options to tackle the recurrence of religious conflict in Nigeria.

The International Dialogue Centre (KAICIID) is an inter-governmental organisation set up by Saudi Arabia. In 2017 the International Dialogue Centre (2019) sought to build bridges between diverse communities. The Interfaith Dialogue Forum for Peace (IDFP) was the result of consultations with over 80 stakeholders and local partners to promote sustainable peace. It funds projects working with marginalised groups, such as women and young people, and advocates for policy change and the targeting of policy-makers in this process. It succeeded in an interreligious action plan to support social cohesion through:

- interfaith education;
- the freedom of religion and the protection of holy sites;
- interfaith exchanges and media sensitisation; and
- countering hate speech.

The activities of International Dialogue in peacebuilding in the areas affected by violent conflicts has included:

- Visits to communities in Kaduna State, Plateau State, Taraba State, Benue State and Zamfara State affected by tensions between farming and pastoralist groups.
- A high-level intrafaith roundtable meeting on the deradicalisation of extremist tendencies in Nigeria, resulting in a roadmap and a consensus working document for further implementation by the Muslim community.
- A roundtable for Muslim and Christian students on the prevention of hate speech.
- A workshop for women which raised awareness on hate speech and incitement to violence, and equipped participants with tools to foster peace.
- Training for 120 Nigerian young people on the positive role of religion in peacebuilding within their communities (The International Dialogue Centre, 2019).

It is clear that these initiatives have tried to address some of the criticisms of work done within existing power structures, noting they are often elitist, patriarchal or 'academic' rather than practice-focused (Ahmad, 2011). On the other hand, although events for young people and women were included, it seems as though the numbers of people involved and the level at which they occurred precluded popular participation.

The Nigerian government and non-governmental organisations have also promoted community conferencing, known as town hall meetings, with relevant stakeholders with a view to address violent conflicts in Nigeria. This involves training both religious and traditional civic rulers (such as district heads, ward heads and unit heads) in how to facilitate community conferencing. Local imams have traditionally conveyed messages during daily prayers or through Friday sermons. As many attend these religious gatherings, it is a relatively easy way to extend messages and communicate with the actors in the community space. Traditional leaders have adjudicated on disputes among local people. While there is no doubt that some local people, particularly adult men, may well attend mosque prayers or traditional civic meetings, women and children may be excluded from the traditional forms of civic participation. However, sometimes traditional leaders work in partnership with a neutral or independent third party who can gather evidence to help settle conflicts (Abbas, 2018). A recent example of mediation involved a third party with a group which had been involved in violent activities who wanted to make amends for previous actions, by facilitating the release of students kidnapped by other groups.

Community-based approaches

Community development in Nigeria has a number of distinct origins which may merge, diverge or be in opposition to one another:

- Long-standing practices of collective action and community learning which pre-dated and survived colonial rule.
- Colonial government practices evident from the first years of the 20th century onwards in various guises including colonial development, agricultural extension and mass education.
- Missionary work, particularly in areas such as health and education.
- Decolonisation and other emancipatory movements.
- Post-independence national and international government and non-governmental/civil society initiatives (Smyth, 2004; Onyekwelu, 2018).

Some of these actively fuelled divisions and fomented (violent) conflict; others have ignored them, and some have tried to overcome them. These cleavages included north/south, urban/rural, religion, ethnicity, gender and wealth. The top-down, centre-outwards legacy of colonialism, mission-educated elites and international donor programmes has been hard to overcome (Charles, 2018). A survey of local government officers in Nigeria's northern states carried out in 1980 showed that development officers believed that they knew best, and that development was primarily about doing things for and to people, with their cooperation but not necessarily with them in control (Hay et al, 1990). Many programmes focus on building health, education, transport or housing infrastructures or material outputs such as poverty reduction. A study of community perspectives on peacebuilding in some of the areas most affected by the Boko Haram insurgency found that 'local populations feel their fears, needs and concerns are not properly considered in national and international responses to the insurgency. Communities resent this exclusion and feel it leads to ineffective and inappropriate programming that fails to reach the most vulnerable sections of society, and in some cases makes the situation worse' (Kukah Centre and Conciliation Resources, 2018: 2).

However, a number of programmes have put more emphasis on substantive participation of communities in defining ends and means as well as delivering programmes.

On the one hand there is evidence of how women and young people are marginalised in a lot of development practice in Nigeria (Akpan, 2015).

On the other hand there are good examples of how both groups have been involved in community-led peacebuilding.

Umuada

One instance of how a long-standing traditional community development practice has evolved to meet new challenges including addressing conflict is Umuada (or Umuokpu; 'the powerful daughters') in the predominantly Igbo states of Nigeria (Arogo et al, 2017). Obasi and Nnamani (2015) have argued that these community-level women's associations play an important role in conflict management and development using methods which are recognisable in the global literature of people such as Jean Paul Lederach and John Burton. They argue that the Umuada use both conciliation and dialogue methods but also arbitration and insistence that however serious the conflict is, using force to resolve it, or departure from social rules, is unacceptable (Obasi and Nnamani, 2015).

Women's informal peacebuilding in northeast Nigeria

Another example of women leading a community development approach to peacebuilding is in the Internally displaced persons (IDP) camps in Borno State in the north of Nigeria. Women have been involved in the reintegration of girls who have been abducted and raped by Boko Haram, relief work, protecting men and boys from attacks and capacity building for women to develop skills to earn a livelihood (Imam et al, 2020).

Hope Interactive

Hope Interactive has been in existence for 20 years. It operates in northern Nigeria. It aims to promote economic, social and cultural development through civil society organisations by research, advocacy, community development and learning opportunities. It is supported by the UK peacebuilding organisation, Conciliation Resources, among other international organisations as well as local statutory, private and non-governmental organisations.

Among its many programmes are Women 4 Peace, which has initiated Women Mediators across the commonwealth of Nigeria (WMC) and Smart Peace (Hope Interactive, nda, ndb).

WMC is a network of women with experience of mediating conflicts at the community level to formally mediating conflicts as part of official peace processes. They target the most highly marginalised women within vulnerable communities. These women face stigmatisation, because they have experienced gender-based violence, been accused of perpetrating extreme violence, had children or spouses associated with Boko Haram, or have abused drugs or other substances or been sex workers. The programme creates women-only storytelling and listening spaces across conflict divides. The process therefore provides a platform for reconciliation and greater mutual understanding between different identity groups. The programme aims to develop the confidence and skills of marginalised women to express themselves and challenge societal barriers at the community, local government and state levels (Hope Interactive, nda).

Borno Coalition on Democracy and Progress

Borno Coalition on Democracy and Progress (BOCODEP) is another organisation supported by Conciliation Resources. It was founded in 1993 to promote peaceful coexistence, democracy and human rights in Nigeria (BOCODEP, nd).

One of its projects is called 'Peace by the People', also known as 'Youth Peace Platform' (YPP). The rationale for the project is the exclusion and stigmatisation of young people in northeast Nigeria. Exclusion from political, social and economic decision-making leads to increasing disengagement from society and makes young people prime targets for mobilisation by Boko Haram and other armed non-state actors. They are then blamed by government, security officials and local communities as the architects of violence.

BOCODEP's strategy is to help young people gain control to find their own creative, alternative paths away from violence. The project works by asking young people what they need and what challenges they face.

It supports a network of face-to-face and digital youth coalitions committed to promoting messages of tolerance. Young people receive training, mentoring and other support. The programme works to build young people's confidence and resilience, helping them process the traumas of their past, and their ability to analyse conflicts. By doing this they are better able to voice their needs and concerns to overcome the stereotypes and develop trust and understanding between the young people, their communities and the state (Conciliation Resources, nd).

Conclusion

Nigeria faces considerable challenges to transform people from being ethnic, cultural, sectional or regional jingoists to agents capable of shaping their lives and the lives of others based on shared identity. It is necessary to create justice for the victims of poverty, conflicts and displacement to create a sustainable peace. Best (2007) argues that it is crucial to address poverty, displacement, forced migration and further escalation of violent conflicts.

Community development is a key part of the process of addressing injustice and conflict. Peacebuilding and empowerment requires working with people to raise critical consciousness (Freire, 1993) and with opportunities and power to understand and challenge ideologies, structures and cultural practices that plunge them into violence and conflicts. Lifelong education is central to this. Allman (1999) argued that creating a new ethics of harmonious existence and a lasting transformation can only occur through critical learning, especially when alternative understanding and values are experienced in-depth (seriously, subjectively, and cognitively or intellectually). McLaren (1998) has argued that efforts to engage in the struggle for humanisation with the aim of addressing escalators of conflicts (including social injustice) have many elements. These include, but are not limited to:

- good intentions from both internal and external mediators of peace;
- consciousness of social solidarity and social interdependence;
- international in scope and composition;
- a strong philosophy of critical education for social transformation; and
- a revolutionary movement of educators and students who are informed by the principled ethics of compassion and social justice.

Peacebuilding needs to draw on, or tap into, the skills, energy and motivation of everyone, especially the poorest, most marginalised and excluded communities. It must change the relationship between the most disadvantaged, stigmatised and even demonised, communities and the formal institutions (international, national and local state, private and non-governmental), which typically see these people as the problem, beneficiaries or dependents, and not as partners, or co-producers, in the solution.

Note
[1] Fadama is the Hausa name for irrigable, low-lying plains fed by shallow aquifers found along major river systems.

References
Abbas, A.I. (2018) 'Peace and conflict resolution in Nigeria: An imperative tool for countering violent extremism', Paper presented at the National Conference on Peace Building, Security, Sustainable Development and Reconstruction of North Eastern Nigeria, organised by Nigerian Political Science Association North East Zone, at Federal University Kashere, April.

Adedayo, A. (2018) 'Niger Delta crisis and Amnesty programme implementation in Nigeria, Uyo', *Journal of Sustainable Development*, 3(1): 209–23.

Ahmad, A.T. (2011) 'The importance of interreligious dialogue in Nigeria: (Muslim- Christian relations)', *International Journal of Muslim Unity*, 9 (1–2): 67–102.

Ahmed, I.K and Dantata, B.S. (2016) 'Federalism and national integration: The Nigerian experience', *Historical Research Letter*, 35: 8–13. Available at https://core.ac.uk/download/pdf/234668708.pdf

Akpan, F., Olofu-Adeoye, A. and Ering, S.O. (2014) 'Women and peace building in Nigeria', *African Journal of Social Sciences*, 4(1): 170–82. Available at https://irepos.unijos.edu.ng/jspui/bitstream/123456789/2700/1/ajss2014akpan002.pdf

Akpan, N.S. (2015) 'Women and rural development in Nigeria: Some critical issues for policy consideration', *Social Sciences*, 4(5): 110–18.

Allman, P. (1999) *Revolutionary Social Transformation: Democratic Hopes, Political Possibilities and Critical Education*, London: Bergin & Harvey.

Arogo, A., Ohanaka, O., Diekedie, A., Ephraim-Emmanuel, B. and Apiakise, E. (2017) 'The impact of Umuada Group (The Powerful Daughters) in Umuorah-Umuohiri', *Asian Research Journal of Arts & Social Sciences*, 4(4): 1–10.

Azad, A., Crawford, E. and Kaila, H. (2018) *Conflict and Violence in Nigeria: Results from the North East, North Central, and South Zones*, World Bank/National Bureau of Statistics. Available at https://documents1.worldbank.org/curated/en/111851538025875054/pdf/130198-WP-P160999-PUBLIC-26-9-2018-14-42-49-ConflictViolenceinNigeriaResultsfromNENCSSzonesFinal.pdf

Bagaji, A.S.Y., Achegbulu, J.O., Maji, A. and Yakubu, N. (2011) 'Explaining the violent conflicts in Nigeria's Niger Delta: Is the rentier state theory and the resource-curse thesis relevant?', *Canadian Social Science*, 7(4): 34–43.

Best, S.G. (2007) 'Methods of conflict and conflict transformation', in S.G. Best (ed) *Introduction to Peace and Conflict Studies in West Africa: A Reader*, Ibadan: Spectrum Books, pp 18–34.

Blench, R.M. (2004) *Natural Resource Conflicts in North-Central Nigeria*, London: Mandaras.

Blench, R.M. (2010) *Conflict between Pastoralists and Cultivators in Nigeria: A Review Paper Prepared for DFID, Nigeria*, Cambridge: Kay Williamson Educational Foundation.

BOCODEP (nd) *About Us*. Available at https://bocodep.wordpress.com/about-us/

Brunner, M. (2002) *The Unfinished State: Democracy and Ethnicity in Nigeria*, Hamburg: IAK.

Central Intelligence Agency (nd) *Nigeria*. Available at https://www.cia.gov/the-world-factbook/countries/nigeria/

Charles, S. (2018) 'Problems and prospects of community development in Nigeria', *Infoguide Nigeria*. Available at https://infoguidenigeria.com/problems-prospects-community-development-nigeria-2/

Cheeseman, N., Bertrand, E. and Husain, S. (2019) *A Dictionary of African Politics*, Oxford: Oxford University Press.

Conciliation Resources (nd) *Young People Prevent Violence in Northeast Nigeria*. Available at https://www.c-r.org/our-work-in-action/young-people-prevent-violence-northeast-nigeria

Cooke, B. and Kothari, U. (eds) (2002) *Participation: The New Tyranny?* London: Zed Books.

Fafunwa, A.B. (2019) *History of Education in Nigeria*, Abingdon: Routledge.

Felix, I.O. (2016) 'Violence in Nigeria: Nature and extent', *International Journal of Arts and Humanities*, 5(1): 72–85.

Freire, P. (1993) *Pedagogy of the Oppressed*, 30th anniversary edn, New York: Continuum Books.

Galtung, J. (1969) 'Violence, peace and peace research', *Journal of Peace Research*, 3: 167–92.

Gwary, M.M., Mai-Jir, M.M., Mustapha, S.B., Makinta, A.A. and Galadima, B.K. (2017) 'Influence of socio-economic factors on involvement in conflict among natural resources users in Yunusari local government area of Yobe state, Nigeria', *Journal of Sociology*, 1(1): 8–16.

Hay, R., Koehn, P. and Koehn, E. (1990) 'Community development in Nigeria: Prevailing orientations among local government officials', *Community Development Journal*, 25(2): 147–60.

Hegre, H., Nygard, H.M. and Strand, H. (2012) 'Development consequences of armed conflict', *World Development*, 40 (9): 1713–22.

Hope Interactive (nda) *Smart Peace*. Available at http://www.h-interactive.org/438882770

Hope Interactive (ndb) *Women for Peace*. Available at http://www.h-interactive.org/437975455

Human Rights Watch (2016) *Nigeria: Officials Abusing Displaced Women, Girls Displaced by Boko Haram and Victims Twice Over*. Available at https://www.hrw.org/news/2016/10/31/nigeria-officials-abusing-displaced-women-girls

Ikime, O. (1968) 'Reconsidering indirect rule: The Nigerian example', *Journal of the Historical Society of Nigeria*, 4(3): 421–38.

Imam, A., Biu, H. and Yahi, M. (2020) *Women's Informal Peacebuilding in North East Nigeria*, CMI Brief, Bergen: Chr. Michelsen Institute. Available at https://www.cmi.no/publications/7296-womens-informal-peacebuilding-in-north-east-nigeria#pdf

Independent Evaluation Group (2011) *Implementation Completion Report Review Nigeria: Local Empowerment and Environmental Management Project*, Washington, DC: World Bank Group. Available at https://documents1.worldbank.org/curated/en/231461474484779281/pdf/000020051-20140624191842.pdf

Institute for Democracy and Electoral Assistance (IDEA) (2001) *Democracy in Nigeria: Continuing Dialogue(s) for Nation Building*, Stockholm: IDEA.

International Development Association (2016) *Nigeria: Community and Social Development Project*, Washington, DC: World Bank Group. Available at http://documents.worldbank.org/curated/en/649151467992818774/Nigeria-Community-and-Social-Development-Project

International Dialogue Centre (2019) *Peace and Reconciliation through Interreligious Dialogue in Nigeria*. Available at https://www.kaiciid.org/what-we-do/peace-and-reconciliation-throughinterreligious-dialogue-nigeria

Isidiho, A.O. and Sabran, M.S.B. (2015) 'Challenges facing Niger Delta Development Commission (NDDC) projects in Imo state and Niger Delta region in Nigeria', *International Journal of Humanities and Social Science*, 5(6): 37–48.

Kabir, A. (2020) 'From war to peace: How Ife, Modakeke have been living together 20 years after last bloody conflict', *Premium Times*, 31 December. Available at https://www.premiumtimesng.com/regional/ssouth-west/434152-from-war-to-peace-how-ife-modakeke-have-been-living-together-20-years-after-last-bloody-conflict.html

Kukah Centre/Conciliation Resources (2018) *Through Our Eyes: People's Perspectives on Building Peace in Northeast Nigeria*, London: Conciliation Resources. Available at https://rc-services-assets.s3.eu-west-1.amazonaws.com/s3fs-public/Through%20our%20eyes%20-%20peoples%20perspectives%20on%20building%20peace%20in%20northeast%20Nigeria.pdf

Lere, M. (2020) 'Why we killed Zabarmari farmers: Boko Haram', *Premium Times*, December 2. Available at https://www.premiumtimesng.com/news/headlines/429119-why-we-killed-zabarmari-farmers-boko-haram.html

Lugard, F. (1926) 'Part II: Special Problems – Chapter X – Methods of Ruling Native Races', in *The Dual Mandate in British Tropical Africa*, pp 193–6. Available at http://www.fafich.ufmg.br/~luarnaut/Lugard-dual%20mandate.pdf

Mamdani, M. (1999) 'Historicizing power and responses to power: Indirect rule and its reform', *Social Research*, 66(3): 859–86.

McCaslin, J. (2018) 'Lord Lugard created Nigeria 104 years ago', blog, Council on Foreign Relations. Available at https://www.cfr.org/blog/lord-lugard-created-nigeria-104-years-ago

McLaren, P. (1998) 'Revolutionary pedagogy in post-revolutionary times: Rethinking the political economy of critical education', *Education Theory*, 48(4): 431–62.

McNutt, J. and Boland, K. (2007) 'Astroturf, technology and the future of community mobilization: Implications for non-profit theory', *The Journal of Sociology & Social Welfare*, 34(3): 165–78.

Obasi, C.O. and Nnamani, R. (2015) 'The role of Umuada Igbo in conflict management and development in Nigeria', *Open Journal of Political Science*, 5(4): 256–63.

Obioha, E.E. (2008) 'Climate change, population drift and violent conflict over land resources in northeastern Nigeria', *Journal of Human Ecology*, 23(4): 311–24.

Ojelabi, F.A. (2020) 'A new framework for measuring inequality sheds light on poverty eradication in Nigeria', LSE blog, 4 November. Available at https://blogs.lse.ac.uk/africaatlse/2020/11/04/multidimensional-framework-mif-for-measuring-inequality-sheds-light-poverty-eradication-nigeria/

Okoli, A.C. and Ugwu A.C. (2019) 'Of marauders and brigands: Scoping the threat of rural banditry in Nigeria's north west', *Brazilian Journal of African Studies*, 4(8): 201–22.

Olaniyi, M and Terzungwe, S. (2020) 'Katsina school bandits' invasion: How we spent night inside bush – student', *Daily Trust*, 13 December. Available at https://dailytrust.com/katsina-school-bandits-invasion-how-we-spent-night-inside-bush-student

Onyekwelu, R.U. (2018) 'Rethinking community development: An option to Nigeria's development challenges', *International Journal of Advanced Research in Public Policy, Administration and Development Strategies*, 3(1): 65–80.

Osaghae, E.E. and Suberu, R.T. (2005) *A History of Identities, Violence, and Stability in Nigeria*, CRISE, Working Paper No. 6, January. Available at https://assets.publishing.service.gov.uk/media/57a08c9840f0b652dd00141e/wp6.pdf

Ranger, T. (1993) 'The invention of tradition revisited: The case of colonial Africa', in T. Ranger and O. Vaughan (eds) *Legitimacy and the State in Twentieth-Century Africa*, London: Palgrave Macmillan, pp 62–111.

Reynolds, A. (2006) *Electoral Systems and the Protection and Participation of Minorities*, London: Minority Rights Group International. Available at https://minorityrights.org/wp-content/uploads/old-site-downloads/download-161-Electoral-systems-and-the-protection-and-participation-of-minorities.pdf

Segun, J. (2013) 'Politics, poverty and violent conflicts: Exploring their complex nexus in Nigeria', *Developing Country Studies*, 3(7): 102–8.

Shettima, A.G. and Tar, U.A. (2008) 'Farmer-pastoralist conflict in West Africa: Exploring the causes and consequences', *Information, Society and Justice*, 1(2): 163–84.

Smyth, R.A. (2004) 'The roots of community development in colonial office policy and practice in Africa', *Social Policy & Administration*, 38(4): 418–36.

Tarr, G.A., Williams, R.F. and Marko, J. (eds) (2004) *Federalism, Subnational Constitutions, and Minority Rights*, Westport: Praeger.

Theophilus, A.T., Kingsley, C. and Aondowase, T. (2013) 'Political violence and its effects on social development in Nigeria', *International Journal of Humanities and Social Science*, 3(17): 261–6.

UNHCR (2020) *Nigeria Emergency*. Available at https://www.unhcr.org/nigeria-emergency.html

World Bank (nd) *Nigeria* https://data.worldbank.org/country/nigeria

6

Memory, truth and hope: long journeys of justice in Eastern Sri Lanka

Sarala Emmanuel and P.B. Gowthaman

Summary

This chapter places the community-based work described in the context of civil war in Sri Lanka, with roots traced back to the war of independence in 1948. The war was brought to an end in May 2009 with the use of overwhelming military force by the state, but the chapter mainly focuses on the period before this – 2002–9 – a period that saw a fragile ceasefire agreement signed between the Liberation Tigers of Tamil Eelam (LTTE) and the government of Sri Lanka, but also witnessed the recommencement of armed conflict in 2006.

Describing the challenges faced by communities in East Sri Lanka, that were directly affected by the violence, the authors describe building/developing clusters of grassroot level organisations and collectives based on community development approaches. The chapter describes how the development of sustainable economic activities had to be negotiated in conflict-affected areas as well as examining how the war disrupted gender roles, resulting in community leadership roles being held by women. Finally, the authors share their personal reflections on both the community resilience demonstrated, but also the challenges that remain.

The authors are both writing from the grounded experience of being activist-practitioners – one who worked in a mainstream international development organisation, supporting community-based partner organisations, and the other working with local feminist organisations over the past two decades.

Setting the scene

The roots of the Sri Lankan civil war can be traced back to 1948, when Sri Lanka claimed independence from more than a century of British colonial rule. In 1949, as the new nation was being imagined, close to half a million Indian-origin Tamils working in the tea plantations of Sri Lanka were disenfranchised and denied citizenship rights (Hoole et al, 1992).

This decision was taken by an interethnic elite, motivated by a desire to monopolise power in the emergent nation. In the subsequent struggle for political predominance, the initial alliances between the interethnic elites disintegrated. Despite several attempts at negotiating political autonomy and devolution of power to the northern and eastern regions of the island, which were predominantly populated by Tamil and Muslim communities, these political developments failed.

Over the period of state formation political and economic developments resulted in an escalation of grievances among minority communities. As in many protracted conflicts, the Sri Lankan conflict was rooted in myriad and complex causes. One such cause was the major development programmes, adopted as large-scale state colonisation schemes in the 1950s, through which predominantly landless Sinhala households were given plots of land in the north and east, thereby affecting minority communities (Hoole et al, 1992). This, along with the passing of the Sinhala Only Act (Official Language Act) in 1956, which made Sinhala the official language of the state (Hoole, 2016; Wickrematunge, 2016; BBC, 2019), contributed to conditions for the ethnic conflict and the subsequent protracted war. Sri Lanka is also considered a classic case of ethnic outbidding that fuels conflict – a process of auction-like competition for support within ethnic groups which leads parties or leaders to escalate the extremity of their position (Horowitz, 1985; Devotta, 1995).

There were repeated incidents of brutal communal violence, often with state sanction, against the Tamils and Muslims in the 1950s (Tambiah, 2017), 1970s (Wijayawardana, 2008) and most significantly the anti-Tamil pogrom of 1983 (Samarakkody, 1977). It is in this context that several Tamil groups took up armed resistance, dating back to the 1970s. One such group was the LTTE. Over the war years, LTTE became one of the most powerful militant groups, violently eliminating most of the other Tamil militant groups (Khan, 2017). Since the 1980s there were nine attempts at negotiating a political settlement (Paramanathan, 2007). None of the agreements negotiated proved to be successful.

The civil war finally came to a military end in May 2009, with internationally unprecedented use of military force by the Sri Lankan state. It was a military victory that decimated the leadership of the LTTE. In the final stages of the war the UN estimated that between 40,000 and 70,000 civilians were killed (Darusman et al, 2011). During the war years, civilians were affected by multiple displacements, loss of life and property, massacres, injuries, enforced disappearances, extortions, lack of access to education and employment, torture, child recruitment and sexual violence (Satkunanathan, 2018). Civilians, learning to survive among the multiple armed groups in a highly militarised society, found that social structures of care and safety were destroyed by cultures of surveillance in addition to the breakdown of

Figure 6.1: Map of Sri Lanka

Source: https://d-maps.com/carte.php?num_car=26911&lang=en

traditional support structures – such as kinship networks, religious spaces, performance of cultural events (Kodikara and Emmanuel, 2012).

Community development in Batticaloa in the 1990s

Drawing on the two authors' experiences from 2002 to the present, this chapter focuses on the period 2002–9. In 2002 a ceasefire agreement was signed between the LTTE and the government of Sri Lanka. The ceasefire agreement was extremely fragile, with frequent violations of the terms of agreement by both parties. The LTTE continued recruitment of members, particularly children, and in 2004, the eastern leader, Vinayagamurthy Muralidharan (Karuna), split from the main leadership in the north, establishing his base and headquarters in Batticaloa. Karuna later allied with the Sri Lankan state military forces. Following this, the two leaders in the east, Pillayan and Karuna, came into conflict resulting in further killings and disappearances (Child Soldiers International, 2004; Human Rights Watch, 2004). In 2006, open warfare recommenced in the east leading to massive displacement of communities into camps. Killings by unknown gunmen, abductions and disappearances were commonplace during this time (Sánchez Meertens, 2013).

Batticaloa is a district with a diverse population of Tamils and Muslims alongside smaller pockets of Sinhala communities. The main economy is agriculture and fishing with some contributions from tourism. Over the war years Batticaloa experienced numerous armed groups, comprising different military units as well as paramilitary squads. The 1990s saw horrific massacres in Muslim and Tamil villages, with the involvement of both non-state armed groups and the military (Munas and Lokuge, 2013; Silva et al, 2018; Godamunne, 2019). This is the context within which community groups in the east have functioned since 2002.

The theoretical approach to community development

The authors – one based in a mainstream international development organisation that worked with community-based partner organisations, and the other working with local feminist organisations – have built strong networks in the east over the past two decades. Both their models of work, albeit from different vantage points, involved building/developing clusters of grassroots level organisations and collectives based on community development approaches. These were linked with one another at the district level.

Some of the distinct features of the approach are:

- Recognition that holistic community development is possible and needed in a protracted war context with volatile security/insecurity cycles. That this approach is required to build resilience within communities where episodes of critical emergencies are 'normal' (see also Thangarajah, 2014) – the rescue, relief, recovery, rehabilitation, reconstruction and development needs were envisioned with long-term resilience objectives in mind. While the initial community development followed the classic mobilisation approaches widely pioneered in rural South Asia, the disruption caused by protracted violence as experienced in Sri Lanka made it imperative that protection, relief and recovery were factored into the approach adopted. Early practice accepted that resilience requires

a holistic, multifaceted community approach to negotiate the difficult environment – local practice acknowledged this interlinking of approaches much earlier than many development actors.[1]
- Relentless focus on reaching out to the most oppressed/vulnerable – the 'poorest of the poor' or the 'multiply marginalised'.[2] Prolonged conflict did not undo existing hierarchies within each community which were often manifested in who was able to participate in community mobilisation and access some respite during the war. Thus an intersectional framework[3] was essential to reach those most disadvantaged.
- Intensive mobilisation processes were used with actors from the community adopting a Freirean (through Community Activist Training and Functional Literacy Training) approach and a rights-based framework. Constituted by small groups as basic building blocks, these then were aggregated at the village level as village societies (*sangams*) and federated at divisional levels[4] as community-based organisations. These small groups and alternative community-based structures significantly challenged the traditional modes of community representation and power dynamics in a village while also making possible demands for collective rights.
- Working on individual awareness and empowerment as a necessary condition for informed collective action and subsequent change at community level. The importance of change at individual level and working through aspects of false consciousness as a precondition for collectives' empowerment was stressed.
- Linking such community groups with one another at the district level and building solidarity networks on specific common issues, including negotiating for livelihoods and basic needs, women's land rights or violence against women, and so on.

This chapter documents some of the positive experiences that this community-based approach enabled, and although some were not sustainable beyond a few years, they made a crucial difference when operative during the periods of violent conflict.

Implementing the approach

One important aspect of this approach was the capacity for negotiating sustainable economic activities that were essential to meet the basic needs of marginalised groups. With the main economic base in the east being agricultural, it was important that agricultural activities such as rice production continued functioning, alongside the powerful influence of development agency micro-finance and micro-credit programmes (Gant et al, 2002). The dynamics of war and violence kept changing. Lines of control kept shifting between the military and armed groups, with areas marked as 'cleared' and 'uncleared' (of other armed actors) by the government of Sri Lanka.[5] These boundaries, however, were never stable; consequently, local communities had to negotiate access to livelihoods and land on a regular basis. In this context, farmer, fisherfolk and other community collectives had to negotiate access to lagoons, rivers and other water resources in order to meet the basic livelihood needs of a functioning society.

Regular negotiations had to take place to ensure daily access to work the land, forage in forests, take cattle for grazing, engage in fishing or guarantee access to markets, supplies and traders. Sometimes, 'taxes' had to be paid to armed groups and/or to the military to enable such access. In this context, it was extremely important that there was investment in community groups and structures to enable them to negotiate in a collective manner with the various warring parties.

In the work the authors were involved in, in contrast to what might be practised in some approaches to community development, there was no unquestioning acceptance of the ability of traditional community structures to lead these everyday negotiations given that these structures often entailed discriminatory and patriarchal attitudes. The conditions of war made the facilitation of new social collectives and structures essential to ensure that the more marginalised segments of the communities were able to survive and have voice. These alternative structures were based on principles of equity, participation and transparency. As reflected in this chapter, this was neither idealistic nor a luxury, but was *essential* for survival and sustaining life during war for some of the most marginalised communities.

Another practical example was the collective negotiation of access for reconstructing housing and toilets after the tsunami disaster which devastated the war-torn areas of the east in December 2004. The community-based bodies, that had been created, sustained and supported over the years, were easily mobilised to ensure a transparent and equitable community response in the post-tsunami context. The fact that there was the consciousness to include strong women's representation in these structures was also important. This was in marked contrast to how the traditional decision-making bodies, and government/rebel groups, mediated development programmes prior to the war. Furthermore, these newer representative bodies were prepared to openly talk about what would have been previously taboo subjects such as domestic violence and power relations within the household. In rare instances some of these small groups and *sangams*, primarily made up of women, were also able to discuss issues of sexuality as the war was rupturing the traditional structures and notions leaving in its wake many young widows.

It is essential to highlight that these non-traditional community-based groups were able to play this interlocutor and solidarity role at the time of need. They offered a different dimension and priority to community development to the previous savings and credit-focused interventions, bringing also a different focus to humanitarian intervention. This was not so much changes in the nature of needs-based humanitarian intervention, but more in 'how' humanitarian work was delivered. Intrinsic to this 'how' was the mobilisation of communities on principles of participation, transparency and democratic leadership. The legitimacy that the groups had in the community gave them voice and authority to enable negotiations with both the military and the armed groups at times of crises. Often these were the only institutions that were able to engage in humanitarian interventions in some areas. Carving out such independence and neutrality in a fraught environment was no easy task.

Even more importantly, the 'who' within these groups involved mobilising the most marginalised people within communities to have a voice and take on leadership. This included women and others who traditionally were not in decision-making roles. In Vakarai, for example, the community group prepared the list of beneficiaries, noting what relief materials were coming in, the value and quantities of relief, and shared it transparently with the entire community. This transparency made it difficult for any armed groups, or the military, to monopolise these processes, exert power or engage in corruption.

This is one among many stories that highlighted the importance of investment in community structures which had to be maintained over lengthy periods of time. This long-term investment helped sustain community structures even in the face of the volatile macro-dynamics of war and post-war contexts. During the war years, it was even known for state structures to cease functioning. Equally, international humanitarian actors came and went, leaving local people to negotiate their everyday realities. For example, often community structures helped to negotiate with the LTTE in the 'uncleared' areas which they governed, so that communities could have continued access to state-run essential services, such as health and education.

Another important element of these community structures was that they maintained some connection with other community-based groups, thus resulting in building small networks of support and communication across the district. These networks then collectively worked towards rights-based articulations of peace. Consequently, community-based structures were thought of, and operated, as a web of participation and representation rather than as singular nodal entities. This further strengthened their role in negotiating the practicalities of civilian life during times of conflict.

Rupturing gender norms

As already mentioned, one of the key elements of the community level mobilisation approach was that, counter to default assumptions, such mobilisation *did not* reaffirm existing normative structures of power within communities. One of the most visible and powerful ways in which this 'how' manifested itself was in the realigning of gender norms. The approach empowered women to take on leadership roles in the management of community affairs. The process saw the gradual replacement of male leadership in community-based organisations. The war had disrupted traditional gender roles as men were killed, detained, abducted and arrested. Women were often the sole breadwinners for the household. Many also became leaders of both individual and collective processes to search for people who had been subject to enforced disappearance. These struggles under the leadership of women continue even today. At the same time, women were also talking about violence in their homes, communities and in the highly militarised public sphere – the violence perpetrated by state and non-state armed actors. While giving voice to injustice, women became key actors in ensuring collective peace and justice. They were visible in building bridges at the local level as well as championing coexistence and interethnic cooperation in the border areas. They played a key role in imagining alternatives while countering dominant narratives of ethnic polarisation. The community-based organisations provided the institutional scaffolding to facilitate this greater sense of agency exercised by women.

The focus on a gender perspective and women's rights emerged as an important aspect for reflection. This involved having a gendered approach to livelihood programmes as well as broader advocacy strategies on economic rights. While the need for greater gender equality was recognised in every analysis, it was the rupture of extant traditional socioeconomic structures due to protracted war that offered the opportunity of bringing a gender perspective into local community organising. As the potential of this perspective became increasingly visible, it allowed for new social structures to be both conceptualised and created.

Amidst these ruptures women began to play non-traditional roles and take the lead in economic production. In one area, this took the form of collective farming. In another area that was ravaged by the tsunami, local women became leaders in the camps for internally displaced persons (IDPs), accessing and distributing relief while at the same time responding to gender-based violence within the camp. It was these very same women who took the lead in ensuring gender sensitivity in the reconstruction of housing when they and their communities were eventually resettled in a new area.

Community networking for rights advocacy

While meeting these practical needs, women also started creating and participating in discourses around their right to land and financial resources in the post-tsunami reconstruction process. The networks built across the districts, discussed earlier, came together for the purpose of this advocacy. Local women leaders collected information on land ownership patterns which highlighted matrilineal land-owning practices in the east. This data was then used to prepare a report on women's land rights which was adopted as an advocacy tool at both the district level and nationally (Maunaguru and Emmanuel, 2010). The need to reform the discriminatory Land Development Ordinance (PARL, 2021), which governed all state land distribution and only recognised male land ownership and succession, was asserted through collective advocacy. The report highlighted the connection between gender-based violence and land ownership as the basis to argue for joint legal ownership of land and housing. Based on the case studies, the report further argued that when there had been a history of domestic violence (with multiple police complaints and verification from local government officers, and so on), land and housing should be given in the name of the woman.

The post-tsunami context paved the way to mobilise strong women-led community groups and non-governmental organisations into a dynamic network which was called the Women's Coalition for Disaster Management (WCDM), Batticaloa. Apart from the advocacy work on land rights, the WCDM focused on a range of rights violations that women experienced in the post-tsunami and protracted war context. A case in point was when a young woman was raped and killed in the heart of Batticaloa town (Amnesty International, 2005; Emmanuel and Kodikara, 2016). One of many cases of sexual violence we were responding to at the time was this:

> On the 3rd of August 2005, an unidentified young woman was found raped and murdered in a school near the high security zone in Batticaloa. No one came forward to identify her and she was to be buried in an unidentified grave. The Women's Coalition for Disaster Management (WCDM), a network of which Suriya is a founding member, mobilised around this case and took to the streets demanding justice for her rape and murder. A public statement was issued condemning the rape and murder, which was signed by 19 organisations. Many women attended her burial, lit candles and placed a wooden plaque on her grave and made sure she was not buried alone. As she was never identified, the legal case never proceeded. Later on we were able to make contact with her family. Her mother was distraught that she could not even perform the death rituals for her daughter. She was too afraid to come forward and claim her body, as her daughter had been branded as a part of the LTTE. (Emmanuel, 2008: np)

This coming together as a network, raising voice and bearing witness to injustice, was made possible by the years of slow and sustained work within community settings that had seen women leaders supported, collectives built and alternative social structures envisioned and created.

Reflecting on the gender perspective in our work clearly has much to do with the creation and sustenance of community groups, although we recognised that in the midst of a massive humanitarian crisis there can be difficulties in creating participatory and democratic community groups and corresponding structures. If careful sustained community development work is not undertaken over many years, effective community-based leadership is unlikely, or where it does exist is very likely to be structured along traditional lines that excludes not only women but other oppressed castes and marginalised groups. However, where the necessary foundational work is in place then in moments of crisis women can assume leadership in response. Thus, in a context where ruptures paved the way for non-normative community development the importance of challenging oppressive structures became amply clear in order to facilitate and invest in best practices within humanitarian responses.

Having said this, challenging existing social norms was not an easy task for anyone, especially for those who were marginalised. Local women leaders went through an extensive and prolonged process of awareness-raising and conscientising on power dynamics and exploitation, gender equality, rights, caste, class, ethnicity, and so on. In parallel to this process, these women leaders maintained a strong presence in their community, having an intimate knowledge of the realities of women's lives and those of households in their area. The engagement had to be intensive.

The leaders did not work in isolation but were connected to one another across ethnicity and region. They built relationships of trust and understanding in order to learn to work collaboratively within a rights-based framework. By connecting with everyday experience as their baseline, and coming together – as women, as rural workers, as those who suffered enormous loss – it was possible to build solidarities across ethnic divides. These relationships have, and continue, to strongly contest the fundamental hard-line logic of the war that assumed absolute ethnic essentialism and division. For example in the border villages of Polonnaruwa District and Batticaloa District, where Sinhala and Tamil rural poor lived, women worked together on livelihoods as well as on community-based peacebuilding. They did this even while the hard-line discourses of Tiger 'terrorism' and 'national security' predominated. Through their own experiences of the violence perpetrated by all sides of the war, it was possible for them to connect and build collectives through shared realities.

In 2008, K.P. Vasantha from Jathin Athara Sahayogitha Sangwardena Kamituwa (JSSK), the committee for solidarity and development among ethnic communities in Polannaruwa, said:

> 'JSSK's achievements in this [inter-community relations] regard were outstanding. Both Sinhalese and Tamil women described their long-standing fear of the other community, and how this had previously restricted their mobility. Many said they were no longer fearful, and described how they worked together to solve problems … two women

described how Tamil and Sinhalese members had worked together to rescue abducted youth. Men from JSSK thought that promoting ethnic solidarity was one of the women's great achievements, and reported that there was now more peace between the two communities. There is no distinction between Sinhalese and Tamils here now. We need them [each other] a lot. We interact with them, we have meals with them and share food. ... My son was hit by a gunshot. When they heard about my son's injury, the Tamil people in the village all came to see him and gave support. ... Some of the Sinhalese children were abducted by the rebel group. Both Tamil and Sinhalese women went together to bring them back out. The Tamil community knew where the camps were, so they helped to get them. Tamil and Sinhalese go, but it is more women than men that go. Women negotiate more than men. Men feel more fearful and nervous than the women' (Vasantha, 21 September 2008). (Hunt et al, 2009: 38)

This reflection highlights the importance of sustained work, building community level collectives and structures that go beyond traditional hierarchies of gender, caste, class, ethnicity and region, particularly in the circumstances of war. It was in sync with how people survived and lived; further, in the context of protracted war this process contributed to the ability to envision and create, even if only momentarily, a relatively more equal and peaceful society in the midst of brutality.

Authors' personal experiences and bearing witness to resilience

If the cornerstone of these collectives was trust, a crucial aspect of building it was focus on issues of protection and safety from violence during and after the war years. This has been an important part of our own everyday work which was rarely recorded or made public given the exigencies of those very insecurities that we navigated in order to do our daily work.

Personal tragedies were an everyday occurrence for local community activists. Family members were arrested or detained, while abductions and disappearances were common. Communities faced multiple displacements and lived in IDP camps, while homes and assets were repeatedly destroyed. Many died in violent attacks, bomb blasts and shootings. Unidentified gunmen often came into IDP camps, shot someone and left. In the east specifically, tensions prevailed among Muslim, Tamil and Sinhala communities. Additionally, as described earlier, abduction of children and forced recruitment occurred regularly. The combined violence unleashed by the military and armed actors, as well as resulting from inter-community tensions, had a devastating impact on the livelihoods of the most marginalised families. This, in turn, forced them to take undue risks for survival. When women, and some men, took on leadership roles within their communities, there were also risks attached to assuming such positions.

From our experience we realise that sensitive humanitarian work, with rights-based community development at its core, cannot be achieved by adopting a risk averse procedural approach, or by operating in satellite mode whereby development workers are stationed in distant, safe locations. What is required is personal presence, standing side by side in solidarity during times of tragedy or difficulty; offering whatever support one can offer. In our experience, evacuation procedures, insurance policies and security risk assessments cannot override the imperatives of everyday human relationships; relationships that slowly build networks of trust and solidarity. Where such networks exist across the district they offered the potential to connect with existing support services when there were serious protection issues, as there often were. In real terms this meant connecting with the rare trusted UNICEF officer, whom you had met and worked with; or the International Committee of the Red Cross (ICRC) or Human Rights Commission officer who would pick up the phone when you called in desperation. As trust is slowly built over time with such officials, it brings with it a confidence that allows for the sharing of insights into the details of humanitarian crises and human rights violations from reliable sources. Trusted community leaders, who were trained in gathering verifiable information, can communicate the necessary information. This facilitates a cycle of trust within which protection is mutual rather than unidirectional. Indeed, it was often community leaders, negotiating with armed actors on behalf of humanitarian workers, that protected them when there were threats.

During the protracted war years, advocacy was done quietly, based on confidentiality and trust. We also faced cases of breach of this trust, as when UN international staff were evacuated leaving local staff and their families behind in brutal war conditions. We saw life jackets being taken out of international NGO vehicles as local colleagues were not covered under the agencies' insurance plans. There were instances where the international humanitarian organisations kept silent about the conditions in the camps in Vavuniya in 2009 in order to maintain access and not antagonise the military and the Sri Lankan government (Samath, 2009; Doucet, 2012; Balasundaram, 2019). These were bitter moments where relationships of long-term trust were broken when we needed it the most.

Bitter moments notwithstanding, our practice ethics demanded that we remain present in the midst of the community over long periods of time. Working in this way both strengthened the ability of communities to protect themselves and their ability to protect us, the humanitarian workers. Just as approaches taken in, and by, these community-based organisations enabled a more sensitive humanitarian response, our relationship with them ensured that our advocacy remained grounded and was accountable to those most affected by the issue.

This approach to community development in conflict settings is premised on long-term commitment by all concerned and willingness to work on the slow process of empowerment and institutional strengthening. This is labour-intensive and may not neatly fit into the vagaries of shifting donor priorities. There are also the obvious challenges in terms of community dependence on activists and field workers, where these intermediaries become overly powerful in the process.

Our final reflections were on the connection between community development, issues of protest/safety and the ways in which they are connected to processes of truth and justice with regard to atrocities committed during the war. Looking back at 15 years of work, it was clear that the processes of community development and truth/justice are intimately connected. Local community leaders held histories and memories. We also were witness to many events. As part of our everyday work we protected and hid people; moved people or provided access to medical care; we documented as much as we could; we accompanied representatives of UN bodies; we went to police stations, prisons and camps of armed actors – state and non-state; we attended funerals; we also protested on the streets. The following excerpt from a report offers an example of witnessing and documentation:

> Significant numbers abducted in Batticaloa District and Polonnaruwa District. Almost exclusively boys. Many above 18 but sizable number below 18. Most abductions during the period attributed to Karuna group who are building up their movement. They abducted close to 150 cadres who are currently being trained and parents who went to plead for release had been chased away. LTTE also engaged in abduction in areas under their control. (Human Rights Watch, 2007, np)

As the years pass, files get misplaced and older leaders are no longer there. Histories sometimes got forgotten, particularly given a reluctance to record things on paper, let alone digitally, due to security considerations. We saw it as a fundamental component of community development and humanitarian work to remember in the context of a politics of justice and trust, with the hope for future accountability. Day-to-day work should encompass the idea that one day the truth will be told. Survivors must be supported to keep evidence and documents, to write down witness accounts and narratives of events, storing this information carefully with a view to future accountability.

The hope for future processes of justice and accountability also mean maintaining relationships with all those whom we supported over the years. The woman whose daughter was raped and killed in 2005, whose dignity in death was ensured by local women activists/leaders, is still in contact with one of the authors. Over the years we have helped her face various challenges, including securing housing, educating her other children and earning a living. Currently, she is part of support groups for all women survivors. In January 2020, she participated in a public meeting in Batticaloa, organised by the newly appointed Office for Reparations, to present her recommendations. What she wanted is a death certificate that states that her daughter lived, died and how she died.

Another aspect of memory, truth and accountability was about communicating our multiple histories to the younger generations. It is worrying that young people do not know the histories of war or the experiences of survival and resilience. There was a macro-narrative of the victor which was problematic and was only countered by simplistic counter-narratives that painted black and white histories. Space is lacking to remember and articulate alternative complex histories that are closer to a holistic truth. One of our motivations to write this chapter is to share our experiences with a younger generation of development practitioners. As we are both involved in training young people to critically engage with political concepts and debates in Sri Lanka, this entails critically understanding our histories and politics, critically engaging with patriarchal structures and values as well as with concepts such as national security, ethnicity, democracy, sexuality, and so on. We feel that the documentation of previous work and experience is important to encourage the engagement of the younger generations.

Conclusion

We would like to conclude by focusing on the present – more than a decade after the war ended. What happened to the collectives, networks and women leaders we worked with? Before answering that question, it is necessary to note the current context in Sri Lanka. In early 2022 there was a new government in office, headed by a president who was the Defence Secretary in control during the last stages of the war in 2009. He recently declared that many of those disappeared in the final stages of that war are dead (Srinivasan, 2020). Measures have been taken to strip away the independence and remit of official bodies such as the Office on Missing Persons, established in 2016 (Office of Missing Persons, 2020). Community development has also suffered with increased priority given to extremely harmful micro-finance schemes, primarily targeting poor women in the erstwhile conflict areas.

Simultaneously, there has been growing resistance to these economic strategies, as suicides and deaths due to rising debt have increased (Kadirgamar and Kadirgamar, 2019). Women, particularly those considered to fall outside the traditional norms (women-headed households, former militants, politically active Muslim women, women activists calling for reforms of discriminatory personal laws, women with disabilities, and sexual and gender minorities) are facing a strong re-emergence of controlling social norms in the post-war context (Gomez, 2016; International Crisis Group, 2017;

Kandanearachchi and Ratnayake, 2017). Rising communal hatred against, and the corresponding ossification of regressive practices within, the Muslim community, is evident throughout Sri Lanka (Saroor, 2021). For those in the east, this has meant that women's freedom of dress and their mobility has been severely curtailed (Cegu Isadeen, 2019). The Easter attacks in April 2019 made the local context in the east exponentially worse, with already fragile inter-community relationships becoming increasingly hostile (Saroor, 2021).

So what happened to the women leaders – those voices speaking of rights, coexistence, peace and justice? It is those very same women who worked during the war years that continue to maintain solidarities in the post-war context. NGOs have closed down. Funding has dried up. There is hardly any international presence in the east anymore. It is those activist women community leaders across Muslim and Tamil communities that have yet again taken on the role of articulating rights, justice and peace. The Tamil Muslim Sinhala Sisters Group, for example, is a loose body of community women from different parts of the district who came together to resist the anti-Muslim rhetoric of Sinhala Buddhist fundamentalist forces which led to communal violence in the town of Aluthgama in 2014. Soon after the attack, on 22 April 2014, while curfews were being declared and fear and panic was everywhere, a small of group of these women (including one of the authors, Sarala) met in a home. We strategised as to how to respond in that crisis context (Firthous et al, 2021). We have continued to meet regularly. These same women – Muslim and Tamil – stood near one of the biggest Hindu temples in town, after the bombings in April 2019, offering pilgrims sweet curd to quench their thirst. This is a potent symbol of love and coexistence where much communal hatred towards the Muslim community is articulated through practices of untouchability with regards to food as well as through irrational rumours of food being tampered with.

Speaking from years of experiences, it is heartening for us to see that small victories and slow investments in community development, governance, equality and leadership during the protracted war is transferrable to post-war peacebuilding. In Sri Lanka this gives us hope for future truth, justice and accountability as we still stumble in a time of uncertainty.

Notes

[1] For a latter-day discussion of the conceptualisation of resilience as a link between relief and development in difficult settings see Mosel and Levine (2014).

[2] These targeting approaches were conceptualised and indices for multiple marginalisation were developed and fine-tuned by Professor Arjuna Parakrama and Nalini Kasynathan in a participatory manner with the staff and community groups that Oxfam Australia was working with. These drew heavily from the insights of subaltern studies in Asia as well as from the works of Mahbub ul Haq and Amartya Sen.

3   'An intersectional approach to analysing the disempowerment of marginalised women attempts to capture the consequences of the interaction between two or more forms of subordination. It addresses the way racism, patriarchy, class oppression and other discriminatory systems create inequalities that structure the relative positions of women, races, ethnicities, classes, and the like. Moreover, intersectionality addresses the way that specific acts and policies operate together to create further disempowerment' (Abeseykera, 2003).
4   Divisional level denotes an administrative unit below the district level in the Sri Lankan public administration.
5   'Uncleared' was a term used by the military to refer to areas which were under the control of LTTE and not under the control of the Sri Lankan military forces (Al Jazeera, 2007; United Nations Secretary General, 2007).

References

Abeysekara, S. (2003) 'Racism, ethnicity and peace: Some initial thoughts on intersectionality', *Canadian Woman Studies*, 22(2). Available at https://cws.journals.yorku.ca/index.php/cws/article/view/6484

Al Jazeera (2007) 'Fresh clashes erupt in Sri Lanka: Thousands of refugees flee renewed fighting between government troops and Tamil rebels', *Al Jazeera*, 11 March. Available at https://www.aljazeera.com/news/2007/3/11/fresh-clashes-erupt-in-sri-lanka

Amnesty International (2005) 'Sri Lanka: A climate of fear in the east', *A Report to the OHCHR*. Available at https://lib.ohchr.org/HRBodies/UPR/Documents/Session2/LK/AI_LKA_UPR_S2_2008anx_asa370012006.pdf

Balasundaram, N. (2019) 'How the UN failed Tamil civilians in 2009', *Al Jazeera*, 18 May. Available at https://www.aljazeera.com/opinions/2019/5/18/how-the-un-failed-tamil-civilians-in-2009/

BBC (2019) 'Sri Lanka profile: Timeline', *BBC News*. Available at https://www.bbc.com/news/world-south-asia-12004081

Cegu Isadeen, H. (2019) 'In the name of security how the burqa niqab ban is impacting Muslim women', *Groundviews*. Available at https://groundviews.org/2019/05/22/in-the-name-of-security-how-the-burqa-niqab-ban-is-impacting-muslim-women/

Child Soldiers International (2004) 'Child soldiers global report 2004: Sri Lanka'. Available at https://www.refworld.org/docid/4988062ac.html

Darusman, M., Sooka, Y. and Ratner, S.R. (March 2011) *Report of the Secretary-General's Panel of Experts on Accountability in Sri Lanka*. Available at https://reliefweb.int/sites/reliefweb.int/files/resources/POE_Report_Full.pdf

Devotta, N. (2005) 'From ethnic outbidding to ethnic conflict: The institutional bases for Sri Lanka's separatist war', *Nations and Nationalism*, 11(1): 141–59.

Doucet, L. (2012) 'UN "failed" Sri Lanka civilians says internal probe', *BBC News*, 13 November. Available at https://www.bbc.co.uk/news/world-asia-20308610

Emmanuel, S. (2008) 'Global issues, local realities: A note from a post-tsunami coastal town in Sri Lanka', in D. Zarkov (ed) *Gender, Violent Conflict and Development: Challenges of* Practice, New Delhi: Zubaan, pp 60–74.

Emmanuel, S. and Kodikara, C. (2016) 'Global discourse and local realities: Armed conflict and the pursuit of justice', in K. Jayawardena and K. Pinto-Jayawardena (eds) *The Search for Justice: Sri Lanka Papers*, New Delhi: Zubaan.

Firthous, A., Emmanuel, S. and Ponni, A. (2021) 'Of continuing injustices and continuing conversations: Women's collective support across ethnicities in Batticaloa', in S.A. Saroor (ed) *Muslims in Post-War Sri Lanka: Repression, Resistance and Reform*, Alliance for Minorities/Minor Matters, pp 151–61.

Gant, R., de Silva, D., Atapattu, A. and Durrant, S. (2002) *National Microfinance Study of Sri Lanka: Survey of Practices and Policies*, Colombo: AusAID and GTZ. Available at https://www.findevgateway.org/sites/default/files/publications/files/mfg-en-paper-national-microfinance-study-of-sri-lanka-survey-of-practices-and-policies-2002.pdf

Godamunne, N. (2019) *Understanding Women's Livelihood Outcomes and Economic Empowerment in the Eastern Province of Sri Lanka*, Colombo: International Centre for Ethnic Studies. Available at http://ices.lk/wp-content/uploads/2020/02/Understanding.pdf

Gomez, S. (2016) 'Women in post-war Sri Lanka: Linking policy to reality', in A. Barrow and J. Chia (eds) *Gender, Violence and the State in Asia*, Abingdon: Routledge, pp 52–67.

Hoole, R. (2016) ' "Sinhala only" & its effects on Ceylon's legal tradition', *Colombo Telegraph*. Available at https://www.colombotelegraph.com/index.php/sinhala-only-its-effects-on-ceylons-legal-tradition/

Hoole, R., Somasundaram, D., Sritharan, K. and Thiranagama, R. (1992) *The Broken Palmyra: The Tamil Crisis in Sri Lanka: An Inside Account*, Claremont: Sri Lanka Studies Institute.

Horowitz, D. (1985) *Ethnic Groups in Conflict*, Berkeley: University of California Press.

Human Rights Watch (2004) 'Living in fear: Child soldiers and the Tamil Tigers in Sri Lanka', *Human Rights Watch*, 16(13). Available at https://www.hrw.org/reports/2004/srilanka1104/index.htm

Human Rights Watch (2007) 'Return to war: Human rights under siege', *Human Rights Watch*, 19(11). Available at https://www.hrw.org/reports/2007/srilanka0807/srilanka0807webwcover.pdf

Hunt, J., Kasynathan, N., Yogasingham, S., Fernando, D., Gamage, P. and Roubin, D. (2009) 'Breaking the shackles: Women's empowerment in Oxfam Australia's Sri Lanka program', *Occasional Paper 3*, Oxfam Australia. Available at https://genderevaluation.unwomen.org/-/media/files/un%20women/gender%20evaluation/resourcefiles/oxfamaustralia_breakingtheshackles-0909.pdf?vs=102

International Crisis Group (2017) *Sri Lanka's Conflict Affected Women: Dealing with the Legacy of War*, report no 289. Available at https://www.crisisgroup.org/asia/south-asia/sri-lanka/289-sri-lankas-conflict-affected-women-dealing-legacy-war

Kadirgamar, A. and Kadirgamar, N. (2019) 'Microfinance has been a nightmare for the global south: Sri Lanka shows that there is an alternative', *Open Democracy*. Available at https://www.opendemocracy.net/en/ourecon omy/microfinance-has-been-nightmare-global-south-sri-lanka-shows-there-alternative/

Kandanearachchi, K. and Ratnayake, R. (2017) *Post-War Realities: Barriers to Female Economic Empowerment*, Colombo: International Centre for Ethnic Studies. Available at https://ices.lk/wp-content/uploads/2017/12/Post-War-Realities-For-Circulation.pdf

Khan, F. (2017) ' "Demons in Paradise" review: A spine-chilling testimony to rebel violence in Sri Lanka', *Economic Times*, 30 July. Available at https://economictimes.indiatimes.com/magazines/panache/demons-in-parad ise-a-spine-chilling-testimony-to-rebel-violence-in-sri-lanka/articleshow/59825098.cms

Kodikara, C. and Emmanuel, S. (2012) 'Women's peace work in Sri Lanka: Experiences, impact and expectations', in N. Katjasungkana and S.E. Wieringa (eds) *The Future of Asian Feminisms: Confronting Fundamentalisms, Conflicts and Neoliberalism*, Newcastle upon Tyne: Cambridge Scholars Publishing, pp 247–65.

Maunaguru, S. and Emmanuel, S. (2010) *Penkalin Nilam: A Study on Women's Land Rights in the Post Resettlement and Relocation Process in Batticaloa*, Batticaloa: Suriya Women's Development Centre.

Mosel, I. and Levine, S. (2014) *Remaking the Case for Linking Relief, Rehabilitation and Development: How LRRD Can Become a Practically Useful Concept for Assistance in Difficult Places*, London: Humanitarian Policy Group of Overseas Development Institute. Available at https://odi.org/documents/4371/8882.pdf

Munas, M. and Lokuge, G. (2013) *A Livelihood and Market Study of Resettled Communities in the Eastern Province*, Colombo: Center for Poverty Analysis. Available at https://www.cepa.lk/wp-content/uploads/2020/08/Market-Study-English-Final.pdf

Office of Missing Persons (2020) *Media Release*, 15 January. Available at https://www.facebook.com/ompsrilanka/posts/2491895127736379

Paramanathan, M. (2007) *Peace Negotiations of Sri Lankan Conflict in 2000–2006: The Ceasefire Agreement Facilitated by Norway is at Stake*, master's thesis, Jönköping University International Business School. Available at https://www.diva-portal.org/smash/get/diva2:4488/FULLTEXT01.pdf

People's Alliance for Right to Land (PARL) (2021) *The People's Land Commission Report is Now Online*, 9 August. Available at https://www.par lsl.com/publications/the-peoples-land-commission-report-is-now-online

Samarakkody, E. (1977) 'Behind Bandaranaike rout in Sri Lanka elections', *Ilankai Tamil Sangam*. Available at https://sangam.org/2007/08/Samarakkoddy.php?uid=2517

Samath, F. (2009) 'Sri Lanka: Aid organisations struggle to operate in post-war Sri Lanka', *Inter Press Service*, 14 July. Available at http://www.ipsnews.net/2009/07/sri-lanka-aid-organisations-struggle-to-operate-in-post-war-sri-lanka/

Sánchez Meertens, A. (2013) *Letters from Batticaloa: TMVP's Emergence and the Transmission of Conflict in Eastern Sri Lanka*, doctoral thesis, Utrecht University Repository. Available at http://dspace.library.uu.nl/handle/1874/282359

Saroor, S.A. (ed) (2021) *Muslims in Post War Sri Lanka: Repression, Resistance and Reform*, Alliance for Minorities. Available at https://www.minormatters.org/storage/app/uploads/public/615/69b/d3b/61569bd3b3d59076872669.pdf

Satkunanathan, A. (2018) 'Sri Lanka: The impact of militarization on women', in F. Ni Aolain, N. Cahn, D.F. Haynes and N. Valji (eds) *The Oxford Handbook of Gender and Conflict*, Oxford: Oxford University Press.

Silva, K.T., Razaak, M.G.M., Herath, D., Usoof-Thowfeek, R., Sivakanthan, S. and Kunanayaham, V. (2018) 'Post-war livelihood trends in Sri Lanka', *Background Paper No 5*, prepared by the International Centre for Ethnic Studies as a supplement to the *Socio-Economic Assessment of the Conflict Affected Northern and Eastern Provinces* conducted by the World Bank, Kandy: International Centre for Ethnic Studies.

Srinivasan, M. (2020) 'Sri Lanka civil war: Missing persons are dead, says Gotabaya', *The Hindu*, January. Available at https://www.thehindu.com/news/international/missing-persons-are-dead-says-gotabaya/article30609730.ece

Tambiah, S.J. (1996) *The Anti-Tamil Gal Oya Riots of 1956*, New Delhi: Vistaar Publications.

Thangarajah, P. (2014) 'Forging feminist alliances: A front line struggle of war affected northern women', in S.A. Saroor (ed) *Our Struggles, Our Stories*, Colombo: SA Saroor, pp 67–94.

United Nations Secretary General (2007) *Report of the Secretary-General on Children and Armed Conflict in Sri Lanka* S/2007/758. Available at http://www.securitycouncilreport.org/atf/cf/%7B65BFCF9B-6D27-4E9C-8CD3-CF6E4FF96FF9%7D/CAC%20S2007%20758.pdf

Wickrematunge, R. (2016) 'A tale of two languages: Sri Lanka's efforts to implement a sound language policy', *Himal – South Asian*. Available at https://www.himalmag.com/a-tale-of-two-languages/

Wijayawardana, K.N.K. (2008) 'The anti-Tamil riots of August 1977', *Sri Lanka Guardian*, 25 February. Available at http://www.srilankaguardian.org/2008/02/anti-tamil-riots-of-august-1977.html

7
Brazil: public security as a human right in the favelas

Eliana Sousa Silva and Lidiane Malanquini,
translated by Renata Peppl

Summary

The work of Redes da Maré[1] in the Complexo da Maré favelas is a proud statement that these people exist – referring to the 140,000 residents that were officially invisible for decades. The favela area itself dates back to the 1940s, but it took more than half a century of struggles and achievements to see Maré establishing itself as an acknowledged working-class area in the city of Rio de Janeiro. Despite being described as temporary and experiencing high levels of inequality, racism and violence, such communities continue to innovate and survive with a lot of creativity and intelligence. Every day new alternatives and solutions are devised to challenge the lack of responsive public policies and a state security policy that is characterised by violence. In response a number of locally based non-governmental organisations (NGOs) have worked in support of local residents to demand better living conditions, putting forward evidence-based proposals that have improved access to water, sanitation, education, health, as well as the arts and culture.

The challenges faced by Redes da Maré are indicative of the structural violence described by Galtung (1969). It encompasses forms of violence that harm people by preventing them from meeting their basic needs, invariably based on both direct and/or indirect discrimination, that so often is a casual factor in outright violent conflict. Where such structural violence is preventable it is arguably a particularly pernicious demonstration of social injustice.

This chapter explains how community activists in Complexo da Maré worked to enhance the sense of identity of local residents by recording and celebrating their stories, lives and the social relations that exist, in addition to physically mapping the area for the first time. This participative mapping exercise, undertaken with the support of sympathetic academic and civil society actors, provided an evidence base to make effective demands on service providers. The chapter also refers to the range of strategies adopted by

Redes da Maré, from creative approaches to the training of local volunteers, and from the provision of direct services to advocacy and legal tactics.

Given the levels of violence suffered by residents in Complexo da Maré, specific attention is paid to the community-directed work carried out in the area of public safety and access to justice. The chapter focuses on how Redes da Maré worked with residents to raise their awareness about rights and to enhance their capacity to deal with the militarised violence of the police and security forces in a nonviolent manner. This work has been long-term in nature but gained increased visibility with the launch of Brazil's first collective civil lawsuit in the public security field taken under the Brazilian Constitution – the Public Civil Action of Maré. Such legal and advocacy strategies were based on community mobilisation and conscientisation that reflects a Freirean approach, seeking to shift the narrative about the nature of public security to reflect the lived reality of residents in Maré. Notwithstanding the very difficult conditions that the local communities face, the favelas demonstrate both joy and resistance.

Setting the scene

The making of the favela

Favelas in Brazil emerged as result of poverty and marginalisation but were consolidated by urban development policies characterised by inequality in public investment in different parts of cities. This urban or socio-spatial segregation is the geographical reproduction of a broader social segregation directly related to the division between different social classes and ethno-racial groups. Thus, social groups historically considered as subordinate tend to live in more remote areas with less access to large economic centres and poor access to public services.

The origin of favelas has been traced back to the late 19th century, when they first developed in Rio de Janeiro as low-income, informal settlements. The draw of urbanisation and industrialisation saw the favela population expanding with an in-flow of migration from rural areas, until favela settlements began to be seen as a problem in the 1920s. It was not until 1937, however, that the Building Code (*Código de Obras*) first acknowledged the existence of these settlements in an official public document. A decision was taken to ignore the favelas on the grounds that they were only 'temporary'. A housing crisis in Rio in the 1940s, alongside urban industrialisation in the 1950s, resulted in yet another expansion of the favela population despite being ignored by the municipal authorities. By 1950 it was estimated that some 7 per cent of the population of Rio de Janeiro were favela-dwellers. This percentage increased to 19 per cent in recent years.

A collection of 16 favelas in Rio de Janeiro is known as Maré, an area that borders Guanabara Bay in the North Zone of Rio. Three of the city's most

Figure 7.1: Map of Brazil

Source: https://d-maps.com/carte.php?num_car=4845&lang=en

important highways run through it: Linha Vermelha, Linha Amarela and Avenida Brasil. Considered as the most populous favela in Rio de Janeiro, with 139,073 residents distributed across 47,758 households, the favela covers an area of 4.3km², making it larger than 96.4 per cent of Brazilian cities. Maré, however, remained officially unrecognised, with no street names, no house addresses, no postal codes, just blank white spaces on the city map. This had major consequences for the residents of the favela who could not receive mail to their accommodation, list their address on job applications or bank accounts, or gain access to many essential services.

While the Maré favela dates back to the 1940s, it saw an expansion in the 2000s as a result of government-sponsored housing programmes. Like other favelas in Rio de Janeiro and Brazil, Maré houses working-class people who have historically suffered from the failure of the state to recognise their rights or provide essential services. It cannot be said, however, that the state is completely absent from these communities, given that the favela residents have constantly fought for services, resources and the recognition of rights.

Figure 7.2: Map of Redes da Maré favela in Rio de Janeiro

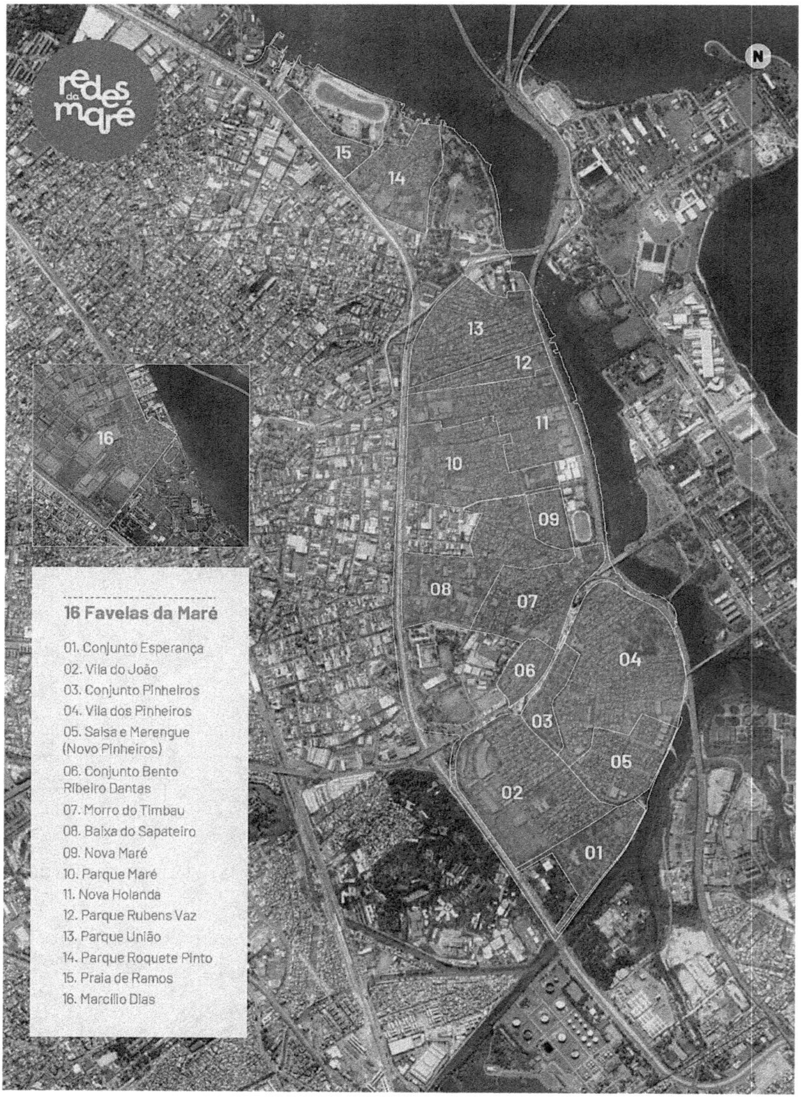

Source: Original map by Redes da Maré

The nature of conflict in Maré

Studies and reports on Complexo da Maré have noted that the population continues to experience much instability in their daily lives in the face of the urban violence they have long lived with. This is both due to armed groups linked to international drug trafficking that manage the territory, and militia groups which are also present in some of Maré's favelas, particularly since the

1990s, exercising control over certain illegal activities, such as illegal transport and security services for the region's traders. However, it is the response of the state, through its armed police and security forces, that have often wrought havoc on the lives of the residents, as the following comment highlights:

> 'My husband picked me up at work because of the demonstration taking place on Avenida Brasil. When we went through Nova Holanda, everything was dark, and we noticed a lot of people at the entrance to Rua Teixeira. We imagined it was an operation. We carried on and entered Parque União: windows down, the inside lights on, hazard lights on. We were afraid of being mistaken for the police or for criminals. As we passed the iron grid, I heard the first shot. I threw myself on the floor and told him to accelerate. Then I heard more shots. When I got up, his shirt was covered in blood, and he was saying he'd been hit.' (Nilzete Duarte, Cláudio Duarte's wife targeted in the police operation on 24 June 2013)

Historically, police operations have been characterised by an excessive use of military apparatus resulting in intense armed conflict that has given rise to deaths and injuries, such as in Cláudio's story. Such operations are the main way that police operate in Maré, impacting negatively on the lives of the community.

With a military dictatorship in Brazil over the years 1964–85, there are long memories of the use of excessive force, but the experience of communities within Maré is more recent in nature. 'Pacification' policies have been adopted over many years to limited success, with the victims of police operations being disproportionately young, Black men. The fact that Maré is located on the direct route from the main airport in Rio to the city centre has warranted particular attention to the area, with a noted security operation in March 2014, seeing its occupation by over 1,000 members of the security forces – police, the Special Police Operations Battalion (BOPE), the Shock Police Battalion and the Brazilian Marine Corps – in the months before the city hosted the 2014 FIFA World Cup.

Human Rights Watch has consistently raised the issue of the use of force by the police and other state forces in favelas which was given added momentum by the election of Wilson Witzel as governor of Rio de Janeiro in 2018, with his muscular approach to favela criminality. Report after report document innumerable cases such as that of the schoolboy, Marcus Vinicius de Silva (14 years) who died after being strafed by police from a helicopter in Maré in June 2018. It is the combination of these incidents, and the policies that give rise to them, that has forced community activists in Maré to adopt the right to public security and access to justice as one of the four pillars of the strategic work of Redes da Maré, the civil society network in the area. It has concluded that police operations fail to guarantee the right to public security, but on the contrary, they appear to be the main instrument of rights violations, especially the right to life of those who live in the neighbourhood. From experience police interventions are characterised by arbitrary entries and searches of homes and the premises of civil society organisations, damage to property, arrest without warrant and even extra-judicial killings. Redes da Maré frames its analysis in the context of a rights-based approach which challenges structural inequalities in the balance of power and a pernicious official perception which characterises Complexo da Maré as a virtual war zone, to be dealt with accordingly.

Community development and peacebuilding

In the face of the intense violations of the fundamental rights of Maré's residents, local community activists concluded that it was necessary to highlight and denounce the violations of rights and to build ways to deal with the abuses committed, seeking to identify strategies to influence policymaking, together with the ruling authorities. It was agreed that security issues would not be overcome by resort to more violent actions. On the contrary, protection of life needs to be the basic principle of security policies and state action should focus on the protection of, and investment in, children and young people in favelas such as Maré. The current militarised public security policy is a direct infringement on the civic rights of local people, in addition to demonstrating structural racism.

Based on the premise that public authorities fail to protect the fundamental rights of Maré's residents, the area development network, Redes da Maré, has sought to put pressure on the state to implement public policies that improve the population's quality of life. The work carried out by Redes da Maré for more than 20 years, based on its 'right to public security and access to justice' area of work, aims to reaffirm legal equality among the city's residents, regardless of their skin colour or place of residence. This links the local response to state violence with seeking to strengthen notions of citizenship and access to fundamental rights. Thus, it is essential to deconstruct the idea that 'the law is different in the favela' and to reaffirm the democratic and republican precepts of legality at a national level.

The pillar of public security and access to justice, however, is only one of four strategic objectives adopted by Redes da Maré (the others focusing on education; arts, culture, memories and identities; and territorial development), with initiatives implemented in these fields seeking to expand the rights of local residents in a holistic and cohesive manner. Indeed, when the creation of Redes da Maré began in 1997, it was access to educational opportunity that was the main driving force. Over

1,200 young people successfully took part in a Maré community course which prepared young people for university. A decade later, when the name Redes da Maré was officially registered, the range of community development activities had expanded to take account of the four priority pillars and showed how Redes da Maré could expand and consolidate public policies relating to the Maré's population, based on joining forces with both territorial and urban agencies.

In line with community development principles the central concept adopted by Redes da Maré was that all those who live in Rio de Janeiro should have the right to access resources, regardless of the region where they live. Lived experience, however, highlighted the fact that the quality of public services offered in the favelas was generally substandard and there was little account taken of either the rights or potential of local people. In February 2010 residents in Maré had been involved in a consultation exercise that produced a report, 'A Maré que Queremos' ('The Maré We Want'; Redes da Maré, 2010). The document made demands on agencies and local authorities for improved services, however it became clear that there was also a need to develop an evidence base to support these demands. Consequently a local census and mapping exercise was decided upon to make the residents visible to policymakers and officialdom. It was saying – people in favelas exist.

It was a major achievement when Redes da Maré, in partnership with Observatório de Favelas, organised a census of the Complexo da Redes and engaged in a participatory mapping exercise. The unofficial census was carried out by more than 100 local people over a period of six years. It found that Maré is home to 660 bars, 307 beauty salons, 138 supermarkets, 69 computer stores, 21 ice-cream shops and 8 dental offices. In total, 3,182 legal businesses employ 9,371 people. The Redes Network used the same methodology as the Government's Institute of Geography and Statistics to conduct the survey in order to ensure the legitimacy of the findings. The census strengthened the case for improved provision of public services, such as education and healthcare, highlighting the number of children throughout the favelas and identifying the needs of residents. Provision, although still lacking, began to improve as the local evidence gathered provided the basis for advocacy with the policymakers.

Alongside this the participatory mapping exercise completed in the area – also known as social cartography or 'insurgent cartography' (see, for example, Stevens et al, 2016) was a major initiative rooted in a commitment to citizen control over the mapping process. The Redes da Maré approach complemented the mapping process with the compilation of the histories of individual neighbourhoods in order to emphasise the sense of belonging, place and social connection. The mapping of the physical spaces, the collection of stories and the community census were all undertaken with the objective of making the favelas visible to policymakers, but as important was changing the official narrative about both the physical neighbourhoods and the residents of these communities. Having mapped the 16 favelas in Complexo da Maré, street names were agreed, and the local art class made blue and white ceramic tiles to attach the names to streets. Local people now had addresses. Redes da Maré printed up a favela guide, which also contained the histories collected that celebrated local identity. The guide offers information about the people some streets are named after, while leaving some blank, to be filled in by residents.

While as a development network, Redes da Maré continues its role of linking the various residents' associations and civic groups throughout the favelas, it also promotes and supports a range of area initiatives. Culture and the arts are important to both offer opportunities and to recognise a sense of place and identity. The Maré Arts Centre was established as was the Lima Barreto Library, and Redes took over management of the Herbert Vianna Cultural Canvas as a performance space in Nova Maré. The Museu Maré opened in 2006, challenging the portrayal of the area in the media as a war zone. It is felt important to encourage a sense of local self-esteem in addition to providing facilities. Culture, dance, sport and memory are valued and valuable as community development strategies.

Redes da Maré describes itself as a civil society institution that produces knowledge, development projects and actions that strengthen the guarantee of rights of the 140,000 residents of the 16 favelas of Maré, and as such it espouses seven key values:

1. defend the rights of residents;
2. recognise the sociocultural, educational and economic potential in the spaces of Maré;
3. defend ethnic-racial and gender equality;
4. action against all forms of violence and discrimination;
5. take full responsibility for the commitments and results to be generated;
6. guide our performance in ethical principles, integrity, honesty and transparency; and
7. defend democracy.

In this context there is a recognition of the problems of inter- and intra-community violence (including domestic violence), but on the understanding that public security is a right. The question posed is why are those who live in favelas automatically perceived as accomplices of illicit and criminal activity?

Developing a community response to state violence

In 2016 Redes da Maré asked school children in the community to write letters describing their experience of police violence seen on their way to school. This was to provide evidence for an ongoing legal challenge to the police, but also to highlight the fact that although important advances had been made in achieving the right to education (there are 50 public education facilities serving more than 16,000 children, many of them still in poor condition), the constant armed confrontations during police operations result in the cancellation of classes on a regular basis. According to the armed violence monitoring carried out by the Right to Public Security and Access to Justice team of Redes da Maré, 129 police operations took place in the area between 2016 and 2019. As a result, 92 people were injured by firearms, 90 people were murdered, schools were shut for 89 days, and health services were halted for 92 days. This was clearly both a public security and a quality-of-life issue for local residents.

Monitoring by the Redes da Maré team on an ongoing basis highlights the scale of the problem faced (Table 7.1). In addition to the toll of deaths and casualties, structural racism in Brazil trivialises death rates among young Black people, as well as of favela residents and people on the periphery of society. The monitoring in Maré takes account of this, recording those killed in both police operations and in conflicts between armed groups (Table 7.2). In 2017, 88 per cent of those killed as a result of armed violence in Maré were Black or mixed race. In 2018, that number rose to 92 per cent. In 2019, 95 per cent of those killed were Black or mixed race, while a year later (2020) all of those killed in police operations belonged to these ethno-racial groups.

This policy of managed killings, resulting mainly from the lack of a public security policy based on protecting life, is a hallmark of racism in Brazil. Regular monitoring highlights the racial dimension of violent death, with the Black population, above all young people and favela residents, deemed worthless, ranked as subordinates and their killings met largely with public indifference. As the youngest are the largest category of victims of violence, an important part of Brazil's future is sacrificed.

Table 7.1: Impact of police operations on Maré's favelas

Year	Number of operations	Deaths	Injuries	Days schools were shut	Days with no health services operating
2016	33	17	8	28	20
2017	41	20	41	27	36
2018	16	19	13	10	11
2019	39	34	30	24	25
Total	129	90	92	89	92

Source: *De olho na Maré* – Redes da Maré

Table 7.2: Violent death rates in police operations and conflicts between armed groups in Maré

2017	Race/colour	Black	Mixed race	White	Total
	Number of deaths	18	10	4	32
	Percentage	56%	31%	13%	100%
	Not given	10			
	Total	42			
2018	Race/colour	Black	Mixed race	White	Total
	Number of deaths	5	7	1	13
	Percentage	38%	54%	8%	100%
	Not given	11			
	Total	24			
2019	Race/colour	Black	Mixed race	White	Total
	Number of deaths	11	31	2	44
	Percentage	25%	70%	5%	100%
	Not given	5			
	Total	49			

Source: *De olho na Maré* – Redes da Maré

Rio de Janeiro has historically adopted a strategy of repression and neglect in relation to its poorest, non-White population, essentially those living in favelas. As community activists, we have observed a police and public security model rooted in a logic of repression and militarised violence which fails to recognise the favela population as citizens of the city. In addition to the quality of public services offered in these territories generally being substandard, the official perception of these areas as being more violent than anywhere else, reinforces, and is used to justify, aggressive behaviour by state forces. This results in the systematic violation of fundamental rights guaranteed by law. The so-called war on drugs does have a direct impact on the daily lives of favelas and working-class districts, but in the name of 'combatting drugs', government decision-makers and agencies justify rights violations against Maré residents, and especially, against young Black people, that have been experienced year on year.

In response to this situation, Redes da Maré has invested considerable time and attention in developing an effective community-based public security strategy. This is composed of a number of reinforcing elements which seek to change the way security forces relate to the residents of Maré. This is based on mobilising people directly affected by the violence, both in terms of ensuring individual support where required, but also in building collective strategies. These include:

- *Production of knowledge about the context of armed violence in Maré*: working to collect data on violence and rights violations using the following methodology: (1) data collection on rights violations in situ, both during armed conflicts and up to 48 hours after they start; (2) connecting with a network of local collaborators who report and validate evidence about violent incidents through an Eyes on Maré initiative; (3) collection of official data from municipal and state government departments as well as from police and research institutes; (4) a survey of mass media and social networks; (5) production and maintenance of database; and (6) annual publication of The Right to Public Security in Maré Bulletin.
- *Assisting victims of rights violations*: free social and legal assistance for residents, in the context of armed violence. Support services provided by social workers, psychologists and lawyers seek to enable and strengthen access to rights, especially to justice.
- *Mobilisation of residents*: activities to raise awareness and disseminate content about fundamental rights. Starting with daily dialogue on the streets, the intention is to strengthen strategies for demanding rights, especially in areas where repeated violations occur.
- *Maximising political impact*: the central idea of this work is to maintain a permanent dialogue with government agencies, researchers, social movements and influencers that allow the effective strengthening of public policies in the territory, especially related to public security and access to justice.

In the context of the community mobilisation work carried out by Redes da Maré, the campaign 'Somos da Maré, Temos Direitos!' ('We're from Maré, We have Rights!') began in 2012, with the aim of informing and strengthening the idea of security as a right for Maré's residents. The first stage of the campaign focused on agreeing content about what is legal and illegal during police operations. This was followed up by stage two which engaged residents in dialogue about the impact of police operations on their daily lives. Conversations were held in public spaces and volunteers delivered leaflets door-to-door to some 47,000 households. This consultation work resulted in the idea that the network could be a channel for denouncing violations, but it could also support dialogue with public security agents to protect rights during police activities. Consequently, local residents turn to Redes da Maré to seek support in crises and violent situations during interaction with the police, as well as to formalise legal complaints in the case of rights violations.

Based on the work of social workers and lawyers, the Right to Public Security and Access to Justice team's area of work began to accompany residents at different stages of the legal system: at police stations or the offices of public defenders and public prosecutors, for example. It was on the basis of these experiences that we realised the power of strengthening individual demands and facilitating access to justice, while promoting the construction of collective strategies for demanding rights.

Training support is also available through a course on 'Talking about Public Security in Maré'. The course is basically a series of meetings with interested residents to reflect on aspects of daily life related to human rights and public security. Topics include drug policy, gun control, high homicide rates, access to justice and the right to public security from a perspective that considers gender and race issues. It is intended to promote exchanges of experiences between participants, building strategies to cope with violence as well as to engage in discussion with various specialists, activists, other residents and professionals working in Maré. A complementary Textual Production Workshop encourages and skills local participants to write about their experiences in articles that are then published in the pages of *Maré de Notícias* online. A professor working on Redé's Pre-College Admission Programme teaches in the workshop to help develop the necessary writing skills. This approach facilitates the process of local people taking ownership of the public security narrative.

Public Civil Action of Maré: a case study

A Public Civil Action is a procedural and legal tool provided for in the Brazilian Constitution that deals with diffuse and collective rights. The purpose of this class action is to protest for the rights of people in the same situation. The Public Civil Action of Maré was Brazil's first collective lawsuit in the public security field that obliges the police to submit to a series of measures to reduce harm and risk during its operations in favelas. The public civil lawsuit (known as ACP Maré) that was brought in Rio de Janeiro's Court of Justice in June 2016 was in direct response to the rights violations experienced as a result of police actions overseen by the Public Security department of Rio's state government. Its aim was to protect residents' rights during police operations. The case was brought by Redes da Maré, in conjunction with the Public Defender's Office, the Public Prosecution Office, residents and representatives of other associations and NGOs. Almost a year later, in June 2017, a preliminary injunction was granted by the judiciary determining that public security agents adopt a series of measures for any police operations in Maré, including the requirements that:

- police operations comply with court orders and are prohibited at night;
- vehicles should be installed with video cameras and Global Positioning Systems;
- vehicles should be installed with audio equipment;
- ambulances should be made available on police operation days; and
- a Violence Reduction Plan should be made for police operation days.

Although legally approved, these measures have never been fully complied with by the state, but they still constituted an important tool to give visibility to the ongoing violations of rights and to mobilise people around demanding a security policy based on the defence of life and the protection of citizens in Maré. This was celebrated as a success, but also heralded an improvement in the public security situation over the next period. The latter was presented in the third *Right to Public Security in Maré Bulletin*, published by Redes da Maré, which highlighted that between 2017 and 2018 there had been a reduction in the number of police operations, which resulted in fewer days of school closures and health services disruption; also, fewer armed conflicts, deaths and injuries. For example, when 2017 and 2018 are compared, it can be seen that there was a 61 per cent reduction in police operations, which dropped from 41 in 2017 to 16 in 2018. Similarly, conflicts between armed groups fell by 43 per cent, days without schooling by 71 per cent, and days when health services were disrupted by 76 per cent.

However, local monitoring saw the situation deteriorating again in 2019, when between 10 and 12 June 2019, the Military Police Special Operations Coordination (COE) entered, and remained in, Maré for three full days. On 19 July 2019, less than a month later, the ACP Maré public civil lawsuit injunction was suspended. Soon after, the Public Defender's Office for Rio de Janeiro state filed an appeal for it to be reinstated and, at the same time, Redes da Maré started a series of mobilisations in the area, with local partners, in order to reverse this decision. One of the proposed actions was for residents, especially children and young people, to write letters to the judges expressing how they live and feel when armed conflicts take place in Maré and how this recurring situation affects their lives and limits their daily activities, such as going to school or playing outdoors.

This campaign, carried out between July and August 2019, resulted in 1,509 letters being written by residents in Maré in just one month. On 12 August, the same day that the Public Defender's Office formally lodged a case to reinstate the ACP Maré decision, a group of residents went to the state's Court of Justice to deliver these letters to the court president but were not granted an audience. The letters were filed and the following day they were archived. However, the 'Letters of Maré' gained coverage across all national and international media and eventually managed to make an impression on Judge Jessé Torres, who decided, on 14 August, to reinstate the ACP Maré injunction temporarily until the case could be judged.

As already noted, ACP Maré was the first collective legal case dealing with the right to public security in the favelas. Recognising the importance of involving the judiciary in this debate, the 'action against the violation of constitutional fundamental right 635' (ADPF das Favelas) was filed with Brazil's Federal Supreme Court in late 2019. Like the ACP Maré, the ADPF das Favelas is a legal instrument, with the aim of preventing the state authorities from behaving in ways that violate the constitution and undermine the rights of the population living in favelas and working-class areas, during police operations in Rio de Janeiro state. It was lodged at a time when the impact of armed violence began to rise again due to the politics of the elected Rio de Janeiro state government which favoured a militarised public security policy, the consequence of which was an increase in the number of police operations in favelas and the exacerbation of rights violations in these areas.

Comparing 2018 and 2019, the impact of this policy as according to the fourth *Right to Public Security in Maré Bulletin*, the number of police operations more than doubled, rising from 16 to 39. The impact of these operations on local people rose more than 100 per cent over those years, with victims of firearm injuries rising from 13 to 30, and school and health service closures rising from 10 to 24 days and from 11 to 25 days, respectively. The death toll as a result of the operations increased 79 per cent, from 19 in 2018 to 34 in 2019. As in previous years, those that died were racially either Black or Brown.

Based on the ADPF das Favelas, on 5 June 2020, Minister Edson Fachin, of the Federal Supreme Court, issued a preliminary injunction suspending police operations in Rio de Janeiro's favelas during the pandemic period, except in exceptional cases. According to the minister, in these cases, care must be taken not to put the population, the provision of public health services and humanitarian aid efforts carried out by residents and organisations working in those territories at even greater risk.

According to Redes da Maré's records for armed violence, the minister's decision has had a significant impact on the figures. When comparing the months of June and July 2019 and 2020, we noticed that in June 2020, after this decision, the number of police operations dropped by 75 per cent, which resulted in a decrease from five deaths in June 2019 to none in June 2020. In July 2020, the impact was even greater. In 2019, there were five police operations in that month, resulting in six deaths, while in July 2020, there were no police operations or deaths in that month. By comparing the same period over the two years, we estimate that the measures as a result of the ADPF das Favela saved at least 11 lives among Maré's residents in the COVID-19 pandemic period. The Redes Maré Right to Public Security and Access to Justice team continues to monitor the situation and it is noteworthy that the resurgence of violence led to a community mobilisation which mounted a protest for life in Complexo da Maré that was covered in the network's Rio on Watch[2] communications site in February 2021. Placards carried by local people asserted that 'Peace without Voice isn't Peace, it's Fear'.

Conclusion

For residents of a poor, marginalised area, who suffer high levels of violence on a daily basis, peacebuilding is a mix of visibility, the assertion of rights and envisioning a more equitable and just future for themselves, their families and their community. Redes da Maré has created space and opportunities for this in favelas that have long experienced endemic violence, demonisation in political and public perceptions and a militarised state security response that has resulted in loss of life, injuries and a breakdown of trust in the concept of law and security. Through a mixture of bottom-up reframing of the narrative of public security and adopting approaches that raise local awareness and confidence about the feasibility of asserting individual and collective rights, Redes da Maré has effectively combined community mobilisation with alliance building and effective advocacy strategies. It has also drawn on the ability of residents to tell their own story, whether through the writing and drawings by school children or the newsletter blogs and letters by adults impacted by the violence.

For the activists that work through Redes da Maré the central question remains how the state makes itself present in their favelas and what regard it has for people living on the periphery. The constant armed conflicts that happen systematically in favelas continue to have an impact on many aspects of daily life, including affecting the school life of children and adolescents through the cancellation of classes on the days of police operations as well as the disruption of other essential services. The state, for its part, fails to offer effective public policies that can break the cycle of armed violence. The so-called 'war on drugs', inherited from the United States, shows itself to be an ideology of criminalising poverty, which has intensified the process of militarising police actions in Maré. In this scenario, all rights violations committed during police raids against residents are justified by a discourse on combatting drugs and crime. Armed violence is the greatest expression of our inequalities as a society, as it is supported by a vision of favelas and their residents that defines them as 'dangerous' or as an 'enemy army', as already pointed out by Silva (2015). This framework of violence and lack of respect for basic rights, such as the right to life and freedom, affects the present and threatens the future of Maré's residents.

The importance of shifting the narrative about public security became linked to the need to defend democracy as experienced by local people in Maré. Brazil has a Federal Constitution that was introduced in 1988 on the back of a national struggle for the reinstatement of democracy from the rule of the military (1964–85). The progressive character of this Constitution has, in theory, consolidated the democratic rule of law, however it is clear that the poorest people, who are mostly Black and live in favelas, have rarely experienced the benefit of this democracy in practice. On a day-to-day basis public security policies appear to be one of the main instruments for violating these people's fundamental rights. The reality of life in Complexo da Maré can be assessed from the number of days of school and health service closures, house raids, constant physical and psychological violence, especially the violation of the right to life, resulting from armed violence that has become the norm in this area. The policy of shoot-to-kill policing as a public security approach is not a one-off phenomenon that is contrary to the rule. It is the rule, despite being out-with the law. The routine practice has both normalised it and sends out a clear message that the state has little regard for the wellbeing of those living in favelas and working-class areas.

As a result of this experience, Redes da Maré has realised the importance of mobilising residents, producing knowledge and creating new narratives that come from people who experience violence directly. Through collective discussion and dialogue, based on everyday reality, it has been possible to think of alternatives and possibilities that change the way in which public policies can operate in these areas. It is also essential to involve the whole of society, and the different spheres of power, in the debate about the dynamics of violence as well as identifying strategies to overcome an establishment logic of combatting crime through militarised approaches that have extracted a heavy toll in the favelas for many years.

Work is ongoing to build mechanisms that expand ways to access justice, democratic spaces and social participation in order to win a new narrative of public security that can encompass a rights-based approach. Experiences such as the legal ACP Maré and the ADPF das Favelas cases have been shown to be effective instruments for reducing police violence in favelas (despite the periodic setbacks) when based on a broad societal alliance and where a central role is given to those people directly affected by the violence experienced.

Notes

[1] www.redesdamare.org.br
[2] www.rioonwatch.org

References

Galtung, J. (1969) 'Violence, peace and peace research', *Journal of Peace Research*, 6(3): 167–91.

Maricato, E. (2015) *Para entender a crise urbana*, São Paulo: Expressão Popular.

Redes da Maré (2010) *A Maré que Queremos*. Available at http://itdpbrasil.org.br/wp-content/uploads/2016/05/Relato%CC%81rio-Mare%CC%81-que-queremos.pdf

Redes da Maré (2016) Boletim *Direito à Segurança Pública na Maré*. Available at https://www.redesdamare.org/

Redes da Maré (2017) Boletim *Direito à Segurança Pública na Maré*. Available at https://www.redesdamare.org/

Redes da Maré (2018) Boletim *Direito à Segurança Pública na Maré*. Available at https://www.redesdamare.org/

Redes da Maré (2019) Boletim *Direito à Segurança Pública na Maré*. Available at https://www.redesdamare.org/

Silva, E.S. (2015) 'Eliana Sousa', in *Testemunhos da Maré*, 2nd edn, Rio de Janeiro: Mórula.

Stevens, J., Barbosa E. and De Meulder, B. (eds) (2016) *Insurgent Cartography: Mapping Occupied São Paulo*, Leuven: KU Leuven – Faculty of Engineering Science.

8

Nepal: working with community-based women to influence inclusion and peacebuilding

Susan Risal

Setting the scene

Nepal's political history has always been unstable. The authoritarian Shah dynasty ruled over Nepal for 240 years from 1768 to 2008. Between 1846 and 1951 Nepal was dominated by the Rana family who institutionalised and controlled oligarchic rule in the country. In 1951 the Shah dynasty again regained power with the support of a number of political parties. A period of democracy followed but was again undermined by the Shah dynasty in 1960, which augured in the Panchayat era (Khadka, 1993). This regime, described as 'guided democracy', in reality concentrated power with the monarchy. Three decades later – in 1990 – the popular 'People's Movement 1' restored multi-party democracy in the country. Despite the hope of the general public that the 1990 democratic restoration in Nepal would usher in an era of improved governance and social inclusion, none of the post-1990 incoming governments met the expectations of the people for social change (Lama, 2009). The main victims of this failure have been the majority Nepali population, but particularly disadvantaged women, the poor, the vulnerable and the marginalised given the dominance of upper-caste men.[1] Such dominance applied not only to state institutions but also to civil society. Any sense of meaningful participation by people who were from poor, vulnerable and socially excluded communities in the state and non-state institutions was frustrated by the elite capture and exercise of power. Equally, participatory democracy for social change remained confined to the realm of rhetoric.

As a result of this situation, in 1996 the Maoist Party initiated the armed conflict that they named 'the people's war' by presenting a 40-point demand that included the call for Nepal to be reconstituted as a republic. The origins of the Communist Party of Nepal (CPN) date back to 1949, with the movement led by the CPN (Maoist) emerging in the late 1960s. Various different tendencies and factions were established and became

Figure 8.1: Map of Nepal

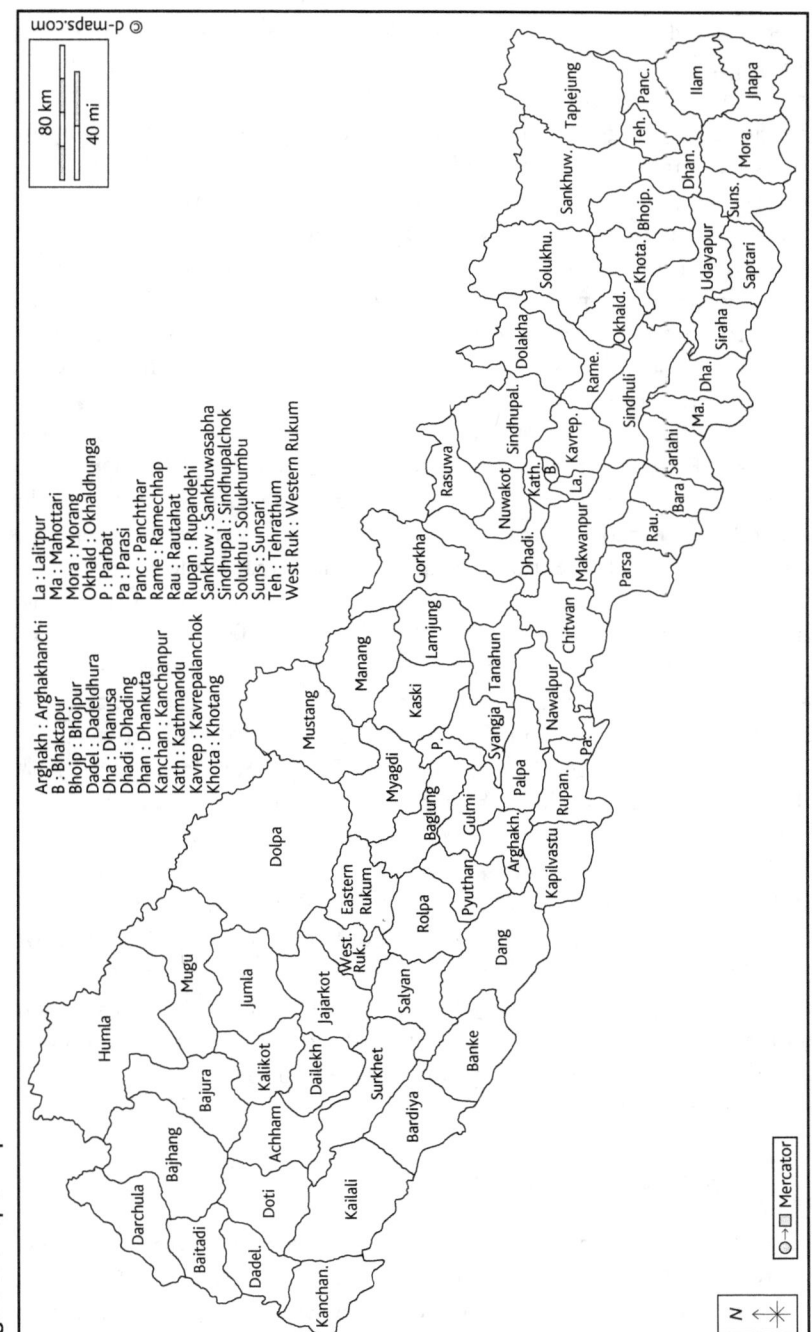

Source: https://d-maps.com/carte.php?num_car=26991&lang=en

active over the years. Some of these differences focused on whether an armed struggle strategy should be adopted versus those who advocated a more gradualist approach to the idea of revolution. In March 1995 the party named the CPN (Maoist) formally adopted the doctrine of armed struggle. This struggle, which included the targeting of those categorised as 'class enemies', started in the hill districts of Rolpa and Rukum, in the Western Region: a particularly disadvantaged region with a long history of communist organising. It was led by relatively small groups of young people from middle and lower middle-class backgrounds. The government responded with a repressive security operation, Operation Romeo, which often served to increase local alienation and garner sympathy for the Maoists. The scene was set for a conflict that developed into one of the worst periods experienced in Nepal.

By 2001, the year of the Palace massacre, which claimed the lives of nine members of the royal family, it was reported that the Maoist insurgency had spread to all 75 districts of the country. Data shows that the violence escalated considerably after the royal massacre. Human rights organisations documented both the extra-judicial executions, rape and arbitrary arrests by the police and the killings, extortion and destruction of property by the Maoists. The brunt of the impact of violence was felt in remote rural and hill areas, with limited impact on life in the capital, Kathmandu. In 2001, after the failure of a first attempt at peace talks, the government declared a state of emergency and promulgated the Terrorist and Disruptive Activities (Control and Punishment) Ordinance (TADO) which declared the Maoists to be terrorists and provided the security forces with extraordinary powers of arrest and detention. This law was in place until 2006.

In 2005 King Gyanendra assumed direct control of the government by dissolving the parliament and abrogating absolute power to the monarchy. This action by the king sparked the 'People's Movement II' which forced the reinstatement of democracy. As part of this development an alliance of seven political parties came together with the Maoists to end the war by negotiating and agreeing a consensus based on a 12-point agreement. In November 2006 the Seven Party Alliance (SPA) and the Maoist party signed a peace accord – the Comprehensive Peace Agreement (CPA).

Putting in place a peace process

The CPA laid down the basic framework for the country's political transition, however there were difficulties to be faced. In 2007, a number of groups whose grievances had not been addressed in the Agreement made their voices heard. People such as the Madhesis, *janajatis* (indigenous peoples) and the Dalits (categorised as 'untouchable' by the caste system) had long been discriminated against and excluded. The representatives of the Madhesis, who constitute about one-third of Nepal's population, questioned the peace process. It took further negotiation between their representatives and the Nepali government to reach an understanding that allowed elections to take place to the Constituent Assembly. When these finally were held in 2008, the Maoists emerged as the largest single party within the 601-member Assembly. The Maoist leader Pushpa Kamal Dahal, widely known as 'Prachanda', became prime minister. The first meeting of the Constituent Assembly declared Nepal as a Federal Democratic Republic State and abolished the monarchy.

While the CPA has been largely applauded as an achievement to end the violent conflict, there have been criticisms that there was a failure to implement the Agreement's commitments on justice and accountability. Alongside the lack of accountability of those, from all sides, who were alleged to be guilty of abuses during the conflict, there were delays in putting in place a promised Disappearances Commission and a Truth and Reconciliation Commission. It was not until 2014 that an Act was passed to establish the Commission of Investigation on Enforced Disappeared Persons (CIEDP). The Truth and Reconciliation Commission was also established in 2015. There has also been criticism of the limited compensation measures for the relief of the families of victims of the conflict. During the insurgency in Nepal, 17,625 people were killed, 78,675 people were displaced, 1,302 people were disappeared, 4,305 became disabled and 9,000 women became widowed (Ministry of Peace and Reconstruction quoted in NIPS, 2013: 2). Many women were sexually abused and physically tortured during that period but, as is the case in many conflicts, there is no exact data on those cases.

At the time of writing, Nepal is still going through the transition period, experiencing increased instability in the government and the market and widespread impunity due to legal failings. Despite almost 15 years since the CPA, there has not been any significant action taken by the state to improve the status of conflict-affected communities, and especially the position of women affected by conflict. The basic needs of these communities and the issues of justice have still to be addressed, a situation that is leading to increased frustration and anger among the conflict-affected peoples, which has the potential to further conflict. Democracy is still fragile given ongoing political, social, cultural and economic crises and the sudden announcement of elections in 2021. As has been argued (Robins, 2016) there is a real danger that the transformative ambitions of the CPA have been sacrificed in favour of a process constrained by an ideological and global understanding of liberal peace that has been used instrumentally by Nepali elites to their own advantage. Recent government action has once again sidelined the promises made in Article 3 of the CPA which envisages the 'progressive political, economic and social transformation in the country, eliminating the current centralised and unitary form of the state and ending discrimination based on class, caste language gender, culture, religion and region' (Government of Nepal, 2006, 2011).

The failure to translate these promises into government action have resulted in a situation where issues of structural violence remain unaddressed by both the governments in power and the larger political parties. The prevalence of the COVID-19 pandemic is exacerbating this experience of structural violence among the most disadvantaged communities, while at the same time being used to legitimise the actions of the state and political parties in the name of responding to the current crisis situation. However, there is still a need to acknowledge and respond to those issues that contributed to the context of the violent conflict if peace is to be sustainable and peacebuilding effective.

Despite the fact that there has been large-scale suffering as a result of the conflicts experienced in Nepal from 1990 to the present day, many local organisations contributed to peacebuilding over the years. This chapter recognises that although the main impact of the conflict has been felt by women, they were always neglected in the peacebuilding process in Nepal and excluded from any peace dividend. Notwithstanding this, it was the importance of strengthening women's agency at the community level that proved to be essential in peacebuilding. Nagarik Aawaz, as a women-led peacebuilding organisation, is an example of community peacebuilding as well as working to impact the national peace process in Nepal through the inclusion of local conflict-affected women.

Nagarik Aawaz: strategy and principles adopted

Nagarik Aawaz was established in 2001, in the midst of the crisis of violent armed conflict in Nepal. It was conceived and set up as a locally based peacebuilding organisation to respond to the immediate causes of the armed conflict. Motivated by a vision of a just and peaceful Nepal, Nagarik Aawaz believes that youth and women play a key role in turning this aspiration into reality. Consequently it has consistently invested in the personal transformation of young people and women, helping them to become leaders with a strong belief in nonviolence. The initial years of the organisation's work focused mainly on responding to the immediate needs resulting from the conflict, which involved it in establishing a weekly peace kitchen, providing meals, in 2004.

The organisation was founded under the leadership of Rita Thapa, who responded to the urgency to put in place support for women and young people impacted by the ongoing violence. Rita had already initiated Tewa (officially registered in 1997) as a Nepali Women's Fund. Reflecting on the period when she was moved to set up Nagarik Aawaz in a period of escalating violence that followed the Palace massacre, Rita spoke of how trust seemed to be disappearing on all sides, consequently, the mission of Nagarik Aawaz was to work on issues of conflict transformation and peacebuilding, although this area of work was also impacted by the prevailing climate of suspicion. It was agreed that the vulnerability of women and youth from outside of Kathmandu Valley was the most acute with attacks being experienced from both sides of the warring parties. Many were displaced from areas across Nepal and were coming to Kathmandu seeking greater safety, however, they were not being supported by any government or non-governmental structures. Nagarik Aawaz began its interventions without any clear knowledge of how to do peace work but adapting the maxim 'save seeds in the time of famine', it propounded its own philosophy of 'save women and youths in the time of war'. This formed the basis for a programme of work that focused on youths and women who were affected by the violent armed conflict.

If Nagarik Aawaz lacked a peacebuilding analysis, it rooted its understanding of need in the direct experience and local knowledge of the conflict-affected people themselves. Interestingly, current peacebuilding framing validates this approach, with reflective practitioners such as John Paul Lederach asserting that the experiences and knowledge of local people should always be at the heart of peacebuilding interventions (Lederach, 1996). Alongside this, sensitive and responsive community-based peacebuilding work draws on important values, such as egoless aptitude, empathetic approaches, the component of care and safe spaces, listening to unheard voices, building trust and relationships, groundedness and creative hearts as central to strategic peacebuilding interventions. Furthermore, as a feminist organisation, Nagarik Aawaz always believed in the philosophy of feminism that the 'personal is political', and while initiating its peace work the organisation espoused this philosophy, convinced that 'peace work is also not only personal, but political as well'. From the time of its establishment during violent conflict to the current period, Nagarik Aawaz contributed to peace work through a multiplicity of activities, informed both by unfolding events and through the adoption of conflict resolution/transformation approaches (Orjuela, 2008).

Realising how the framing of ongoing events can significantly affect the intractability of a conflict, particularly where a mutually incompatible interpretation of events exists, Nagarik Aawaz tried to reframe a unifying worldview among its team members as well as the conflict-affected youth and women that it worked with. The emphasis was on experiencing transformation at both the individual/personal level and the sociopolitical level by applying various strategies and creativity (Kaufman et al, 2003). Further, as argued by Lederach, it worked to promote constructive processes of transformation within both these levels (Lederach, 2003). By analysing the systemic relationship between various factors in its peacebuilding work, Nagarik Aawaz identified five principles which became intrinsic to the

Table 8.1: The foundational principles of Nagarik Aawaz

Care	This value guides us to practice empathy in our actions and serve people from our heart. We care for human dignity and frugal utilisation of resources, and manage conflict through nonviolence.
Everyday peace	Peace has to be felt by each individual in a way that is defined by them. We help promote peace which exists in everyday experiences of people and help them to live with dignity and justice.
Safe space	Developing physical and psychological space where people can feel safe and secure to express, engage and strive for a better future. Additionally, practise transparency, accountability and responsibility to manage conflict through nonviolence.
Human relationships	Human relationships are the foundation for peace and harmony. It enhances relationships and trust between individuals and groups. This, in turn, creates a favourable environment for individuals and groups to work together, to accept each other's differences and heritage, and to bring them closer together for sustained peace and harmony.
Listening to unheard voices	We plan our responses keeping people in our heart, listening to their voices and dialogues, and valuing their needs and aspirations in relation to fostering peace and harmony among people, groups and the society as a whole.

effectiveness of the organisation and contributed to the clear understanding that contribution to one system will have ripple effects on others (Table 8.1). Peacebuilding thus became both internal and external.

In addition to clarifying the five organisational principles, Nagarik Aawaz moved over time from its initial response to expressed need to combining these interventions to examining the causes of the conflict as well as addressing the deep-rooted structural fissures that contributed to violent conflict.

Community development approaches and peacebuilding
Investing in local women affected by conflict

Gender is the socially determined expectations for what it means to be male and female, it is caused by the psychological and social development of individuals within a society (Ojha et al, 2005). In times of violent conflict, men and women face new roles and changing gender expectations. It has been further argued that violent conflict offers opportunities for reshaping both public and private relationships between men and women and in taking positive steps towards gender equality (Schirch and Sewak, 2005). Women and men experience the impact of the war very differently. Without taking gender into account, real conflict transformation will not occur. Women are more affected by war, and they face multiple forms of violence. Warring parties use women as weapons and as targets of sexual violence, which often goes unacknowledged. There is also a tendency to see women solely in terms of war victims, ignoring their potential for building peace as change agents within their societies. When a country enters into a phase of peacemaking, and post-war peacebuilding, there is a real danger that the contribution and potential of women is overlooked and neglected. However, Nagarik Aawaz believes that if peace and security is to be sustainable at every level, women must be included in every plan, policy and peacebuilding process, facilitating them to contribute to peace writ large.

However, in Nepal's peacebuilding process, the country has failed to acknowledge the women's contribution for system change; there has been little or no effort made to include them in the peacebuilding process nor to provide holistic justice to conflict-affected women by adopting a gender lens. Despite the fact that ten years of violent conflict in the country opened up avenues towards gender equality, the status of conflict-affected women has not changed. At the time of insurgency, many women lost their husbands either by killing or by enforced disappearance; many experienced intense gender-based violence; others were forcibly displaced from their hometown; as well as those who either joined, or were forced to work, as frontline combatants, leaving their family and societal roles as daughters, mothers and wives. During the period of post-conflict reintegration, most of the women who were combatants returned back to their accustomed social roles and the household chores. Many of the women who were adversely affected by the conflict are still living with a sense of victimhood, due to the lack of strong justice mechanisms or any access to accountability or compensation for the hurts suffered.

As an organisation rooted in feminist ideology and believing in the grounded notion that women can be catalysts for change, Nagarik Aawaz invested its initial peace effort in prioritising support for conflict-affected women, working with them to create and strengthen the culture of peace. We recognised the core primacy of basic human needs as an essential requirement for human development (Burton, 1990), and that the failure to satisfy these needs leads to dysfunctional development, frustration and protracted conflict. Identity and security are important needs requiring both physiological security and identity, as well as the need for self-esteem. Nagarik Aawaz initially provided the opportunity to meet these basic needs as expressed by conflict-affected women who were struggling for survival, both physically and mentally. The programmatic approach adopted by Nagarik Aawaz reflected the nested paradigm suggested by Lederach, where peacebuilding is divided into four phases:

1. immediate action/crisis intervention (2–6 months);
2. short range planning/preparation and training (1–2 years);
3. decade thinking/design of social change (5–10 years); and
4. generational vision/desired change (20+ years). (Lederach, 1997: 80)

According to this scenario, conflict transformation should be seen as a long-term progression in which we can distinguish timeframes appropriate for planning and action, so that specific intermediate interventions are connected to movement towards a long-term outcome goal. This framing addresses the structural and relationship challenges that generate systematic conflict and helps move in the direction of desired change. It is accepted that without building the necessary capacities at the individual level, as well as within the communities who experienced the direct impact of armed conflict, desired social change cannot be achieved. This then inhibits the potential to achieve sustainable peace. Nagarik Aawaz's programming was informed by Lederach's theories when it initiated the holistic intervention that helped women to become change agents, building their self-esteem and supporting their advocacy in asserting their rights.

The initial interventions were primarily focused on providing immediate relief to meet the basic needs identified. Later on, when a relationship had been established, the focus shifted to empowering the conflict-affected women through various capacity building training, such as conflict transformation and peacebuilding, gender equality, nonviolence, peace education, storytelling and listening skills, social inclusion, governance and democratic practices, composite heritage in peacebuilding, and so on. This acquired knowledge was applied first by women and youth in their personal lives, and then within their community. This helped the women start their own initiatives to challenge gender hierarchy, gender inequality, patriarchy, normative understanding of violence and asymmetrical power relations. They were also better equipped to question, and raise their voices against, the structural discrimination within their communities. From long-term experience, Nagarik Aawaz has learnt that when women are provided with capacity building training in an appropriate manner and over a period of time when they are most receptive, then they can emerge as community leaders who can contribute to maintaining peace in their communities. However, simultaneously, investment has to be made in their personal transformation, given as Galtung (Galtung, 1969) suggests that attitude, behaviour and the context contribute to an individual's ability to be an effective peacebuilder. This is also Nagarik Aawaz's understanding as it found that it was preferable to work more on aspects of personal transformation first before strengthening the capacities for community leadership and societal transformation. Focus on personal transformation also helped in building a sense of ownership and respect for shared values and the acceptance of others that are the main variables for building a culture of peace.

Working at this personal transformation level requires interventions that seek to achieve a mental shift from those cultural values that exacerbate intolerance and violence. This shift does not happen instantly, and indeed requires time and the use of creative processes. Thus, women were provided with the opportunity for long-term engagement and a range of support strategies, including those that helped them come to terms with trauma and psychological issues, as well as practical financial and social empowerment. Women are encouraged and supported to express their feelings and to build sufficient trust to share their experiences of hurt. With this focus on the individual, many conflict-affected women came to realise that they were not the only person to have been subjected to sexual and other forms of violence in a conflict situation where all too often women's bodies became a battleground. Alongside this approach, as a women-led organisation, Nagarik Aawaz adopts a feminist approach to peacebuilding by raising the awareness of conflict-affected women about power relations in different structures and the position of women in a public domain that has consistently undervalued their contribution. This helps promote visibility of issues but also builds their leadership potential.

Another important aspect of the work is the effort to collectively shape the peace together, drawing on the diverse past histories and experiences of conflict-affected women. Nagarik Aawaz has learned over the years that we cannot destroy or ignore past stories in an effort to replace them with new narratives. Instead, we need to listen to each other in an open and receptive manner. This, often sensitive and difficult, peacebuilding work rarely requires hardcore technical or intellectual skills (which can sometimes actually inhibit the understanding) but does need heart, creative arts and soul to encompass and deal with the deep-rooted impact of the conflict that was experienced and is shared. This collective process has the potential to create a sense of solidarity between diverse conflict-affected women, enhancing their understanding of each other's stories and breaking down feelings of fear and suspicion. The importance of humility and softness as a basis for empathy is highlighted as an essential ingredient for effective peacebuilding. The capacity to take risks when engaging in challenging conversations is also recognised given that the path to peace is complex and often uncertain. This very uncertainty necessitates regular reflection and assessment of what is working and where approaches were less effective make changes. Consolidating and building capacity means taking risks, and meaningful intervention often uses creative arts. It also requires the moment of standstill whereby we can assess what went wrong and what went right to consolidate the existing best practices as well as to learn from difficult situations. On many occasions Nagarik Aawaz has managed tense or risky situations by encouraging women to use creative art forms, like poetry, peace songs and theatre for peace, as interventions that are inclusive and non-threatening in nature. Reflection is also encouraged to take stock of the impact of programmes of intervention.

Creating safe space

The second area of intervention that Nagarik Aawaz invested in is creating a safe space for women, community groups, local and national political leaders and other stakeholders. In both the time of the conflict, and in the post-conflict period, these essential spaces shrink. As an inevitable consequence of the large-scale violence and concentrations of power, ordinary people suffer and face the breakdown of social relationships. This results in an increasing sense of fear and deep-rooted mistrust of the 'other'. This prevailing uncertainty and fear further contributes to destabilising the social and cultural fabric of the society. In conflict transformation terms, the conflict affects physical wellbeing, self-esteem, emotional stability and damages the physical, spiritual and psychological integrity of the individual. By extension, the integrity of the family and community is adversely affected. Therefore conflict transformation requires interventions designed to minimise these destructive effects and maximise the potential for individual growth at the interrelated physical, emotional and spiritual levels (Hamber, 2009).

The creation of safe and inclusive spaces for individual women, and their communities, is very important to facilitate the building of relationships, as well as hosting dialogue and discussion on the individual and collective impact of the violence of the conflict, as well as about issues of structural violence. Alongside this, the creation of safe spaces allows communities to come together, in both the conflict and post-conflict periods, to share and understand each other's identity, sense of belongingness and the need for greater mutual understanding and thinking in terms of each other's security. All these elements are essential if there is to be any opportunity to build a greater sense of tolerance or to build a culture of peace that might contribute to sustainable peacebuilding at the community level. In the many communities and districts where Nagarik Aawaz works, in partnership with other organisations, there is evidence that opening up these safe spaces provides women and their communities with the ability to effect individual reconciliation by ventilating their stories through dialogue with previously divided groups. There is also the potential for communities to come together to challenge the legitimacy of established power structures.

As an organisation that offers a feminist analysis, Nagarik Aawaz works with conflict-affected women in these community spaces to support critical conversations that challenge the structural inequalities/violence and to question prevailing social norms, belief systems, values that promote patriarchy and a normative framework of violence. It is in these spaces that Nagarik Aawaz encourage women to express their feelings in the form of songs, peace drama, poetry and dance; creative forms that Nepal is culturally very rich in. These approaches also help to spread messages of peace and harmony to the larger community, making them aware of their roles and responsibilities in sustaining peace. Besides this, participative artistic initiatives help to heal trauma, drawing on Nepalese traditions of cultural healing which reduces dependency on the Western style of trauma management. It has been found to be important to ensure that local peacebuilding activities should not ignore the psychosocial effects of violent conflict; the experience of trauma and other less visible effects of violence can be very damaging both to individuals and communities.

Nagarik Aawaz recognises that underpinning all these initiatives and approaches is the critical element of trust. Constructive individual and community communication helps to build bridges between people and develop a healthy nonviolent response to injustice by generating greater community trust and promoting positive leadership. The security that safe space provides gives women the opportunity to participate in discussions/activities and to gain greater acceptance and the trust of their communities. The confidence to share their stories of past suffering is also critical for collective democratic change in the structure of power. Social opportunities are opened up for women to come together and challenge the legitimacy of current power systems. In addition to this, Nagarik Aawaz is always mindful about intersectionality and the complexities of both social and power systems, which include many diverse actors. The safe spaces provided allow broader engagement with a range of these actors – youth and women affected by armed conflict, non-affected communities, government stakeholders, traditional leaders, students, security personnel, as well as women-led organisations. Sensitively handled, these intersectional meetings can contribute to further building the necessary trust and relationships among people.

In short, common space enables people to come together to talk about their problems, traumas and sufferings and to seek alternatives to their problems through the use of creative approaches that serve to develop self-esteem and build relationships for, and with, those who were most impacted by violent conflict. The safe spaces can be in the form of rooms or as open places where diverse groups of people can meet, talk and express their opinions and feelings. While peacebuilding is inevitably a difficult and lengthy process, it is particularly important in the specific context of South Asian nations to empower women and local communities to address the basic human need for justice and reconciliation in the aftermath of conflict. This entails talking about issues such as unequal power structures, lack of good governance, corruption and serious deficits in the rule of law, which are all underlying causes of conflict. Safe spaces are essential if such issues are to be considered and discussed.

Building collaboration, networks and linkages

Another crucial consideration in the strategic approach adopted by Nagarik Aawaz is time invested in building collaboration, networks and linkages for individual, societal, political and cultural change. A conflict or war impacts on all aspects of human experience, from the personal to the social, and from the political to the cultural. For this reason peace work cannot be done in isolation and it requires the engagement of multiple stakeholders if we want to see the change necessary at different levels to create a culture of peace. Evidence tells us that where programmes only focus on change at the individual/personal level, without regard to the social/political dimensions, they inevitably fall short of having an impact on the larger goals (Collaborative for Development Action, 2016). Consequently, Nagarik Aawaz encourages women to build the necessary linkages between different levels so that they are better placed to achieve real change.

The linking of the various dimensions of the long-term peacebuilding work also ensure that no political or strategic goals can be pursued without addressing the basic human needs for safety, wellbeing and a more secure livelihood for those people who suffered most during the conflict. A conflict transformation approach needs to be based on this premise. People on the ground, and their legitimate aspirations, should be an integral part of any political or strategic considerations. Therefore our effort to ensure inclusion in local peacebuilding has to engage multiple stakeholders by building collaboration, networks and linkages so that these issues can be heard and addressed in the interests of contributing to a culture of peace. Nagarik Aawaz is committed to supporting peacebuilding to network beyond the local and parochial by engaging with multiple actors and facilitating the engagement of conflict-affected women with such actors.

Trauma healing circles

The importance of recognising and addressing the issue of trauma has been noted in this chapter as a core aspect of the work of Nagarik Aawaz. The fact that many women are still experiencing post-traumatic stress disorder (PTSD) as a result of the impact of political violence undermines their sense of self-esteem, gives rise to mistrust, reduces social connections and isolates them due to the sense of humiliation. It also undermines their identity and their sense of belonging in both their community and society. As Hamber argued (Hamber, 2009), trust and a sense of connection are essential to social interaction and wellbeing. The erosion of social ties and the collapse of connection and confidence results in both individuals and communities becoming less tolerant of 'the other' and less able to cope with difference.

There are also the very real practical problems experienced when conflict-affected women and their children are abandoned by their family members. This inevitably undermines their sense of identity and belonging and can result in these individuals starting to see their family members as 'others'. Nagarik Aawaz is delivering a current programme called 'Building Leadership for Women, Peace, Security and Equity' (supported by German funders) to work with women who faced sexual violence, torture and whose husbands disappeared during the conflict. In a number of cases such women were also disowned by family members. The work is being implemented in the Dang, Rolpa, Kailali and Bardiya districts of Nepal, all areas that were badly affected by the violence. In the spirit of collaboration, Nagarik Aawaz is working in partnership with the Nepal Women Community Service Centre (NWCSC) based in Dang and Tharu Mahila Uthan Kendra (TMUC) based in Bardiya. Both the cultural and the psychological empowerment of the women are priorities, as is the challenge of raising broader societal awareness about what the women have suffered.

Forty conflict-affected women are engaging as 'Women Peace Facilitators' (aged from 18 to 50 years), with the facilitators being drawn from different ethnicities: Chaudhary, Dalit and other marginalised communities who were adversely impacted by the conflict. These women, in turn, are reaching out to another 60 women who are conflict-affected to engage and work with them in community-based peace centres. This survivor-to-survivor approach helps consolidate social and psychological empowerment by building trust and relationships. The opportunity for vocational training is also provided through this programme to support women's economic security which is found to contribute to peace and reconciliation. The safe space provided by the peace centres that are located in all four districts offer confidential space for women to ventilate their trauma and receive psychosocial counselling as well as a referral service for legal counselling. Where required, access to medical support is also put in place. Alongside addressing PTSD, different empowerment initiatives encourage women to develop their leadership potential. Feelings of revenge and anger are worked through in a transformative manner to focus on reconciliation and forgiveness. After receiving the counselling services, participating in peace circles and dialogue sessions with other non-affected communities is encouraged. These are supported when the women feel empowered, socially and psychologically, to become involved in advocacy for peace, security and equity.

Peace circles and dialogue

Another crucial intervention that Nagarik Aawaz invested in is peace circles and dialogue between conflict-affected communities and non-affected communities that involves the participation of extended family members of conflict-affected youth and women. These include community leaders, male leaders, representatives of youth and women groups, representatives of government bodies and of other organisations and agencies, by giving a space for everyone to voice their opinions. The dialogue approach adopted is a small-scale communication process in which participants may say or hear something that is either new to them or that they have never said before, and which may completely change their perspectives and views. The approach emphasises listening, learning and the development of shared understanding (Maise, 2003). When conducting a dialogue between the groups, the methodology adopted is for the participants to sit in a circle. The circle represents a non-hierarchical position, where all participants can feel comfortable in communicating their views and feelings. It also creates a space where all participants can be equally heard as they speak to one another. Women, and other people who might not be used to having their voices heard, are particularly encouraged to speak openly, as well as to listen respectfully and attentively. This helps the stakeholders from non-affected communities to hear and understand the struggles faced by the conflict-affected women.

Nagarik Aawaz has found that this type of peace circle and dialogue helps to break the cycle of violence and transform the identity of the conflict-affected women from victims to agents of peace and social change. The open sharing and dialogue strengthen communication between the women and the community groups which, in turn, plays a vital role in bridging the gap between previously opposed and/or fragmented communities. With an emphasis on seeking healthy nonviolent responses to injustice, the approach contributes directly to peacebuilding. On a broader basis, the sharing of past suffering through dialogue can be critical in identifying priorities for collective democratic change in the structure of power. It offers space for communities to come together to critique and challenge the legitimacy of current power structures and to seek positive alternatives that can contribute to the sustainability of peacebuilding.

Conclusion

There are undoubtedly different strategies which can be applied to transform the conflict in our communities by engaging women, but the approaches adopted have to be contextual and acceptable to the communities themselves. This consideration needs to be balanced with the priority of ensuring the inclusion of women directly affected by conflict. Their experiences and knowledge need to be taken into account to contribute to the community peacebuilding process with the objective of achieving durable peace. This requires attention to long-term processes as transformation does not occur instantly. The processes adopted involve multiple actors, time and techniques, as well as attention to sensitivities, hurt and silenced voices. Strategies consist of a state of art which can contribute to reconstituting the broken relationships, building trust among individuals and groups in the divided society as well as fostering the social fabric of that society by addressing the impact of direct cultural and structural violence.

While working to these objectives, Nagarik Aawaz has a clear understanding of the systemic relationship between various factors that might impact on effective peacebuilding outcomes, given that societies are built around various systems that are relationship-based. If there are changes in one system, we experience ripple effects in other systems as well. Therefore we need to be mindful about systemic intersectionalities and complexities given the range of diverse actors involved. Bringing conflict-affected women together with these different stakeholders can reduce antagonisms and enhance mutual understanding, particularly where the women have been supported by prior access to trauma healing services, peace circle dialogue and collective analysis of issues. The building of collaboration, networking and linkages between policy decision-makers and the women can also highlight the importance of these support programmes. Consequently, Nagarik Aawaz needs to constantly reflect on its work in order to identify both opportunities and gaps in provision that can be addressed in a timely manner, but also to learn from the insights and experience of the youth and women that it is working with.

Note

[1] The national census of 2011 lists some 26 caste/ethnic groups, with the largest being the Chhetri (16.6 per cent), 12 languages and four major religious groups, with a population of some 26 million.

References

Burton, J.W. (1990) *Conflict: Human Needs Theory* (Vol. 2). New York: St Martin's Press.

Collaborative for Development Action (2016) *Reflecting on Peace Practice (RPP) Basics: A Resource Manual*, Cambridge, MA: CDA Collaborative Learning Projects. Available at Reflecting-on-Peace-Practice-RPP-Basics-A-Resource-Manual.pdf

Galtung, J. (1969) 'Violence, peace and peace research', *Journal of Peace Research*, 3: 167–92.

Government of Nepal (2006) *Comprehensive Peace Agreement between the Government of Nepal and the Communist Party of Nepal (Maoist)*. Available at https://peacemaker.un.org/nepal-comprehensiveagreement2006

Government of Nepal (2011) *National Action Plan on Implementation of the United Nations Security Council Resolution 1325 & 1820*, Nepal: Ministry of Peace and Reconstruction. Available at https://www.lse.ac.uk/women-peace-security/assets/documents/2019/NAP/Nepal-NAP-2011-2016.pdf

Hamber, B. (2009) *Transforming Societies after Political Violence: Truth and Reconciliation and Mental Health*, New York: Springer-Verlag.

Kaufman, S., Elliot, M. and Shumeli, D. (2003) 'Beyond intractability: Frames, framing and reframing', *Beyond Intractability*. Available at http://www.beyondintractability.org/essay/framing

Khadka, N. (1993) 'Democracy and development in Nepal: Prospects and challenges', *Pacific Affairs*, 66(1): 44–71.

Lama, S.S. (2009) *Decentralized Local Governance: Rhetoric and Practice in Nepal since 1950s*, Thesis, Tribhuvan University, Kathmandu.

Lederach, J.P. (1996) *Preparing for Peace: Conflict Transformation Across Cultures*, New York: Syracuse University Press.

Lederach, J.P. (1997) *Building Peace: Sustainable Reconciliation in Divided Societies*, Washington, DC: US Institute of Peace.

Lederach, J.P. (2003) 'Conflict transformation', *Beyond Intractability*, October. Available at http://www.beyondintractability.org/essay/transformation

Maise, M. (2003) 'Dialogue', *Beyond Intractability*. Available at http://www.beyondintractability.org/essay/Dialogue

Nepal Institute for Policy Studies (NIPS) (2013) *Nepal's Peace Process: A Brief Overview*, Kathmandu: NIPS. Available at https://issat.dcaf.ch/download/111494/2023947/Nepal%D5s%20Peace%20Process_A%20Brief%20Overview_Eng%20(2).pdf

Ojha, H., Cameron, J. and Bhattarai, B. (2005) 'Understanding development through the language of Habermas and Bourdieu: Insights from Nepal's Leasehold Forestry Programme'. *International Development Planning Review*, 1(27): 479–97.

Orjuela, C. (2008) *The Identity Politics of Peacebuilding: Civil Society in War-torn Sri Lanka*, New Delhi: SAGE.

Risal, S. (2019) 'Music for peacebuilding and conflict resolution in Nepal', *Peace Review*, 31(3): 297–301.

Risal, S. (2020) 'Defining justice and dignity through gendered peace building: A case study of gender-based violence during armed conflict in Nepal', *Social Inquiry Journal of Social Science Research*, 2(1): 56–81.

Robins, S. (2016) 'Transition but not transformation: How Nepal's liberal peace fails its citizens', in P. Adhikari, S. Ghimire and V. Mallik (eds) *Nepal Transition to Peace: A Decade of the Comprehensive Peace Accord (2006–2016)*, Kathmandu: Transition to Peace Initiative.

Schirch, L. and Sewak, M. (2005) *'Women': Using the Gender Lens*, Boulder: Lynne Rienner.

9

Palestinian storytelling: authoring their own lives

Patricia Sellick

Summary

Storytelling can transform power relations. It is an optimistic act which presumes solidarity between teller and listener and breaks down isolation. Storytelling is also an activist endeavour because it is an opportunity to remake the world and imagine what might have been (Solinger et al, 2008; Senehi, 2009).

This chapter explores the transformative potential of stories that are told and recorded by Palestinians living in the South Hebron Hills.

The chapter begins by showing the inadequacy of international law to protect the Palestinian population of the South Hebron Hills from dispossession by state-backed Jewish settlers, who are turning an area of high plateaux, slopes and valleys, seasonal pasture and bountiful springs into a militarised place of danger to human and non-human life. The chapter then explains the Palestinian experience of progressive and violent dispossession, displacement and fragmentation before introducing the collection of stories which are at the heart of the chapter. These stories were recorded during 2018–19 by Palestinians aged 18–30 living in the South Hebron Hills as part of an externally funded programme to protect cultural heritage in countries affected by conflict. From more than 100 hours of recordings, two interviews are considered more closely. The stories demonstrate how the dialogue between the tellers of the stories and the listeners encompasses both the pessimism related to the ongoing dispersal and dispossession of the Palestinian population and the optimism which comes from constructing community through collective action and solidarity across differences of age, gender, location and nationality.

In the final section, the author analyses the relationship between the external funding and management of the project and the people of the South Hebron Hills. In conclusion, she reflects on her own position as a researcher based in a UK university and how the stories being told in the South Hebron Hills relate to stories being told by other people in other places who also experience the militarisation of borders, the confiscation of land, and the brutalisation and incarceration of bodies.

Setting the scene

Historical context

The South Hebron Hills fold down from the elevated West Bank to the more arid Naqab desert. Proof that this land has supported people who have both cultivated crops and practised pastoralism can be found in the aerial photographs taken at 15,000 feet by the Royal Air Force in 1945. The photographs show both stone dwellings and irrigated fields as well as clusters of black tents.[1] In 1948, those Palestinians living in the Naqab were forced to flee and many found refuge on the higher ground of the West Bank. If they fled with their animals, they preferred not to be confined in refugee camps, but instead to find pasture for their flocks, establishing their homes on the edges of villages or in the plentiful caves. In 1967 the Israeli army occupied the West Bank. Since then, the imposition of severe restrictions on movement not only between Israel, the Gaza Strip and the West Bank but also within the West Bank has threatened the livelihoods of herders who are dependent on pasture for their flocks, and the most vulnerable are those Palestinians who have been forcibly displaced many times.

To add to the pressure on the Palestinian inhabitants, the South Hebron Hills are targeted for permanent settlement by Jewish Israelis who take for granted that they have a God-given right to be there. Their state-backed expansionist logic of dispossession structures prevent the possibility of Palestinians continuing to live in the area. This dispossession is progressive: first the settlers target the land, depriving the Palestinian farmers of access to sufficient forage and water for their flocks and fields to cultivate crops, then the Palestinian farmers become indebted to Israeli commercial forage and water suppliers, and finally the landless Palestinians are faced with the stark choice of working for the settlers as daily labourers or moving to seek work elsewhere (Nawaja, 2018). This slow process of prising away the Palestinian population from the land and the livelihoods associated with it not only dispossesses the Palestinian population of material assets, but also of the intangible practices which bind them together. The Palestinian population risk not only physical dispersal but also the loss of their shared cultural heritage.

Living under occupation

Under International Humanitarian Law an occupying power may not relocate its own citizens to the occupied territory or make permanent changes to that territory, unless these are needed for imperative military needs, in the narrow sense of the term, or undertaken for the benefit of

Figure 9.1: Territories occupied by Israel since June 1967

Source: United Nations, Department of Public Information, https://www.un.org/unispal/document/auto-insert-201336/

the local population. In contravention of the Fourth Geneva Convention 1949, the Israeli occupying power has enabled the establishment of Jewish Israeli only settlements in the occupied Palestinian territory (International Committee of the Red Cross, nd). Additionally, since the early 1980s the Israeli military have declared an area of about 3,000 hectares in the South Hebron Hills a restricted military zone, 'Firing zone 918'. Under the pretext of military needs, Israel has prevented Palestinians from any new construction in the area and facilitated their expulsion (B'Tselem, 2020).

'Invasion is a structure not an event' (Wolfe, 2006: 388). The state-backed impunity of the Israeli perpetrators of discrete human rights violations is part of a logic of dispossession. The invasion is incremental and ongoing: under occupation the Palestinian territory is fragmented and everyday life contained; surveillance by air and from high ground is routine and the occupier's needs for infrastructure are prioritised over those of the occupied people. Despite the activities of a minority of human rights activists who uphold the equality of both Palestinians and Israelis, the violence of the state-backed settlers against the Palestinian inhabitants of the South Hebron Hills continues unchecked. Legal recourse to Israeli military law designed to protect the settlers provides Palestinians with little protection. As long as it is state-backed, the logic of dispossession trumps the reflexivity and equivalence of human rights. The South Hebron Hills are a case study in the inadequacy of International Humanitarian Law as a means of challenging Israeli state policies (White, 2018: 24).

The context of violence

It is within this context that young Palestinians from the 33 hamlets and villages of the South Hebron Hills were trained to record the life-stories of their elders. The stories told in these encounters between generations all confirm that violence routinely mars the everyday lives of the Palestinian inhabitants of the South Hebron Hills.

During the project, one of the Palestinian youth researchers was chased, run over and seriously injured (his leg was broken in two places) by an Israeli settler driving a quad bike. The attack near Al Twaneh was reported to the Israeli police but no action was taken. Other examples of state-backed settler violence are documented on the website of the Israeli human rights organisation B'Tselem (B'tselem, nd) or can be found in the testimonies of the international human rights observers present in the South Hebron Hills (Ecumenical Accompaniment in Palestine and Israel, nd; Pope John XXIII Community Association, nd).

Surveillance and control are an everyday reality. As one of the interviewees said: "Every week there is a small jet that flies over to take photos. Even if you built a chicken coop, you find them in front of you [the] next day" (Najjar, 2019).

As Hannah Arendt conceded even the 'power-with', or solidarity of numbers, cannot withstand the instruments of violence: 'in a head-on clash between violence and power, the outcome is hardly in doubt' (Arendt, 1970: 52). The Palestinian storytellers are clear-eyed about this too: "If you get me out of here by force ... I can't do anything about it. I can't fight a plane or a car!" (Najjar, 2019).

Despite this violent context, violence is not the focus of the stories told.

Community development in practice

The power of storytelling

Storytelling can transform power relations. It is an optimistic act which presumes solidarity between teller and listener and breaks down isolation. Storytelling is also an activist endeavour because it is an opportunity to remake the world and imagine what might have been (Solinger et al, 2008; Senehi, 2009).

Storytelling is accessible to everyone, regardless of gender, unlike playing an instrument or practising a craft, no implements are needed, just the voice and a listener. Because storytelling is accessible, story-based interventions can be a way of allowing more voices into the public transcript.

Between the storyteller and the listener there is a bond based on the willingness of the teller to share the story with the listener and the curiosity of the listener to hear the story. It is this encounter that generates power. 'Power springs up whenever people get together and act in concert, but it derives its legitimacy from the initial getting together rather than from any action that they may follow' (Arendt, 1970: 52). Hannah Arendt's observation is critical: to generate power, as she defines it, the storyteller and listener must willingly tell and listen. 'Tell me the story of your life' is a different invitation from a request to complete a questionnaire or a victim report. The storyteller can choose how to tell the story and the listener does not know in advance where the story will end. One interviewee in this project described her experience of telling a story in this way: "You are holding a treasure in your hand that you can pass on from one generation to the next" (Hureini, 2018). It is in the moment she realises she has a treasure and decides to give it to someone else whom she sees as a worthy recipient of that treasure, that community develops between the two generations. Once they had heard the stories, the young interviewers also saw themselves as custodians of the stories. "I am here today in this village, tomorrow I may not be here. Who will then talk about it? I am the only one who talked about it. I am the only one here who studied university and who is interested in this village" (Hamamda, 2018).

In addition to creating solidarity, stories told between generations can be restorative of self-respect and life's purpose. The act of storytelling fills silences and overcomes singularity. This is apparent in the two stories discussed in more detail later in the chapter. As the first storyteller remembers the past, she remakes the past: caves fill with people, sheep and goats multiply, crops and trees grow. There is also a hint of potentiality in each story: the second storyteller could have stayed and succeeded in school, and his life could have been different.

Storytelling is not normative of itself: it can be either constructive or destructive. The second interview (in the 'In the orchard' section) mixes what Lederach describes as the cycles of relational dignity and respectful engagement, with cycles of destructive relational violence. 'The flows of fear destroy. Those of love edify' (Lederach, 2005: 42).

Practices

Over two years, young Palestinians from the 33 hamlets and villages of the South Hebron Hills gave up their weekends to record the life-stories of their elders. They were trained in the skills of setting up the interview, seeking consent, listening, asking open questions, video-filming and transcription by an experienced and inspirational Palestinian oral historian, Mahasen Rabus.

The research output included a 20-minute film, *On Our Land*. It was funded by the British Council's Cultural Protection Fund, in partnership with the Department for Digital, Culture, Media and Sport (On Our Land, nd).

Despite routine harassment, the Palestinian youth researchers voluntarily picked up their cameras and walked miles to knock on doors and go up to tents and caves, to ask their elders to tell them stories of their lives, convinced of the significance of their endeavour. Why was that?

Ahmad Abu Jondya, like a number of the youth researchers, had been taught by both Palestinian and Israeli human rights organisations to document human rights violations perpetrated by Israeli settlers against Palestinians in the South Hebron Hills. He had grown used to documenting discrete events according to international human rights standards in which Palestinians are defined as occupied people and victims of aggression.

> 'A week ago, my aunt was over at our place and she was working on weaving something and before I even came up to say hello to her, I thought of going to get my camera. I used to pick up my camera to document what the Israelis are doing.' (Jondya, 2019)

Since 2018 he has also been recording the stories the Palestinian inhabitants choose to tell him. These stories are different from the testimonies given in reaction to settler violence and questions from human rights observers. They derive their meaning neither from the settler-colonial logic of dispossession nor the logic of international governance and human rights. Instead, their meaning is made in the encounter between the Palestinian storyteller and the young Palestinian listener.

'I don't want to interview someone dressed in a suit, I want to meet the person as they are and that's how I should conduct the interview with him. When you conduct an interview, it needs to be natural without any "photoshop". I can't tell the person I am interviewing where or how to sit – for the camera angle that's different. I shouldn't try to change the person I am interviewing.' (Mudalal, 2019)

An emancipatory process

In addition to developing community across generations, the storytelling enabled the young people to act in concert and work collectively. They came to see themselves as the generation that had the energy and the skills to look after 'the treasure' they had been given. Even before they asked the storyteller to tell a story the young people were working together: one person would take the video and the other would be the interviewer. If a group met with a storyteller, then each person would contribute a question. After the youth researchers were trained, they continued to receive constructive feedback on their interviews from each other. Together they learned the art of asking questions so that the stories told grew longer and longer.

> 'My first experience with this project was an interview that lasted five minutes and I thought that it was more than enough, however as we developed further and took more trainings, I wanted to conduct more interviews that would reach an hour and more. And each interview would be different, and it would motivate me to carry on.' (Makhamra, 2019)

Encouraging people to tell their stories was not easy; Tagrid Najada said that her throat 'dried up' trying to convince people in her community of Tgayga to consent to be interviewed (Najada, 2019).

The young people describe too how through listening to life-stories their views about knowledge changed, coming to see that knowledge was not the monopoly of formal education and books but that valuable knowledge was held by their neighbours and family members. "I had a different view about our history from what we read about in books, the history we learn about in books differs from oral history, to understand history from someone who lived it is very different" (Mudalal, 2019).

Two stories

The choice of two stories to retell here from the hundred hours of interviews is based on a discussion with the team of youth researchers. Each youth researcher chose a recording they had made which they wanted the rest of the group to watch and listen to.

Lederach emphasises that, in his experience, people who have suffered greatly and are living through the worst cycles of violence are, generally speaking, pessimistic, caught up in the destructive flows of fear (Lederach, 2005: 51–64). These two stories combine pessimism related to the ongoing dispersal and dispossession of the Palestinian population with an optimistic construction of community, beginning from the relationship between teller and listener, but also founded upon the collective action of the young researchers who made the recordings. The process of inviting, listening to, telling, recording and sharing stories transforms the power relations between people of different genders, generations, locations and nationalities. In other words, it generates solidarity.

In the cave

Zhour Mohammad Awad was interviewed by Ahmad Abu Jondya and Ali Awad in her home in Tuba (Awad, 2019). She had been living in the same cave since she got married 60 years earlier. The interviewers asked her to tell the story of her life in the cave. They were accompanied by Mahmoud Makhamra with a camera.

Zhour began by telling the story of how her grandfather built the cave. He had to build it quickly so that he could make enough room for himself and his camel before nightfall. There was no sand blade, so he dug the sand out by hand until he got the camel in. He got the camel in by sunset and slept on the ground. People in the past used to steal, so he kept digging until he managed to get himself in.

Zhour repeatedly expresses surprise at the ignorance of the young men, saying "go and ask your father" when they are unfamiliar with the names of tools and measurements. As she warms to her story, Zhour expresses no complaint or regret about her life. On the contrary, as the two young men ask more questions, many of which are technical about how the cave was built and how people and animals lived, she responds to each question with an emphasis that the cave was beautiful and that the people who lived there were happy. "This cave was full of life. The walls were plastered with mud, and it was something. It looked so bright" (Awad, 2019).

In Zhour's eyes, even the *mitwaa* where the women would store their possessions was "better than the cupboards of today". According to Zhour, the people were not only happy with the level of comfort but also in their relations with each other.

> 'We used to stay here, and goats would come from outside and stay here. My mother-in-law, who was blind, would stay there. My kids would sleep, shower, eat, and relax there, and we were happy, thank God. We spent really good time and days, better than that of today.

When my son got married, we moved the goats there [to Hatta cave], my son got married here next to us. ... Life in the past was better, and today, if we sit in a gathering, you will find people playing with their phones, in the past, people would chat, and we would listen to a story. Everyone is talking to their phone today.' (Awad, 2019)

As she tells the story she seems to gather the family back into the cave. So vivid are her descriptions that it is possible to imagine the people and animals living in the cave. Similar physical arrangements inside the caves are recounted by other interviewees. Figure 9.2 was drawn from the interview with Abu J'at Qubaitat who grew up in a cave in Al Qaryateen.

Zhour narrates her own story of which she is the hero, bearing nine children without the help of a doctor.

'Believe me, I gave birth to all my kids, and none of them were born at the hospital. And the last one of them was Awad, as you know. The women came to the cave, and the last thing I did was carrying the lamp and I went to the family of Hasan Awad, and the girls started asking, where is my aunt? They prepared dinner and all of a sudden, I gave birth to Awad. ... Let me tell you something. In short, when women don't have their period [due to pregnancy], they go to the doctor, and the doctor asks them to come back again a week later, then come back after two weeks, and every time he would charge them money!! I brought all your uncles without paying a single penny, praise be to Allah! I didn't pay money for delivery at the hospital.' (Awad, 2019)

Zhour connects with her own story assured of her knowledge, resilience and ingenuity. There is a benevolent teasing tone in places, as she admonishes the young men, telling them to sit down, stop asking questions and listen to her. She says in a number of places, "surely you know this?" She sees the young men as belonging to her community and expects them to have a shared knowledge or at least shared access to knowledge. This expectation is both of technical knowledge (for example that a *baa* measures almost two hands) and the tacit or practical knowledge that payment is made not only in money but also in food and drink: "Yes. From here to there is ten *baa*. They did it for 40 dinars, and they ate and drank here too" (Awad, 2019).

During the course of a story about the time when a snake entered the cave, Zhour points out the *rouzaneh* overhead. The *rouzaneh* was a hole which served both as a chimney to let smoke out and as a window to let light in. Other interviewees had a similar pride in the ingenuity of their forebears and pointed out *rouzaneh* when we were walking above ground, parting the grasses to show where an opening still existed into a disused cave dwelling.

Figure 9.2: Rebecca Bubb's illustration of growing up in a cave

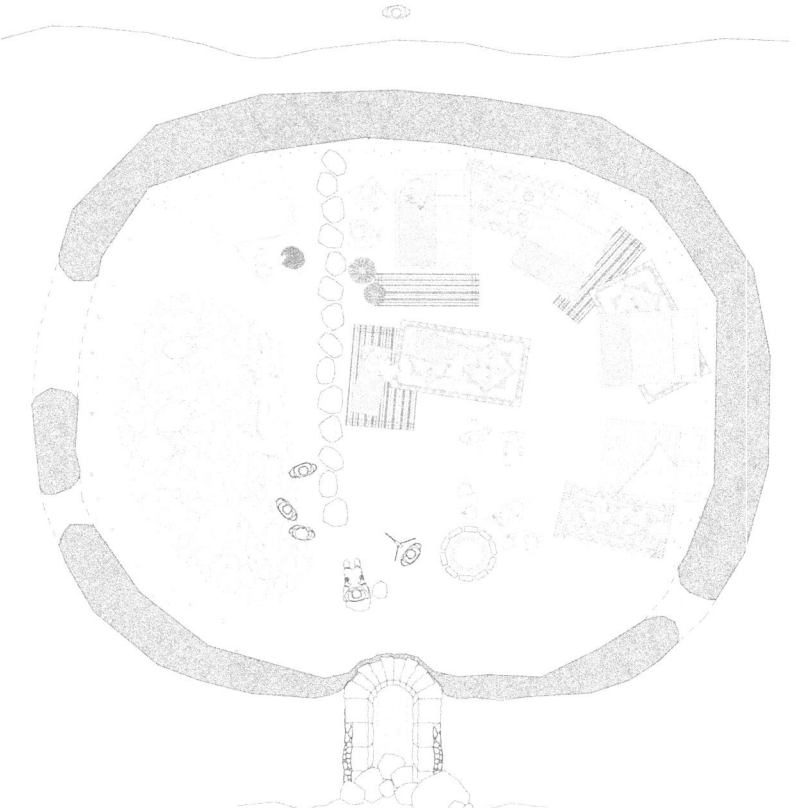

In the orchard

The second interview was chosen by Mahmoud Makhamra and took place in an orchard. "Tell us a story", said Mahmoud Makhamra and Fatima Al Nawaja. This was the story that Ziad Yousif Isma'il Najjar told in response (Najjar, 2019). The three of them were in Sha'b Al-Butom, a hilly area named for its pistacia trees, useful for their wood but with inedible nuts (*butom* in Arabic). Mahmoud and Fatima were curious and ready to listen, and Ziad wanted to speak.

> 'I was born in 1983. We are five brothers and I studied until the fourth grade. That was a long time ago, exactly in 1992. In my family we are sheep-herders. I was born to a grandfather and a father that used to breed sheep. I happened to be the only one in the family who is suitable to herd [in other words] take the sheep out to pasture. I was in the fourth grade when my father came and told me that I have to take the sheep out to pasture. It was six in the morning. I was around

ten back then and I was doing well in school. I was good but he pulled me out of school. I was forced to leave school and I was only ten; I didn't know much back then.' (Najjar, 2019)

Implicit in Ziad's story is the imagined possibility of what his life could have been; that he too could have completed his schooling and been as educated as the young people approaching him with the video recorder. As the interview progresses it becomes clear that he has a different form of education: he has a lifetime's knowledge of trees.

Ziad: Of course, you need to preserve it. Your love of trees and land is represented in keeping the land decorated with trees. You need to follow them and preserve them. At the end of the day, you raise a tree the way you raise your own son. You plant it small, then it grows in front of you while you are raising it like a son. I don't know if you are married and have kids or not.
Interviewer: No.
Ziad: Alright, it's the same way when you have a newborn that grows a bit by bit as you raise him until he becomes a man, it's the same with a tree. You need to give it care to be a tree. (Najjar, 2019)

As they walk and talk Ziad introduces the young people to the different trees in the orchard: the apricot tree, vine, *nabali* olive, plum, *lycium shawii* tree (used to treat sheep), pomegranate, almond, pine (for firewood), cactus, sycamore, pistacia, fig and, around the well, eucalyptus, palm, almond and sumac trees. The trees are important not only to Ziad but are a source of support to others in the community. After taking the olives to the mill he gives part of the oil as *zakāt*, the compulsory gift of 2.5 per cent of wealth Muslims are required to give to charity.

'When you get home, you start counting families in need. Pardon me, not all families have olive orchards and not all families have oil. You do your best to give oil to all families in need, and what is left is a blessing from God. We then divide it into shares for yourself, your brothers and sisters.' (Najjar, 2019)

Mixed in with Ziad's stories of how to care for the trees and how the abundance of crops provides for the needy, stories of nurture and charity, are also stories of destruction and dispossession. Ziad's story of love of his trees and his community is edifying and is constructive of social change within his Palestinian community. At the same time Ziad describes the Israelis as 'grabbing the land slowly and over time the land we control is shrinking'. His story details how Palestinian land is atomised; surveillance by air prevents development; and bypass roads prioritise the needs of settlers.

Even while Ziad is encouraging Mahmoud and Fatima to love the trees, and to sustain the needy families in the community, he is at the same time warning them against the settlers.

Mahmoud and Fatima:	Don't you go to the town?
Ziad:	No, it is hard. If you left your house in Sha'b Al-Butom for a month, it is hard to be allowed back. That is because of the evil settlement of Afigal; it is only 500 metres far. From the south, there is Mitsvi Iar [another Israeli settlement]. Then comes road 317 from Susya settlement to the west. Therefore, we stay where we are all day long to preserve the land where we live. (Najjar, 2019)

Conclusion

The power of storytelling to make and extend community

By putting in the effort to walk in all seasons through mud, under the sun, to find all the caves, tents and houses of the Palestinian inhabitants of the South Hebron Hills, the young people strengthened relations between the Palestinian population of the South Hebron Hills and demonstrated that each inhabitant's story was a valuable addition. Even if each young person did not know all the stories from all the places, they each know someone who did. "What I liked most, was that we were a group from various areas, and we got to know each other through the project" (Jondya, 2019).

Participation in the collection of these stories also changed gender relations: storytelling was as accessible to women as to men. Three of the young women researchers have used their experience to win scholarships for university studies to Bir Zeit University which they might not otherwise have undertaken. While the heritage that emerged from these strengthened chains of connectivity to people, objects, places and practices spoke of deep adversity it also spoke of 'the interactive collaboration of others which gives the less powerful potential for resistance' (Haugaard, 2020: 39).

The role of external funding and programme management

Would these Palestinian stories have been recorded without the impetus of an external funding programme and the participation of a UK university? Paying attention to cultural heritage has become a low priority for Palestinians who, physically threatened and faced with landlessness, struggle to meet their basic needs. Yet, the protection of cultural heritage is understood by many to be as important to sustainable development, as meeting the needs of the present and future generations through economic growth, social inclusion and environmental balance (British Council, 2020). The memory and evolution of shared intangible practices are indivisible from continued Palestinian habitation of the South Hebron Hills. Free of the pressure of immediate survival, outsiders can play a facilitating role in identifying and sustaining community resources of value to future generations. In this example, the UK government set the terms of the grant and rewarded the grant-management and reporting skills of a UK university at the expense of Palestinian priorities and Palestinian capacity. In many ways the relations between the UK funder and university and the Palestinian participants were asymmetrical but it is important to note that the Palestinian participants still found scope to assert their own contradictory priorities.

On the one hand, it is UK government policy to support a two-state solution, with an independent state of Palestine existing alongside Israel, within the 1967 borders. On the other hand, the British Council Cultural Protection Fund also allowed the Palestinian participants to work together to preserve and project a national identity that overflowed the 1967 state borders. It encouraged its partners to focus on the heritage that people themselves value, whether or not that material or intangible heritage ever appears on a national or international list for protection.

In his critical approach to heritage studies Rodney Harrison suggests that heritage emerges from the relationship between people, objects, places and practices. He describes the way in which 'humans and non-humans are linked by chains of connectivity and work together to keep the past alive in the present for the future' (Harrison, 2017: 4). State resources are routinely dedicated to strengthening selected chains of connectivity to produce a national identity that may or may not coincide with state borders. Even though the UK government funding had to be spent in the occupied Palestinian territory, the heritage that emerged was based in the relationships that the Palestinian participants in the South Hebron Hills valued with people, objects, places and practices beyond the borders imposed by the UK government's diplomatic position.

Finding gaps in the wall

The project was able to overcome or work round the formal constraints of the context in at least three ways. Firstly, the trainer employed by the project was a Palestinian living in Israel who drove three hours from her home each weekend to share her skills and experience with the group in the occupied Palestinian territory. Secondly, when an interviewee in the

South Hebron Hills chose to take the group back to his place of birth, he showed the group where to find a break in the Separation Wall and cross the Green Line to reach the cave from which his family had been evicted by the Israeli army in 1948. Finally, the 20-minute film produced from a selection of the interviews was most enthusiastically received by Palestinian students living in the diaspora (Centre for Trust, Peace and Social Relations, 2020).

The diffusion of power

In addition to reshaping the terms of the British Council Cultural Protection Fund, the Palestinian participants adapted Coventry University practices. The research was developed in accordance with Coventry University ethics committee requirements: the number of interviews was specified, participants were to be informed about the purpose of the research in their own language, and recordings were only to be made with consent. However, from the beginning of the project the research team had to continuously renegotiate consent. It has not been a one-off permission giving, but a process of ongoing dialogue, conducted through visits and WhatsApp conversations with the three mayors, the chair of the women's committee, existing youth organisations, and the extended family of the interviewers and interviewees, with frequent interruptions from participants asking questions about the research, shifting their participation, withdrawing entirely or confirming their desire to continue on their own terms. Chazan and Baldwin (2020) have described this as a process of upturning power. Power has also been diffused. After the planned number of interviews had been made, the young people took their own decision to record more stories.

> 'I was once walking with a friend in the valleys in South Hebron, and I noticed he had a camera and beside me was a shepherd, so I told him, since you have a camera with you how about we go document the shepherd if he agrees. So, we went to him and he said that would be fine. So, we put the camera on a stone, because we didn't have a stand, and we started talking with the shepherd. This went on for more than an hour.' (Ali, 2019)

Community development, conflict and peacebuilding

Where power relations are asymmetric, peacebuilding requires a change in those power relations so that actors can come together and recognise each other as equals. In the case of the occupied Palestinian territory, the Israeli occupying forces wield coercive power over the occupied people. There is also another form of power at work: much of the world takes for granted that it is justifiable for one group of people to structure out another.

Privileged groups (usually organised as nation states) build walls, confiscate land and natural resources, incarcerate bodies, and profit from a market in health and education. Within this context, conflict is necessary to transform unequal power relations underpinned not only by coercive force but also by prevailing norms.

Community development, of the kind described here, can create power for the group of people who are being systematically structured out. This power does not depend on coercive violence, instead it springs up in the willing encounter between the storyteller and the listener. The stories told between generations from the same community bring both male and female voices into the public transcript and contain both the possibility of what might have been and the gift of what aspects of the past the storyteller would like to see preserved in the future. This storytelling is resistant to the settler colonial logic of dispossession and escapes the logic of international governance by connecting one individual to another to construct a community that spills over state borders. The young people involved felt power spring up as they acted collectively with and for their community, and they were able to communicate this power to audiences outside the South Hebron Hills through speaking tours and the film they made (Centre for Trust, Peace and Social Relations, 2020). They found strength in numbers, in the way in which they spoke from personal experience, and in the clarity of their message (Sellick, 2020).

The links between academics and activists

The stories have not only changed the Palestinian community in the South Hebron Hills, they have also had their impact on the UK-based researchers. These stories told by Palestinians living in occupied territory are pessimistic. They could not be otherwise given the overwhelming violence of the state-backed invasion of the South Hebron Hills. The knowledge generated here comes from people confronted with the prospect of becoming landless labourers living under military surveillance. How can university-based academics make their living from listening to these stories and respond, not only as researchers working within university structures, but as people of conscience? If there is an answer to this question, it may lie in the constructive power of these pessimistic stories to make and extend community. As Timothy Seidel has identified, 'a growing theme in peace building and development studies relates to a kind of boundary crossing that sees academics and activists drawing linkages across spatial and temporal divides' (Seidel, 2016). The construction of walls, the militarisation of borders, the confiscation of land, and the brutalisation and incarceration of bodies is not only taking place in occupied Palestinian territory but wherever it has become acceptable for one group of people to be structured out. Within this global context, people of conscience can respond to these Palestinian stories by challenging a natural-order-of-things in which it makes sense for one group of people to have power over another group of people because any such justification is a block to community development internally and to the development of positive sum relations between communities.

Note

1. Photographs taken by the Royal Air Force (RAF) 1944–8 as part of a project to systematically map Palestine in the Aerial Photography Archive, the Department of Geography, Hebrew University, Israel, http://ccg.huji.ac.il/aerialphotos/

References

Ali (2019) Interview, Tuba, 20 July.
Arendt, H. (1970) *On Violence*, London: Harvest Books.
Awad, Z.M.A. (2019) Interview, Tuba, 17 July.
British Council (2020) *The Missing Pillar: Culture's Contribution to the UN Sustainable Development Goals*. Available at https://www.britishcouncil.org/sites/default/files/the_missing_pillar.pdf
B'Tselem (nd) *State-backed Settler Violence*. Available at https://www.btselem.org/settler_violence_updates/during-corona-crisis
B'Tselem (2020) *B'Tselem Firing Zone 918: An Exercise in War Crimes*, 28 October. Available at https://www.btselem.org/video/202010_firing_zone_918_an_exercise_in_war_crimes#full
Centre for Trust, Peace and Social Relations (nd) *On Our Land*. Available at http://onourland.coventry.ac.uk/the-project/
Chazan, M. and Baldwin, M. (2020) 'Learning to be refused: Exploring refusal, consent and care in storytelling research', *Postcolonial Studies*, 24(1): 104–21.
Ecumenical Accompaniment in Palestine and Israel (nd) *Where We Work: Southern West Bank: Bethlehem & Hebron Governorates*. Available at https://eappi.org/en/where-we-work/locally/southern-west-bank
Hamamda, S. (2019) Interview, Al Mufagarah, 8 August.
Harrison, R. (2017) *Heritage Critical Approaches*, Johanneshov: MTM.
Haugaard, M. (2020) *Domination, Empowerment and Democracy: Exploring the Four Dimensions of Social and Political Power*, Manchester: Manchester University Press.
Hureini, N. (2018) Interview, Al Twaneh, 8 August.
International Committee of the Red Cross (nd) *Convention (IV) relative to the Protection of Civilian Persons in Time of War*, Geneva, 12 August 1949. Available at https://ihl-databases.icrc.org/ihl/385ec082b509e76c41256739003e636d/6756482d86146898c125641e004aa3c5
Jondya, A.A. (2019) Interview, Tuba, 20 July.

Lederach, J.P. (2005) *The Moral Imagination: The Art and Soul of Building Peace*, New York: Oxford University Press.
Makhamra, M. (2019) Interview, Khirbet Jinba, 20 July.
Mudalal, H. (2019) Interview, Wadi Rakheyn, 20 July.
Najada, T. (2019) Interview, Al Twaneh, 20 July.
Najjar, Z.Y.I. (2019) Interview, Sha'b Al-Butom, 2 September.
Nawaja, N. (2018) Interview, conducted by Mahasen Rabus, 9 June.
On Our Land (nd) *On Our Land*. Available at http://onourland.coventry.ac.uk/
Pope John XXIII Community Association (nd) *Operation Dove*. Available at https://www.apg23.org/en/operation_dove/
Seidel, T. (2016) '"Occupied territory is occupied territory": James Baldwin, Palestine and the possibilities of transnational solidarity', *Third World Quarterly*, 37(9): 1644–60.
Sellick, P. (2020) 'From nonviolent practice toward a theory of political power', *Journal of Political Power*, 13(1): 41–59.
Senehi, J. (2009) 'Building peace: Storytelling to transform conflicts constructively', in D. Sandole, S. Byrne, I. Sandole-Staroste and J. Senehi (eds) *Handbook of Conflict Analysis and Resolution*, Abingdon: Routledge, pp 201–14.
Solinger, R., Fox, R. and Irani, K. (eds) (2008) *Telling Stories to Change the World*, Abingdon: Routledge.
White, B. (2018) *The Settler Colonial Present: Palestinian State-Building Under Apartheid. Palestine and Rule of Power*, Cham: Springer International.
Wolfe, P. (2006) 'Settler colonialism and the elimination of the native', *Journal of Genocide Research*, 8(4): 387–409.

10

Community-based action in Northern Ireland: activism in a violently contested society

Monina O'Prey

Summary

The chapter considers community development practice in the sharply divided society of Northern Ireland/the North of Ireland – where even the appellation is contested. The political context and landscape is described to offer a context for community development and conflict transformation approaches adopted over some five decades. The author is herself a long-term activist who has worked in a wide range of local communities as well as in support of marginalised groups. She examines the politics of peacebuilding as well as outlining community development practice at various phases of the conflict and emergence from overt violence. She also focuses specifically on learning drawn from work undertaken by, and with, victims/survivors of the violence and political ex-prisoners.

The chapter also offers an insight into how development work was undertaken with those communities that were in danger of being 'left behind' in terms of community organising. The sensitive and difficult work of addressing inter-community divisions is also described, with an examination of the application of Putnam's theory of social capital (2000) (bonding, bridging and linking) to frame the important task of building relationships among divided communities. The chapter concludes with some pointers for funding organisations that are interested in resourcing community development approaches to peacebuilding.

Introduction

The proximity of the island of Ireland to Britain has meant an interwoven relationship which spans over 800 years and continues to impact today. In 1921 Ireland was partitioned under a treaty between the British government and representatives of Sinn Féin, combatants in a War of Independence (1918–21). The treaty provided for the majority of Ireland (26 counties)

Figure 10.1: Map of Great Britain, Northern Ireland and Ireland

Source: https://d-maps.com/carte.php?num_car=5545&lang=en

becoming the Irish Free State (later the Republic of Ireland in 1949) and the remaining six northeastern counties, established as Northern Ireland, remaining part of the United Kingdom. Legally, the new statelet is called Northern Ireland. Nationalists and Republicans often refer to it as the 'North' or the 'Six Counties'. Unionists generally use the term 'Ulster'.

The new Northern Ireland was constituted with a population that was two-thirds Protestant in faith and British in identity and allegiance. It was also an area with strong economic ties to Britain. Many in the Catholic minority maintained an Irish identity and favoured the unification of the island.

Although under the overall rule of the Westminster parliament in London, a devolved parliament was established in Stormont (Belfast) where the Ulster Unionist Party governed from 1922 to 1972. This single party rule attracted allegations of structural discrimination against the minority which, in turn, gave rise to the mobilisation of the cross-community Northern Ireland Civil Rights Association (NICRA) in the mid-1960s. Peaceful protest marches to call for equal rights and treatment for all was met with violence from the police and an uncompromising response from the state. In 1969 British troops were deployed to try to maintain control. There was a rapid growth of paramilitary organisations that were reinvigorated to 'defend' their communities whether that was mainly Protestant/Unionist/Loyalist (PUL) or Catholic/Nationalist/Republican (CNR). By late 1969, many working-class areas were barricaded off, almost 2,000 people had been intimidated out of their homes (over 75 per cent from the CNR community) and there were increasing numbers of deaths and injuries from gun attacks. The first of Northern Ireland's now famous 'peace lines' (which later became peace walls) were erected by the army to keep communities apart. The period of violence from the late 1960s to the mid-1990s is often termed the Troubles (McKittrick, 2000).

Combatants included the state forces – the British Army, Northern Ireland police force (the Royal Ulster Constabulary) and the 97 per cent Protestant Police Reserve which was to be replaced by the Ulster Defence Regiment. The Irish Republican Army, and later the Irish National Liberation Army represented militant republicanism. Loyalism saw the re-emergence of the Ulster Volunteer Force (UVF), and later the Ulster Defence Association (UDA), determined to maintain the union with Britain. In an effort to address the deteriorating situation, the British government suspended the Stormont Assembly in 1972 and imposed Direct Rule from London.

The three-sided armed conflict (state forces, Republican and Loyalist) lasted until ceasefires in 1994. Most of the paramilitary groups have complex, far-reaching and deeply embedded structures that remain in existence to this day. The members of the armed groups lived as part of their local community, and were often supported and shielded by them, giving rise to increased politicisation when an often harsh and invasive police and army response was felt at community level.

The Northern Ireland conflict is often posited as a religious/sectarian one; in reality, it is an identity/political conflict, with religion aligning closely with identity and political aspiration. That said, the conflict was intense and, for a small population of 1.8 million people, it left more than 3,500 dead, many thousands bereaved, 48,000+ seriously injured; 25–30,000 in prison for politically motivated alleged offences or interned without trial; plus, massive damage to business, property and the economy. It put huge strain on medical and mental health services and, given the official British government narrative that the conflict was an aggravated crime wave rather than a political struggle, sparse attention was paid to trauma services or counselling. Few families remained untouched. Northern Ireland was a very dangerous place for a long time and remains volatile given the unaddressed legacy of conflict.

The political landscape

Politics and demographics changed significantly over the decades since the founding of the Northern Ireland state. The impact of violence, together with a legacy of systematic segregation and discrimination, resulted in increasing numbers of 'single identity' areas. In 2017:

- 93 per cent of social housing was segregated;
- 93 per cent of nursery, primary and secondary school education was segregated;
- spatial/territorial segregation is visible via harsh physical walls and barriers built between communities as a security solution; some 116 of these 'peace' barriers were still in place in 2017;
- interfaces exist in many urban and rural areas; these may be real (flashpoints and contested space between communities living adjacent to each other) or perceived (no physical interface exists but the territory is contested and generally marked, restricting use or movement);
- many health, social services, sporting and community facilities remain segregated, with the attendant higher cost to the public purse and to good relations, which impacts quality of provision.

Legislative change,[1] imposed in 1976 under London Direct Rule, sought to address the huge disparity in employment opportunities between the two main communities. Improvements were noted over the decades and by 2016 unemployment rates for Protestants and Catholics were 5 per cent and 7 per cent respectively. Equality and human rights remained key demands for the Republican/Nationalist community in the 1998 Good Friday/Belfast peace agreement (Gray et al, 2018).

The decades also saw a significant change in the demographic composition in Northern Ireland. The PUL community who mainly identify as British made up 66.6 per cent of the population in 1922, and now sits at 48.4 per cent (2020); whereas the CNR community, who mainly identify as Irish, were 33.4 per cent in 1922 but are now 45.1 per cent (2020). It is expected that this gap will continue to narrow given the younger profile in the CNR community. Despite growing inward migration into Northern Ireland, this non-binary population remains relatively small.

There have also been changes in the party-political landscape, with the decades of the Troubles seeing a spectrum of parties that included the radically conservative Democratic Unionist Party (DUP) overtaking the traditional Ulster Unionist Party; and the more radical Republican Sinn Féin overtaking the moderate nationalist Social Democratic and Labour Party (SDLP) and the centrist Alliance Party adopting a cross-community liberal position. Entry into the electoral system in the early 1980s saw Sinn Féin garnering increasing support, although there was less electoral success for the Progressive Unionist Party and Ulster Democratic Party which emerged to represent thinking aligned with the Loyalist paramilitaries – the UVF and the UDA respectively. As the peace process progressed the balance of political power shifted dramatically from the Ulster Unionist Party to the DUP, within unionism and from the SDLP to Sinn Féin within nationalism. Current power-sharing governance arrangements provided under the Belfast/Good Friday Agreement see the DUP and Sinn Féin holding primacy of position in the devolved Northern Ireland Executive.

Setting the scene

The politics of peacebuilding

Despite a number of attempts to provide a negotiated settlement to the Troubles over the 1970s and 1980s, it was the Republican and Loyalist ceasefires of 1994 that offered the best opportunity for peacebuilding and the negotiation of a peace settlement. The Good Friday/Belfast Agreement of 1998 was the culmination of protracted negotiations, chaired by the US Senator George Mitchell, and followed years of prior covert negotiations that resulted in the ceasefires.

Importantly, this highly complex political agreement (among other progressive strands) recognised the need for a new set of relationships between Ireland, Northern Ireland and the UK for the first time. These included:

- the development of a power-sharing devolved government in Belfast;
- formal relationships between Northern Ireland and the Republic of Ireland (Belfast/Dublin; north/south);
- formal relationships between Britain/Ireland and Northern Ireland (east/west).

Alongside provision for governance a range of other important issues were provided for, including:

- *Identity*: the Agreement recognised each citizen's right to parity of esteem in terms of holding either a British or Irish identity (or both) with the attendant cultural aspirations and allegiances. On the question of the reunification of Ireland, it allows for the Secretary of State (UK) to call a referendum on unification 'if at any time it appears likely to him that a majority of those

Figure 10.2: Map of Northern Ireland

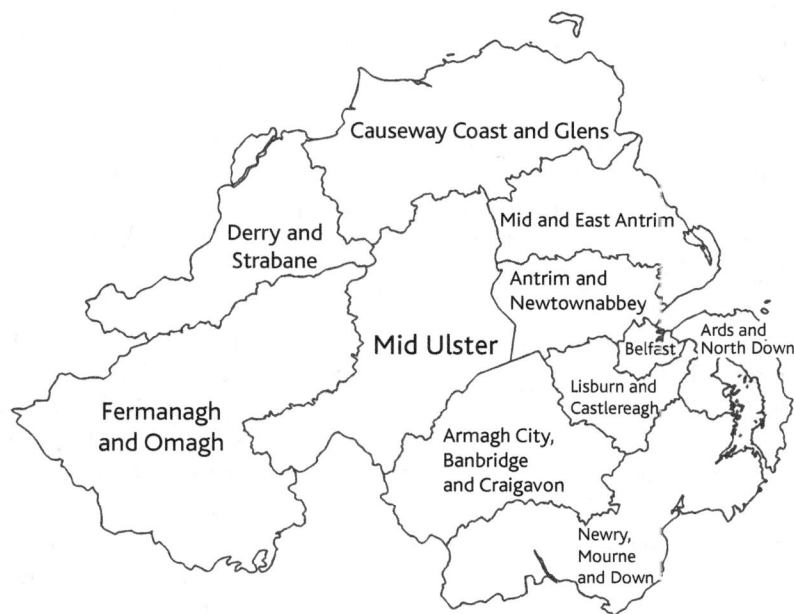

Source: https://d-maps.com/carte.php?num_car=5545&lang=en

voting would express a wish that Northern Ireland should cease to be part of the United Kingdom and form part of a United Ireland'. While a significant number of requirements would have to be met to enable a referendum, the issue of Brexit has prompted increasing interest in this discussion.

- ○ Brexit – introduced as a result of a UK referendum in 2016 – means Northern Ireland staying as part of the non-EU UK, while simultaneously, under a Northern Ireland Protocol, remaining in the EU Single Market (unlike Britain) in order to avoid customs infrastructure along the current Irish land border. The Northern Ireland Protocol has raised fears within Unionism/Loyalism that a semi-detached relationship with Britain will result from the newly imposed customs border between Northern Ireland and Britain in the Irish Sea. This change, together with provision for a possible future border referendum and increasing prospect of demographic changes, exacerbates Loyalist/Unionist fears of constitutional change. However, the prospects for reunification of the island of Ireland in any future referendum remain uncertain.
- *Policing reform*: the Agreement made provision for a commission to examine and take forward reform of policing which set out the path for a new Police Service of Northern Ireland (PSNI). This new service was

established in November 2001 and, according to the PSNI Press Office, by 2021 had a 65 per cent PUL/32.17 per cent CNR profile of police officers and 77.4 per cent PUL/20.3 per cent CNR police staff. Provision was also made for oversight by a Policing Board and a complaints procedure managed by the new Police Ombudsman.
- *Prisoner early release scheme*: the Agreement provided for a controversial early release scheme for Republican and Loyalist prisoners sentenced prior to April 1998. The majority of these prisoners had been sentenced by Diplock no-jury courts under special emergency provisions over the course of the conflict.

There were of course drawbacks to the Belfast/Good Friday Agreement. Two issues of particular concern were its failure to specify and address the 'causes of the conflict', which left mutually exclusive narratives in place, nor did it set out an implementation timeframe for the delivery of its many positive aspirations to build peace and equality. Despite the fact that the Agreement won the support of the vast majority of the electorate in a back-to-back referendum held in both Northern Ireland and the Republic of Ireland, the implementation process has been flawed, with political cherry-picking on the interpretation of commitments and many aspects of perceived agreement floundering along the way. Alongside this, many elements of the Agreement have been renegotiated over five further sets of crises talks. The devolved government agreed for Northern Ireland has also collapsed several times requiring the reintroduction of periodic Direct Rule from Westminster.

In this uncertain context, paramilitary groups continue to exist and impact significantly on communities, despite the main organisations decommissioning their armaments. There has been splintering within paramilitary organisations and the emergence of a number of smaller groups that are opposed to the Belfast/Good Friday Agreement. For many disadvantaged communities, most impacted by the 30-year conflict, it appears that little has changed. Some paramilitary factions continue to engage in armed conflict, while others have become heavily engaged in criminality and coercive control of communities. Efforts to tackle this have had limited impact to date.

With all of this said, even in the ever-changing overt conflict and peace process phases, space was, and continues to be, found for community-based activism that addresses community need and participation, social justice, economic, equality and human rights issues, and legacy issues as well as locating them within a peacebuilding framework.

Community activism during the period of overt violence: 1968–94

Conflict impacts disproportionally on poor people and on local communities that are already disadvantaged. At times of conflict, suspicion and tensions rise. Human rights are increasingly seen as expendable, which was the experience of many working-class communities in Northern Ireland during the conflict: this legacy remains. Ongoing violent conflict made mistrust, fear and trauma the norm. As the conflict escalated, positions hardened; mutually exclusive narratives of cause and effect took root with each community, dehumanising the 'other' as the enemy.

State violence interacted with both Republican and Loyalist violence. Legislation enabled punitive Emergency Powers Acts, which provided for non-jury trials. There was a lack of accountability that gave rise to allegations of state collusion in murders and 'shoot to kill' policies. Local organisations worked to document thousands of human rights abuses (*inter alia* the Association for Legal Justice and the Committee on the Administration of Justice). The 1990s saw the expansion in those organisations that continued the documentation of rights abuses and work to support victims of state and non-state violence. Documenting was a very important process and these essential records have enabled many families to seek justice in more recent years.

Armed Republican groups, with their objective of removing the British presence from Ireland, targeted security force personnel and initiated a major bombing campaign that destroyed businesses, property and left many injured or dead. People perceived to give information to the state were either 'disappeared' or left dead by roadsides as an example to others. Armed Loyalist groups engaged in actions against Republicans, arguing the need to protect 'their' state and its union with Britain, which often translated in practice into a sectarian murder campaign against many innocent Catholics.

During these two decades, community development embraced activism in response to the ongoing violence. This work primarily took place 'within' single identity communities rather than between communities as inter-community work was both dangerous and difficult. Mobility was severely constrained by army roadblocks, regular withdrawal of public transport and fear of the 'other'. People were being intimidated out of homes located in the 'other's' territory; they lived in fear of the heavy police and army presence and constant house-raids, as well as the persistent danger of shootings and bombings, arrests and imprisonment/internment. Personal safety was a key issue for many community workers and activists and, like the communities within which they lived and worked, survival was key (Kilmurray, 2017).

However, often in the absence of, and disruption to much-needed services, local people came together to organise their own provision to meet community needs. Volunteerism was strong, particularly among women, with a focus on supporting families to survive and keeping young people safe and engaged within their own areas. Solidarity was built on the common cause of survival and looking out for each other. It was 'a given' in these communities that armed groups were active and living among them – they were part of the community and part of the struggle. Rarely were they involved in community support groups, other than where the work was in support of the large number of politically motivated prisoners.

The community infrastructure of organised activism that developed included residents and tenants, community councils, women's groups and centres, youth centres, independent advice centres, groups for those with disabilities, community resource centres as well as issue-specific campaigning groups and networks. Primarily located in the increasingly 'single identity' communities, these groups focused on building internal community solidarity and resilience in what can be seen as 'bonding social capital' (Putnam, 2000). It was noted at the time that this 'community infrastructure and solidarity' was more extensive in CNR areas than in PUL communities, partially attributed to the former having lower expectations of state assistance and so relying on self-organisation (McCready, 2001).

The conflict impacted across the North in different ways, but disproportionately impacted on poor working-class urban and rural areas where poverty, neglect and unemployment/under-employment were already facts of life. The direct impact of the violence experienced through bereavement, injury and imprisonment added to the toll of issues to be addressed. There were few statutory services designed to meet the needs of those impacted by conflict although, over time, a number of government programmes were put in place to focus on socioeconomic issues at both regional and community level. Many of these paralleled UK developments rather than being tailored with the impact of conflict in mind.

Notwithstanding the challenges faced, local community workers/activists managed to develop a level of inter-community connection from the mid-1980s, sustained by mainly working on common issues of concern and on efforts to tackle ongoing interface violence. Again, this fledgling inter-community contact work was initiated and led mainly by local women who recognised the societal need to broker relations with their neighbours from the 'other side'. They built common agendas around issues like the need for childcare resources, access to health services, facilities and services, as well as joint campaigns on anti-poverty issues (Rooney and Woods, 1995). This issue focus was functional in nature, enabling activists to come together in joint campaigns. Inter-community networking built important personal relationships over time, but often maintained momentum through the avoidance of potentially divisive issues directly related to the conflict. This 'bridging social capital' was facilitated by a number of networking organisations who were careful to work at the pace of local acceptance and were acutely conscious of language, symbols or campaigning that might run the risk of them being seen as aligned with either community (Cockburn, 1998).

In the later period leading to the ceasefires of 1994, this inter-community work was augmented by the engagement of many local activists and leaders who had a focus on conflict reduction and the need for peacebuilding and reconciliation work. A number of initiatives were taken to give 'voice' to communities as to the type of society that they aspired to. In addition, a number of specific organisational structures were designed which very deliberately reflected an inter-community dimension, often achieved by involving individuals that were former Republican and Loyalist prisoners. The intent behind this design was to create space for hearing the views and position of the 'other side', which could then be reflected back and discussed as a form of confidence-building prior to the paramilitary ceasefires. This was community action as a form of peacebuilding 'cover'.

What approaches worked for communities during the violent conflict?

Given the multiplicity of challenges over the initial decades of violent conflict, it was imperative that a community development approach spoke to people's needs and that collective action was seen to be effective and independent. It also required a belief that developing local solutions to local problems was critical as was the investment in building credible local leadership.

The focus was therefore on a variety of community approaches adopted, including those articulated in Table 10.1. The nature of funding sources available from the mid-1980s onwards served to increase the professionalised non-governmental organisations and voluntary sector organisations, often at the expense of local community organisations, despite the fact that thematic and regional organisations had been a largely missing component in those working-class communities most impacted at the height of the conflict. In addition to placing an emphasis on professionalism, the new funders (both statutory and independent) often minimised the contribution of the lived-knowledge and active experience of local activists. Many viewed this development as a push to control community action, while government funding policies explicitly privileged those organisations and agencies that were seen as 'safe hands' in political terms. Many community organisations struggled to survive and most lost their activism edge when they engaged in competing for funds to deliver programmes within the funder's constraints and agenda.

Activism following the 1994 ceasefires: community development and peacebuilding

The 1994 ceasefires, followed by the Belfast/Good Friday Agreement (1998) opened greater space for inter-community activism between the two main single identity communities. It was timely for an analysis of the essential building blocks for such engagement. This entailed examining the community

Table 10.1: Some community approaches adopted in Northern Ireland

Participation and representation	Service provision	Solidarity and resilience	Campaigning and advocacy
Credible community leadership using representative approaches (including community elections)	Advice and support on welfare rights; housing; health; education and so on	Documenting rights abuses; assessing/utilising community assets	Making demands on inadequate services and poor housing
Use of community newsletters; door-to-door leafletting; community radio	Youth provision as diversionary activities; services for children and older people	Provision of community festivals to enhance/celebrate community spirit	Use of drama and other creative forms to highlight issues
Organising participative community enquiries into priority issues	Women's centres; community councils; residents'/tenants' associations	Support for prisoners and their families; tackling poverty and exclusion	Engagement with political and policy decision-makers
Assessment of security issues and challenges experienced by local people	Delivering locally based training; awareness-raising programmes	Action to combat anti-social behaviour (often taking punitive forms administered by paramilitaries)	Organising protests, public meetings; press articles; issue-based campaigns
Space for reflection, assessment, planning and review of community issues	Support for victims of violence; social inclusion work	Celebration of effective actions and small 'wins'	Amplifying evidence-based resource needs; agency engagement

infrastructure in existence in terms of the confidence, capacity and structures that enabled people to participate and engage collectively in approaches to address local issues while building inter-community relationships. It also required an assessment of what was lacking or in need of both support and investment to enable the building of bridges between communities. Two other areas became increasingly important: the need for more focused work with those who had been engaged in the conflict as well as those specifically impacted by it; and development work in those areas where community infrastructure was weak or non-existent.

In addition to a small number of longer-term independent philanthropic funders, such as the Joseph Rowntree Charitable Trust and the Community Foundation for Northern Ireland, new sources of financial support for local activism and peacebuilding were a game-changer. Space was created for new initiatives, a much better understanding and articulation of the longer-term impact of the conflict, and the resourcing of new approaches to community development and activist peacebuilding work. The European Union PEACE programmes offered major financial support, which was complemented by the more flexible and responsive Atlantic Philanthropies, International Fund for Ireland and the International Committee of the Red Cross. This allowed a sharper focus on community-based peacebuilding and social justice issues (Logue and Kilmurray, 2012). Specific programmes of work developed with both victims/survivors of the Troubles and with the political ex-prisoner and ex-combatant groups.

Activism with and by victims/survivors

The fact that the needs of victims had been unacknowledged over the course of the conflict was a cause of hurt and anger. A small number of self-help groups were established in 1991 (prior to the ceasefires) that provided counselling and support to those bereaved or injured, as well as campaigning for justice and recompense. With the needs of victims being recognised in both the Belfast/Good Friday Agreement and the EU PEACE programmes, a much larger number of groups emerged in the post-Agreement period; many of which were single identity in composition, while others were cross-community and inclusive. A statutory Victims and Survivors Service (established under the Victims and Survivors (Northern Ireland) Order 2006 was put in place to support organisations delivering help to victims. But even the term 'victim' remains contested in Northern Ireland, as in many other areas of conflict. The whole area of legacy and recompense continues to be politically contentious, making this work frustrating for both the individuals and organisations affected. This remains one of the key unresolved legacy issues of the conflict.

Activism with and by political ex-prisoners and ex-combatants

While fledgling work had been undertaken within the prisons pre-1994, more overt work was enabled after the ceasefires with the support of the EU PEACE programmes. It has been estimated that there were some 25–30,000 politically motivated Republican and Loyalist prisoners over the period of the conflict, the vast majority male and republican, but also including a small number of women. Although there were no mainstream statutory programmes put in place to support the reintegration of political ex-prisoners, the various phases of the EU PEACE programmes enabled the Community Foundation for Northern Ireland (CFNI) to support work in this priority area. The approach taken by CFNI was to work directly with representatives of the five main paramilitary groups to enable the establishment of self-help political ex-prisoner centres and services.

CFNI ensured buy-in to the design and delivery of this sensitive programme by inviting each organisation to have two representatives sit on the Advisory Committee with responsibility for making grant awards, based on funding applications. This participative approach was effective in facilitating relationship-building between groups of former armed enemies, which stayed in place even over periods when ceasefires were either under strain or had broken down. This was an important peacebuilding dimension to the community-based work. Emerging from 30 years of censorship, conspiracy theories and counter-narratives, prisoner insights and relationships were essential. Notwithstanding criticism from many politicians and parts of the media, the importance of maintaining communication and building peace among former combatants was a crucial step forward in the overall Peace Process.

The self-help centres established offered information and advice services, drop-in provision, training and educational opportunities. They addressed the individual needs of ex-prisoners and their family members, but also contributed to policy and advocacy. Given their location in disadvantaged areas, the centres quickly became responsive to community needs resulting in ex-prisoners gradually undertaking a role in community development and peacebuilding work generally within and across communities. This work was not without its local critics. Established community activists who were not politically aligned often questioned the role of political ex-prisoners, accusing them of exerting a 'controlling influence' in the community and complaining about the resources being awarded. As against this, it was suggested that political ex-prisoners brought a proven credibility to argue against continuing violence and were often motivated by the drive to 'give back' in a positive manner to their communities.

The conflict transformation work engaged in by political ex-prisoners and ex-combatants included work both within and between their respective communities, as well as between groups. Within 'single identity' communities work was carried out to enhance understanding of 'the other' community and to deal with inter-organisational tensions that were in danger of sparking violent feuds. There was ex-prisoner involvement in the community-based restorative justice initiatives developed to replace paramilitary kneecappings and beatings that had been used to 'police' local 'anti-social' offenders. There were negotiations over the display of flags, emblems and other aspects of territoriality; and efforts were made to address community-level social issues (Shirlow et al, 2005).

On an inter-community basis, dialogue sessions were organised between former ex-prisoners from different political perspectives. There was conflict alleviation at interfaces and at 'peace walls' segregation barriers. There was work with young people to dissuade them from the glamour of paramilitarism. Cross-community projects were developed, such as joint political tours of local areas, and the preparation of a 'Prison to Peace' School Pack delivered jointly by Loyalist and Republican ex-prisoners in schools to share their experiences of being a combatant, to serving a long time in prison, to now supporting the peace process. It also required community activism to engage with those political perspectives who continued to demonise political ex-prisoners as symbolic of the violence of the Troubles. This often took the form of positing the ex-prisoners in opposition to the needs and interests of victims/survivors of the conflict. The fact that many political ex-prisoners were also victims/survivors was often conveniently overlooked.

Community action and peacebuilding in areas experiencing development shadow

When a review was carried out of the capacity to increase inter-community peacebuilding work, analysis showed that 'community infrastructure' appeared to flourish in situations where there was a combination of three key elements:

- social capital (activists/groups/networks/collective processes);
- human capital (local leadership/relationships/knowledge/confidence); and
- physical capital (meeting space/resources/equipment/finance).

Belfast and Derry cities, both of which had been significantly impacted by the conflict, showed relatively strong community infrastructure and it was clear that earlier activist work within communities had supported this development. The advent of the first of a series (currently numbering four) of EU PEACE programmes in 1995 supported interface work and inter-community activities, all with varying degrees of success. Government-funded programmes supplemented where needed. The main issue, however, was that much of the funding available was bureaucratic in nature and required relatively sophisticated capacity within the applicant group to manage it. Further analysis showed that there were areas that had been badly impacted by the conflict where community infrastructure was weak or non-existent and consequently failed to benefit from the funding available. These areas became known as 'areas of weak community infrastructure' (WCI).

There was a high correlation between WCI areas and local government bodies who had limited interest in community development or who did not reach out to communities where there were competing paramilitary organisations or evidence of strong coercive control. Such areas were viewed as 'hard to reach' and support was limited. The research also showed that areas of weak community infrastructure were disproportionately (although not exclusively) found in PUL communities, and that due to lower levels of capacity were less likely to engage in community development or inter-community activity (Healy and O'Prey, 2006). Table 10.2 highlights factors and indicators of weak community infrastructure.

The International Fund for Ireland and Atlantic Philanthropies partnered to fund the Community Foundation NI to deliver a Communities in Transition programme targeted at Areas of Weak Community Infrastructure (AWCI). It worked proactively in areas significantly impacted by conflict, and that were continuing to experience community tension and division in the post

Table 10.2: Factors and indicators of weak community infrastructure

Conflict-related factors	Geography: infrastructural support	Other factors
Political or paramilitary gatekeeping or control	Physical isolation (outside support organisation's priority areas)	Cultural barriers (reluctance to take state or external money)
Intra- and/or inter-community tensions	Lack of community meeting space or venue	Religious or ideological barriers
Areas deemed 'difficult to work with' by agencies	Development shadow – agencies claiming to work in areas but neglecting/avoiding some	Alienation from perceptions of the community/voluntary sector
Fear of failure – due to previous experience; fear to risk robust opposition	Small areas of deprivation with no access to money due to location in the shadow of wealthier areas	Community development seen as ideologically or politically aligned
Lack of human capital – leadership – due to political context	Current funder criteria does not relate to local needs	

Belfast/Good Friday Agreement period. This delivered an intertwined community development and peacebuilding approach. It was designed to assess if positive change could be delivered for local residents in such a manner that they would not feel left behind or ignored by the ongoing peace process.

Key to this approach is the belief that peacebuilding in divided communities needs to be community-led and community-owned. A belief that confidence and capacity must be built from the ground up for it to be sustainable. It was essential from the outset that difficult and potentially divisive issues were not avoided but dealt with in a way that neither further endangered people nor exacerbated tensions. Sensitivity and reassurance were needed at all stages of the engagement process while maintaining the momentum to build inclusivity. Inclusivity requires reaching out to people who are apprehensive of involvement as well as communicating with local 'gatekeepers' (whether party political, paramilitaries or strong local personalities) on the basis of developing honest relationships.

The programme design required proactive identification of local communities where the challenges for the work included:

- little evidence of community development, activism or engagement;
- clear evidence of ongoing community tensions and divisions, both within the areas themselves and on an inter-community basis;
- strong evidence of community control through ongoing paramilitary activity or other gatekeeping resulting in lack of broader community participation; and
- clear evidence of social need coupled with statutory neglect, resulting in lack of services, engagement and investment.

Programme staff had to have the ability to engage in a non-judgemental manner as well as being politically aware of local perceptions, nuances and dynamics. They required the confidence to build and sustain relationships (both within and between communities) and to be committed to inclusive peacebuilding and social justice. Equally, local people had to be convinced that the programme was long-term in nature and that support would be accessible and dependable irrespective of periodic setbacks. It was understood that peacebuilding is not a linear process and is often beset by challenges and back-steps.

The programme implementation

The model adopted had three main steps to initiate the work in each selected programme areas:

- area profiling: mapping of social need; community tensions; challenges; and opportunities/community strengths;
- engagement with local people, agencies and groups to develop relationships; and
- assessing interest and support – as well as potential opposition.

The approach focused on building relationships with people living in and/or who knew or worked in the area; identifying needs and opportunities with local people and developing an action plan that would be implemented at a pace that local people felt comfortable with. There was no pre-set agenda, apart from a commitment to the values of community development and peacebuilding. There were no specific inputs/outputs to achieve and no rigid funding-agency requirements such as year-end spending deadlines. All project areas were allocated a notional five-year programme budget, with all eventually supported for more than seven years within budget.

The initial area assessment established not only the infrastructure and nature of assets/deficits in each area, but also assessed the political profile and nuances – the 'who was who' in terms of influence, controls and power, gatekeeping and the barriers/challenges faced to date. This assessment was made through participant observation, as well as by talking with both external and internal agencies and individuals, that included key actors within paramilitary and political groups.

A transparent process to engage with people and encourage participation was then initiated. This essentially meant talking directly to people to build a relationship of trust. Alongside the social and economic needs that were identified in these conversations, peacebuilding issues also emerged. People spoke about the reasons why things either happened, or didn't happen, within the neighbourhood. Once trust was slowly established, programme staff were able to probe and understand some of the more sensitive issues relating to the conflict that were holding back engagement and progress.

When this initial work was complete, a development process could then be agreed and put in place. Essentially, this meant:

- motivating people to set up and participate in a local development group;
- agreeing an initial action plan based on area needs, opportunities and priorities;
- providing development support and capacity building;
- helping the group develop and build sustainability of both the local activism and achievements; and
- recording the small wins and providing space for reflection, learning and evaluation.

The animation and development phase

This entailed assessment and documentation of local needs and priorities (as well as assets), public meetings, one-to-one resident contact, engaging with agencies, offering training opportunities and access to courses, identifying projects and activities that could deliver 'quick wins' to build credibility and confidence, and the development of flexible action plans and targets for the work. Development was often slow, and the pace varied in the different areas where the programme was being implemented. All, however, established a local action group and either sourced meeting places or opened community offices. Effective engagement was the key and was promoted through public meetings, newsletters, local family events, engaging schools, youth services, churches, community nurses, the local post office and other small businesses where people met. There were attempts, from time to time, by statutory agency workers or local politicians to block the engagement process, whether for vested interests or resentment at external intervention, and this had to be worked through by keeping local people informed and supported to address attempted blockages.

Local programme visibility and accessibility were important, as was organising non-threatening and inclusive activities like community fun-days, taster workshops or local history projects. Opportunities for ideas generation could be informal in nature and include different age groups. It was important to be conscious of any section of the community not participating (such as young people, minority ethnic groups, and so on) and to design proactive activities to reach out to them.

By the nature of the communities targeted for the programme, some of the work was within single identity areas, dealing initially with intra-community tensions. These could take the form of factionalism and feuding between different paramilitary groups. Other areas might have people from different community identities living side by side on interfaces. In these situations, there were often overt sectarian community tensions and divisions. The skills required for both circumstances were the same – building trust and relationships, breaking down negative perceptions of 'the other' and creating opportunities to enable difficult conversations which eventually led to a greater understanding of 'the other' and the development of inclusive processes.

As the capacity of the action groups developed, it was important that they continued to actively participate in decision-making about their areas while taking responsibility for engaging with decision-makers and lobbying for the changes needed. They needed to encourage further local participation by keeping people informed of developments, opportunities and challenges. While paramilitary structures remained in place in many of the areas, the power/control dynamics changed when the local action groups included people with paramilitary connections as well as those who didn't. This was critical to progress. Both worked together as residents and activists on an equal basis, making positive contributions for area improvement, but also discussing negative incidents as they arose, and holding people to account in ways that enabled relationships to be sustained. This was invariably a sensitive process of trial and error, and often required support from external facilitation. There were ups and downs, starts and stops, but learning came from all activity and review/adaption was built in.

Addressing inter-community issues

The challenge of building inter-community relationships needed the hook of safe spaces to meet and a staged approach to naming and addressing sensitive issues. Attention had to be paid to building the confidence of local activists to articulate their fears and aspirations as bringing groups together that have very different levels of confidence and capacity can be an alienating experience for those with less self-assurance. There were also issues about how individual participants were seen by people from 'the other' community, given that local groups often included well-known political ex-prisoners and/or ex-combatants.

The work involved sounding out the willingness for activists to meet on a cross-community basis which was facilitated by highlighting shared community-level interests and concerns. Convenings could then be organised, involving several groups supported through the programme, which offered training workshops, activities, information sessions with external speakers and residential events that included team-building exercises in safe spaces. As confidence grew, site visits were organised so that activists were exposed to the conditions in other areas. In short, there was a strong emphasis on breaking down stereotypes and challenging perceptions. Much of this was achieved by giving people the time, and relaxed space, to mix and network.

Encouraging people to work in small groups, with membership drawn from different local areas, allowed them to work through a range of 'local scenarios' that raised a variety of sensitive issues which required negotiation between the group members as to what the solution(s) might be. These sessions were generally facilitated by external people who could keep an eye on appropriate levels of challenge and discomfort. In practice, it was found that this approach strengthened the building of positive relationships and seeded collaborative follow-on work that was undertaken on an inter-community basis. Undertaking this work within the framing of the overall shared programme helped build confidence in the process.

Many of the sensitive issues identified and addressed had profound effects on the local communities. They included:

- Disaffection with the peace process/potential for a return to armed conflict.
- Dissatisfaction, and in cases disaffection, with policing/security which included the perceived failings of community policing.
- Uncertainties over decommissioning of weapons that impacted on both intra- and inter-community tensions.
- Vulnerability of marginalised young people in areas that continued to feel the impact of the conflict, compounded by the lack of opportunities/hope and vulnerability to both drugs/mental health issues and potential paramilitary/gang recruitment or intimidation.
- Concerns over issues of identity and unaddressed issues arising from the legacy of the conflict.

While discussed, rarely was there consensus of opinion either within local groups, or on an inter-community basis, about many of these issues. However, the fact that they were discussed was, in itself, progress – a step forward. Participants felt that they were being heard – that their views were valued.

The insights derived from this work allowed the design of more tightly tailored programmes grounded in social justice, human rights and inclusion. Whether at area or group level, the work was conceptually framed in terms of the three layers of social capital adapted from Putnam (2000):

- Bonding – building internal relationships and capacity to encourage participation and sense of ownership of the process.
- Bridging – with other communities to encourage greater understanding and collaborative work.
- Linking – with external agencies, organisations and political decision-makers.

As noted earlier, this was never a linear process and required programme review and flexibility in order to take account of the external macro-political environment which was itself often uncertain/changeable and contested.

At programme end, enhanced infrastructure and capacity was in place with investment in local community leadership and a strong contribution to peacebuilding and social inclusion work. All programme areas drew down external monies to regenerate their areas, which would not have happened without the initial investment in the work, but which was much deserved and helped to counter previous statutory neglect. Much-needed new resources, facilities and services were put in place to enable growth and development.

A relatively small investment that was flexible, adaptable and committed to building local leadership and capacity, that believed local people to be core to progress and sustainable peacebuilding, that was carefully managed and reviewed, enabled people in these marginalised areas to have voice, input into decision-making and an opportunity to contribute to peacebuilding and social justice (Feenan et al, 2021).

Conclusion

There are a number of key learning points that can be drawn from the community development approaches to peacebuilding that were adopted. These include:

- Long-term commitment with flexibility around budgets and work programmes and an assurance that the funding won't be pulled when the going gets tough.
- Ongoing moral support in difficult times: people need to know community development workers/funders have their back and won't bow to political and other pressures/criticism.
- Trust, respect and understanding for both local activists and the importance of the work undertaken.
- Ongoing engagement for the purposes of reflection on progress, learning and adaption when change is needed.
- Providing cover for organisations to undertake sensitive and complex work, particularly when they may be open to criticism or security risks.
- Enabling international connections with like-conflict areas that can give guidance and support and potentially be a vehicle for opening up conversations that are too difficult for local actors.
- Enabling safe space for convenings which provide opportunities for external expertise to share experiences, challenge and push boundaries; people can be overwhelmed by their own situation and hearing how obstacles have been overcome/tackled in other situations can be inspirational and help to move things forward.

Community development practitioners need to maintain a strong commitment to the community development principles of empowerment and inclusion. Respect for local people and an understanding that, with support, they are best placed to develop and deliver local solutions to local problems, while conscious of the impacting macro-political circumstances. Peacebuilding also needs to draw out the connections between community-led and owned activism and the overall peace/conflict analysis, so that local communities have the information to engage in broader advocacy.

Community development and peacebuilding work is more successful and sustainable if it develops organically, with support. An 'Adaptive Management Approach' allows programme design to be tweaked to meet new or emerging challenges, or indeed to take on board quickly new opportunities as they arise.

This allows for goals to develop as the programme grows, but also to change as and when necessary. Apart from the essential capacity building and development that is an ongoing feature of the work, regular action planning enables local people to be involved in decision-making, becoming gradually more confident and ambitious for the outcomes.

Training opportunities in approaches to peacebuilding, social justice and human rights have been useful in introducing concepts and issues that people may be worried are potentially divisive. Again, it is important to move at a pace that people are comfortable with. Site visits to others who have delivered peacebuilding work resulting in positive change are useful tools, but it is also good to expose people to examples of when things did not go well. Where there is sensitivity or fear, seminars or events to hear from others can be useful to enable difficult or challenging conversations to commence.

There is also learning for funders. It is crucial that they invest the time and resources to listen (and hear) in order to learn from local people impacted by conflict. They need to accept that small steps on issues identified as important to communities are essential in building confidence and relationships. Sustainable peacebuilding is slow and sensitive work that cannot be rushed just to meet a funder's deadline. Again, it is helpful to approach programmes for peacebuilding with an adaptive management framing rather than a pre-set outputs and outcomes framework. Funders may also find that peacebuilding programmes can best be delivered if they can identify delivery partners with similar ethical-base and values and who have strong local reach and credibility (Knox and Quirk, 2016).

Action research and evaluation can be included in programme design from the outset to facilitate learning and analysis as the work progresses. However, monitoring, evaluation and learning should be treated as an opportunity for participative reflection and learning (iterative evaluation approaches) with local people, offering opportunities for people to review progress and learn together. It should not be solely an external intervention but an integral part of the development process.

Finally, both funders and practitioners need to adopt a 'do no harm' approach to ensure that the work does not make things worse or even more difficult for local people/communities. Ongoing reflection and assessment of risk is essential, as is the need for flexibility to change approach/programmes/priorities in consultation with local partners. When local people engage with the work, it is them that are taking the risks to build peace. What is important is that people feel that they are being supported through both the worst as well as the best of times. This is what builds sustainable community-based peacebuilding in practice.

Note
[1] Fair Employment Acts (NI) 1976 and 1989, followed by Fair Employment and Treatment (NI) Order 1998.

References

Cochrane, F. and Dunn, S. (2002) *People Power? The Role of the Voluntary and Community Sector in the Northern Ireland Conflict*, Cork: Cork University Press.

Cockburn, C. (1998) *The Space Between Us: Negotiating Gender and National Identities in Conflict*, London: Zed Books.

Dixon, P. (2008) *Northern Ireland: The Politics of War and Peace*, Basingstoke: Palgrave Macmillan.

Feenan, S., O'Prey, M. and Kilmurray, A. (2021) *Activism across Division: Peacebuilding Strategies and Insights from Northern Ireland*, Belfast: Social Change Initiative. Available at www.socialchangeinitative.com/resources-for-peacebuilding

Gray, A.-M., Hamilton, J., Kelly, G., Lynn, B., Melaugh, M. and Robinson, G. (2018) *Northern Ireland Peace Monitoring Report*, Belfast: Northern Ireland Community Relations Council.

Healy, K. and O'Prey, M. (2006) *The Communities in Transition Model: Challenges to Community Development in Areas Affected by Community Tension*, Belfast: Community Foundation for Ireland & International Fund for Ireland.

Kilmurray, A. (2017) *Community Action in a Contested Society: The Story of Northern Ireland*, Oxford: Peter Lang.

Knox, C. and Quirk, P. (2016) *Public Policy, Philanthropy and Peacebuilding*, Basingstoke: Palgrave Macmillan.

Logue, P. and Kilmurray, A. (2012) *Then, Now, The Future: Community Foundation for Northern Ireland Learning as We Go 1979–2012*, Belfast: Community Foundation for Northern Ireland.

McCready, S. (2001) *Empowering People: Community Development and Conflict*, Belfast: Stationery Office.

McKittrick, D. (2000) *Making Sense of the Troubles: The Story of Conflict in Northern Ireland*, Belfast: Blackstaff Press.

Putnam, R. (2000) *Bowling Alone: The Collapse and Revival of American Community*, New York: Simon & Schuster.

Rooney, E. and Woods, M. (1995) *Women, Community and Politics in Northern Ireland: A Belfast Study*, Coleraine: University of Ulster.

Shirlow, P., Graham, B., Hadhmaill, F.Ó., McEvoy, K. and Purvis, D. (2005) *Politically Motivated Former Prisoner Groups: Community Action and Conflict Transformation*, Belfast: Northern Ireland Community Relations Council.

11

Everyday peace: after ethnic cleansing in Myanmar's Rohingya conflict

Vicki-Ann Ware, Anthony Ware and Leanne Kelly

Summary

The theory of everyday peace and its relevance at a theoretical level to community development in conflict-affected contexts was presented in Chapter 2. In this chapter, the authors explore and build on this theory to discuss their attempts to operationalise it into community development practice in Rakhine State, Myanmar – a region that has seen significant intercommunal and armed conflict in recent years, resulting in two-thirds of the Rohingya population being driven into Bangladesh in an act of ethnic cleansing. This chapter explores ways in which the principles and typologies of 'everyday peace' are being translated into community development practice by Vicki-Ann and Anthony Ware and evaluated by Leanne Kelly, in a programme working to strengthen peace formation between villages of Rohingya Muslim remaining in Myanmar and their Rakhine Buddhist neighbours. The authors draw from both their academic perspective and their grounded experience of the practice put in place during this programme of work. The case study demonstrates the conclusion that community development approaches can offer a strong foundation on which to scaffold an everyday peace framework that, in turn, supports the building of inclusive relationships and more peaceful coexistence.

Introduction

Our earlier chapter in this volume explored the concepts of 'the everyday' and 'everyday peace' in depth. We argued that the key innovations of everyday peace make it ideal for community development in conflict contexts, to achieve peacebuilding outcomes in the process of development. By definition, everyday peace adopts a bottom-up view, so community development's focus on locally led initiatives, active participation and subsidiarity provide theory and tools that support the strengthening of everyday peace. Everyday peace redefines behaviours usually perceived as negative, such as avoidance, ambiguity or blame-shifting, as potentially positive practices, and recognises that even in the most violent conflict situations a majority of ordinary people already resist the most extreme narratives and engage in some conflict-calming measures. Both of these directly facilitate appreciative inquiry (see Chapter 2 and Elliott, 1999; Bushe, 2011) and fit well with community development principles. They also break down the false dichotomy that wants to distinguish between negative and positive peace, focusing instead on agency and resistance. Everyday peace thus offers a robust framework with a range of innovations that fit very well with community development practice.

'Everyday peace' is defined around the social practices ordinary individuals and groups utilise to navigate everyday life in deeply divided societies, in order to avoid or minimise both awkward situations and conflict triggers – and thereafter perhaps consider active steps to engage with the other. Everyday peace recognises a spectrum of social practices, depending on the individual and contextual factors. These range from simply eking out safe space in which a façade of normality prevails, to allow people to conduct activities crucial to daily living without triggering conflict or violence, through to actively seeking to build sustainable peace and restore damaged relationships. Everyday peace may be the first peace, or inter-group contact after violence, or the last peace before total rupture or return to violence. But it may also evolve into much wider and deeper peace formation. Everyday peace offers a strong foundation for intra-communal work to establish conflict-avoiding practices, upon which intercommunal engagement and social cohesion may be rebuilt.

This chapter presents a case study of our attempts to operationalise awareness-raising of everyday peace social practices, within a community development programme in Rakhine State, Myanmar. In 2016 and 2017, violence in Rakhine State resulted in two-thirds of the Rohingya population being driven across the Bangladeshi border. Over 740,000 Rohingya refugees fled in a matter of months, in an act the UN has labelled ethnic cleansing (Westcott and Smith, 2017). Over a million Rohingya now shelter in Bangladesh, others in internally displaced persons' (IDP) camps inside Myanmar. Nonetheless, an estimated 400,000 Rohingya continue to live in villages across the northern parts of Rakhine State. Their situation is precarious; they remain marginalised, lack citizenship, and have either survived violence or are acutely aware that most other Rohingya have been subjected to ethnic cleansing. Notably, for our study, many live in close proximity to ethnic Rakhine (Buddhist) villages.

The authors have been involved long-term with a local non-governmental organisation (NGO) led asset-based community development programme in this region, working across Rohingya and Rakhine villages. The programme utilises a Freirean consciousness-raising (awareness-raising) approach, to strength both locally led community development and peacebuilding agency. This is explored in detail in this chapter. We argue that everyday peace provides a useful framework for individuals and communities to become critically aware of the issues they face, their degree of agency and the repertoire of potential peace-supporting actions they can take.

The remainder of this chapter is divided into five sections. The first very briefly summarises the concept, principles and typologies of everyday peace detailed in Chapter 2. The second documents the Rohingya conflict context within which we attempt to apply everyday peace. A third section outlines the community development programme and explores our approach to operationalising everyday peace within this. This is the first attempt by anyone to try to translate this theory into practice. A fourth section presents some preliminary evaluation results from the programme, before a final section offers some concluding thoughts and observations.

The concept of 'everyday peace'

This section very briefly describes the idea of everyday peace and how it relates to community development, for anyone reading this chapter as a standalone paper. However, we encourage readers to refer to Chapter 2 in this volume for full details.

The last few decades of research into 'the everyday' frames it as a site of intense micropolitical struggle, a space in which non-elite actors resist cultural narratives, innovate and reclaim as much autonomy and agency as possible (for example, de Certeau, 1984). 'The everyday is regarded as the normal habitus for individuals and groups, even if what passed as "normal" in a conflict-affected society would be abnormal elsewhere' (Mac Ginty, 2014: 550). Hence, our work adopts the definition of everyday peace as 'the routinized practices used by individuals and collectives as they navigate their way through life in a deeply divided society that may suffer from ethnic or religious cleavages and be prone to episodic direct violence in addition to chronic or structural violence' (Mac Ginty, 2014: 549).

Combining the work of multiple scholars, we identify eight social practices that constitute everyday peace behaviour (Ware and Ware, 2021; Ware et al, 2022). These are: avoidance, watching/reading, ambiguity, shielding, civility, reciprocity, solidarity and compromise. As already noted, rather than seeing behaviours such as avoidance, ambiguity or blame shifting as inherently negative, everyday peace reconceptualises them as potentially positive. When applied within community development, everyday peace allows an appreciative inquiry approach which recognises that most people have already rejected personal use of violence, and thus already act in ways that rupture totalising ideas of conflict and division. This holds potential to contribute to peace formation through strengthened agency, and the pooling of individual actions. Such action requires a high degree of bravery, and considerable innovation, creativity and improvisation, even if actions appear minimalistic or negative to outsiders.

Nonetheless, everyday peace is not a panacea. It does not necessarily confront or shift dominant conflict behaviours, attitudes or narratives, and where it institutionalises avoidance-type behaviours and normalises injustice, everyday peace risks helping maintain the moral distance conflict entrepreneurs rely on to perpetuate othering, conflict narratives and sectarian culture (Williams, 2015). In this sense, everyday peace may be less-than-just. However, we argue that while not utopian, everyday peace can generate a stability necessary to support longer-term nonviolent processes to address justice and reform. Where everyday peace brings peace entrepreneurs together, establishes conflict-calming measures, protects or expands neutral spaces, and evokes ground rules or parameters for mutual, respectful, nonviolent coexistence, it can form a foundation for potential wider peace formation. On its own, everyday peace is unlikely to be sufficient to effect transformation of conflict dynamics, unless connected with elite-level processes and longer-term initiatives to address injustice. Nevertheless, even without these, everyday peace has the capacity to support a stabilisation and return to nonviolence in the interim, at both the individual and community level.

Violent context: Myanmar's Rohingya conflict

Conflict has simmered in Rakhine State, Myanmar, for decades, if not centuries. One author of this chapter has elsewhere provided a very detailed account of the conflict, with nuanced analysis going back to the Second World War and earlier (Ware and Laoutides, 2018). Conflict flared in June and October 2012, when ongoing tensions between Rohingya Muslim and Rakhine Buddhists boiled over into intercommunal violence, displacing 140,000 people, mostly Rohingya (UNOCHA, 2013). This was amplified in 2015–17, when armed violence erupted between the Myanmar military and two insurgent groups, one Rohingya and one Rakhine, quickly making this a tripartite conflict. The Arakan Army, an ethnic Rakhine Buddhist insurgency, commenced operations against the Burmese military (led by the Bamar ethnic majority who control Myanmar) in March 2015, and the armed violence has significantly escalated since then. The Arakan Rohingya Salvation Army, a Rohingya Muslim insurgency, attacked security posts in October 2016 and August 2017, provoking massive and disproportionate military responses. As a direct result, violent military 'clearance operations' led to 671,500 Rohingya refugees fleeing to Bangladesh between 25 August 2017 and 18 March 2018 (IOM, 2018), which grew to 740,000 by mid-2018. Médecins Sans Frontières estimates that at least 6,700 Rohingya were killed during this seven-month period alone (MSF, 2017), which involved some ethnic Rakhine nationalists working with the Myanmar military. UN officials have described this as 'a textbook example of ethnic cleansing'

Figure 11.1: Map of Myanmar

Source: https://d-maps.com/carte.php?num_car=4165&lang=en

(Westcott and Smith, 2017), and multiple reports have labelled this genocide, ethnic cleansing and/or crimes against humanity (for example, HRW, 2013, 2017; Al Jazeera, 2015a, 2015b; Green et al, 2015; Lowenstein, 2015; Fortify Rights, 2016; Amnesty, 2017).

Rakhine State was home to just over two million ethnic Rakhine at the time of the 2014 census, and an estimated Rohingya population of 1.3–1.6 million (Union of Myanmar, 2015). After the ethnic cleansing, though, over a million Rohingya now shelter in Bangladesh (UNHCR, 2020), while another 120,000 shelter in formal IDP camps inside Myanmar. Only an estimated 400,000 to 500,000 Rohingya remain in villages in Rakhine State (no more than 30 per cent of the previous population). Meanwhile, an estimated 200,000 ethnic Rakhine Buddhists have also been displaced into IDP camps over the past two years due to violence between the Burmese military and the local insurgent Arakan Army (Aung Nyein Chan, 2020), and the ethnic Rakhine are greatly discriminated against by the Burmese authorities. Nonetheless, the Rohingya have been decimated and subsist now in extreme vulnerability and fear. Decades of discrimination and marginalisation have totally disenfranchised the Rohingya to the point they now lack citizenship, rights and services, confined to their village tracts (approximately ten villages). Additionally, the region within which these two peoples coexist is the poorest part of the country (Ware and Laoutides, 2018), with, for example, the 2014 census finding that only 12.8 per cent have electricity and 72.5 per cent live under thatched roofs (Union of Myanmar, 2015). Both groups live in significant poverty, although this is worse for the Rohingya, who have only limited access to education, healthcare and livelihoods.

So the question for this case study is, how does community development approach a situation like this? How might community development create spaces to commence peacebuilding so soon after such horrific violence, even while there is almost no political will to commence peace talks at higher levels? Very rational existential fears underlie the chasmic social cleavages. Hate speech and narratives urging violence still dominate much of the social media in the region. For months after the 2012, 2016 and 2017 violence broke out, virtually all trade and interaction between Rakhine and Rohingya villages ceased, across the entire state, and security forces policed a hard segregation. At the time of writing, four to five years later, a few villages are reconnecting, although many more remain isolated from one another. In such a context, the idea of bringing people together around mutual interest to rebuild relationships can be dangerous, risking aggravating conflict dynamics and triggering fresh violence. For this reason, our attempts to foster peacebuilding through community development in rural villages affected by this conflict have started with an everyday peace framework.

Operationalisation of everyday peace into community development practice

Operationalising everyday peace is challenging. The theory of everyday peace has grown out of observation of the agency people exert in conflict settings, of their own volition. An external intervention to implement these practices is oxymoronic. We nonetheless argue that it is possible to strengthen everyday peace formation through awareness-raising, helping people become conscious of the social practices they already adopt to minimise or avoid conflict risk, and aware of the breadth of social practices others use elsewhere around the world. This draws on the Freirean concept of consciousness-raising, wherein people can become empowered to act with real agency, through learning to perceive the social, political and economic contradictions driving the conflict, and deliberating together on how to take action against oppressive elements of their reality (Freire, 1972). By working with groups of people committed to peace, to analyse their situation and actions, they can discover real options for resisting violence and dominant conflict narratives. Through deliberation on how they may want to enact new ideas generated through this process, we suggest the process creates real opportunities for them to develop a sense of personal and collective agency, and to make more informed choices to proactively support peace rather than unwittingly perpetuate conflict.

It should be noted that the everyday peace theoretical framework is agnostic to people's motives. People may practice everyday peace social behaviours simply out of self-preservation because they do not want violence, while continuing to hate the Other. Even so, these behaviours should be viewed as positive first steps, however tentative, towards peacebuilding.

As previously mentioned, our attempts to operationalise everyday peace occurs within the context of an asset-based community development programme in Rakhine State, Myanmar. This allows peace to emerge largely as a by-product of another activity. We have worked with one local NGO since 2011, helping them plan and implement a programme built on Freirean consciousness-raising and Sen's (1999) idea that development is the removal of the unfreedoms that prevent people from exercising reasoned agency. The programme seeks to empower recipient communities to analyse their social context, conduct assets and needs assessments, determine priorities, and design then implement their own small-scale, locally led and funded development projects. The programme then provides access to expertise as they need and request it, to address issues and priorities they raise, and help them develop the agency to call on government authorities for additional support. Our local NGO partner identifies potential participant villages through relational networks, then visits them to run awareness seminars that introduce the programme. Where a community indicates interest, the local partner works with village communities to have them nominate a suitable villager to become their paid 'community development facilitator'. Facilitators come to the local partner's centre every 6–8 weeks for training, with at least two sessions per year specifically focused on everyday peace, and much of which we (the first two co-authors) have co-designed and helped deliver with the local partner (Ware et al, 2020). Willing facilitators are chosen because they are respected, natural peace promoters and good community organisers (but not a central leader, because these people culturally tend to dominate community discussions and close down the deliberation). Facilitators then take this training back, training a volunteer representative committee in their own village and leading application of the principles in their communities.

The programme runs for three years in each village, and we are now working with our fourth cohort. The first few cohorts were ethnically Rakhine only, due to sensitivities around contact between them and Rohingya communities. About six years ago, we realised peacebuilding training needed to be coupled with community development training, to generate sustainable positive development and peace outcomes in communities. Because at that time tensions between Rakhine and Rohingya were high, we continued with a Rakhine-only cohort throughout 2016–18, but incorporated novel, arts-based peacebuilding training. Participatory arts are a powerful way to facilitate self-expression, to explore new ideas, and can become a safe, liminal space to engage in difficult conversations. Findings from research into this arts-based component of our peacebuilding approach are reported in detail elsewhere (Ware et al, 2021). Participants almost unanimously report that this approach not only enriched them, but also strengthened their confidence to apply concepts and their ability to remember, process new ideas and communicate difficult messages in home communities.

By late 2018, emerging stories of tentative cooperation between pairs of Rakhine and Rohingya villages living in close proximity pointed towards the potential of a joint Rakhine–Rohingya programme, incorporating a component of everyday peace training with hope of strengthening the emerging peace formation. To our knowledge, this is the first such programme attempting to operationalise everyday peace anywhere in the world, other than for development of indicators or evaluation (Mac Ginty, 2013; Firchow, 2018). After careful consideration and consultation, we commenced this programme with 12 pairs of villages, each comprising one Rakhine and one Rohingya village in close proximity, selected based on their interest in the programme and a history of minimal direct violence between the two. Because the Myanmar authorities' ban on Rohingya travelling outside their village tract means they are unable to attend training workshops, the facilitators are all ethnically Rakhine. This is far from ideal, but necessary in the context. However, both communities self-selected for participation, and the chosen (paid) facilitators are required to organise then work with participatory committees within both communities and lead the planning of projects that benefit both groups equitably. At the time of writing, in late 2021, we have almost completed the three-year programme with these 12 village pairs. Being under local leadership, this programme has slowed but continued during the COVID-19 crisis of 2020–1 and after the coup of February 2021, with the pandemic and political context offering different challenges and opportunities for practising everyday peace.

Everyday peace presupposes people in a single village hold a range of predispositions, which can change. The programme therefore commences work with those already supporting peace, presenting a series of activities to help them reflect on their peace-oriented social practices and deliberate over how they might strengthen these behaviours. By helping natural leaders in the community better analyse and plan their approach to peacebuilding and helping them legitimise these through initiatives of mutual benefit to both communities, we hypothesise a broader uptake of everyday peace social practices. Because each context is unique, we have adopted the idea that nothing they propose or do is automatically wrong, that they are the only ones who can tailor responses to local context. Hence, our training needs to provide them with opportunities to deliberate and devise ways to strengthen peace, which are locally relevant and safe, rather than offering formulaic programmes. The pleasure, safety and ambiguity of arts-based workshops creates spaces where this can take place.

As an integral part of the community development facilitator training, we run three-day workshops twice per year specifically exploring ideas of everyday peace. The activities are very concrete and were co-designed with the local partner organisation and facilitators for their situation, allowing them to draw on local knowledge about what peace and conflict look like in their context. This allows them to explore new ideas intensively and then go away to mull these over and apply them, before returning for further training. Bergh's (2010) work on arts-based peacebuilding suggests this sort of repeated exposure over a long time period – rather than one-off workshops – is crucial for achieving significant impacts. The local partner repeats this training a few weeks later, to allow time to absorb new ideas and work on how to 'cascade' training in their village pairs. Additionally, local staff visit facilitators regularly in the villages to help them work through application in their context. This includes a local arts/peacebuilding specialist staff member, with prior experience as a local facilitator, who rotates through visiting all villages.

Our first everyday peace training workshop starts with recognition and celebration that participants are peaceful people – that is, that they have sought not to engage in violence. We then introduce the concepts of 'the everyday' and 'everyday peace' and discuss why this is important and the agency they have in everyday life. Using creative exercises, we encourage them to dream about what peace looks like, to explore what violence is, and unpack types of violence and its consequences. Blending arts activities with appreciative inquiry, we get them thinking about some of the greatest acts of harmony-building between conflict-affected groups in their region, to help them recognise their own agency as peace-loving people. This leads into a discussion about the basic ideas of everyday peace outlined earlier – including the eight social practices (avoidance, watching/reading, ambiguity, shielding, civility, reciprocity, solidarity and compromise). Using appreciative inquiry, we draw out everyday peace social practices they have already adopted intuitively and help them imagine new practices villagers might adopt to further peace.

In keeping with the strengths-based nature of the community development programme, we repeatedly remind participants that they are already acting towards peace, and that we are here to provide a space to explore ways to strengthen the positive practices that are already happening, and maybe consider others adopted elsewhere in the world. Subsequent workshops further unpack these ideas, and work on conflict resolution techniques, how to build inclusive identities, and other areas that they request, which help them build upon the foundation of everyday peace. To this point, we have played down discussion of renunciation (one aspect of compromise) and blame deferral, given these are more likely to be harmful practices, despite being widely observed in the studies in the literature.

To illustrate the training approach – to get participants thinking about avoidance as an everyday peace social practice, we have them talk about the things they might avoid to improve peace. Some indicative answers we attempt to draw out of the group include: identifying and avoiding high-risk, volatile people; avoiding sensitive places and high-risk situations that might provoke tensions; avoiding speech, behaviour or clothing that might cause offence, or highlight difference; and avoiding contentious, sensitive conversation topics. We then have them break into small groups to brainstorm examples of these practices they have actually seen occur in everyday life, and then brainstorm other examples they have not seen, but could imagine might be helpful in their village context. Creating awareness of behaviours they already engage in and imagining other potentially helpful social practices they could implement, aids the process of consciousness-raising and development of their agency.

Another example in which arts is central, is a carefully planned sequence of activities and discussions used to explore ambiguity. We start with an exercise where participants look at a scene through the eyes of another person, and then debrief them on ways to enact 'non-observance' of aspects of the Other's behaviour that may be offensive. We continue with a series of perspective exercises, including looking at optical illusion illustrations that hold two or more images, both/all of which participants need to try to see. This provides participants with the opportunity to understand and explore the fundamentally important notion that multiple things can be true from different perspectives – and that it is normal for these multiple perspectives to coexist. We then use a mask activity to explore facets of our identity that we may choose to conceal or reveal to maintain peaceful, nonviolent engagement with others. This builds on everyday peace ideas, explored in our earlier chapter, about dissembling as a key act of ambiguity – that is, disguising or concealing some true feelings or beliefs to allow nonviolent coexistence here and now – and deliberately discarding or concealing signifiers of identity, at least in mixed or neutral space. We allow them to explore this through metaphor, in poetry and storytelling, to help them reflect and deliberate on practical ways they can broach sensitive topics ambiguously to avoid offence. Our earlier research also demonstrates that stories, poetry and songs are effective vehicles for codifying their learnings, in ways that can be easily recalled or applied in everyday settings beyond the workshop.

Preliminary outcomes

As previously mentioned, the current programme iteration, the first to fully integrate everyday peace strengthening, is almost through its three-year funding cycle. This section presents the preliminary outcomes documented until the end of year two, based on evaluations conducted in late 2019 and late 2020 by the third author (Kelly and Htwe, 2020). The preliminary data demonstrates the effect that combining an everyday peace framework with a community development approach can have in a highly conflict-affected setting, even over a short time span of two years, and even very shortly after the extremes of ethnic cleansing. In this section, we will explore some of the outcomes reported in our evaluation data, which was predominately captured via interviews and focus groups with facilitators and villagers from participating village pairs. Some positive changes overlap several types of everyday peace social action, so we do not provide a systematic analysis in order of the typology listed earlier. Rather, we describe changes in attitude and behaviour, and explain how these are indicative of certain types of everyday peace social action.

Multiple crises delayed many of the intended activities and trainings during 2020–1, notably the COVID-19 pandemic, the 2021 coup, and prolonged violent engagement between the Burmese military and armed insurgent groups. Despite these interruptions, the crises offered the paired Rakhine–Rohingya villages taking part in this programme opportunities to go beyond practices like avoidance, ambiguity and shielding, to even enact reciprocity as a practice of everyday peace. During 2020, the Myanmar military attacked and damaged two of the Rohingya villages and one Rakhine village, causing residents to run for their lives. In each situation, residents of the paired village provided aid and support to their neighbours. When the Rohingya villages were attacked, the Rakhine religious leaders entreated their own people to provide accommodation, medicine and food to the Rohingya. When the Rakhine village was burned, their Rohingya neighbours provided shelter and care for the Rakhine's animals. Additionally, throughout the COVID-19 pandemic, Rakhine villagers have shared medical supplies, toiletries, food and personal protective equipment with the Rohingya. A local staff member observed that the "Muslims [Rohingya] take care of Rakhine, and Rakhine take care of Muslims". As a result of these crisis events demonstrating positive connections, the staff member noted that "I think Rakhine and Muslims are learning to live together again. We feel very happy to see that".

While blame deferral, an aspect of civility, could be considered a negative practice, in the paired villages this strategy has helped residents conceptualise the conflict as being driven and provoked by the state, and that their Rakhine or Rohingya neighbours are not really the problem. A staff member noted that "if Muslims and Rakhine are fighting, the Myanmar military would be very happy". Identifying the problematic group as lying outside of their immediate everyday vicinity provides the two groups with common ground, captured by the comments of another local staff member who remarked:

> 'We don't want to be victims of political games anymore. We want a peaceful society for all Rakhine and Muslims. We all are suffering from the oppression of the military for too long. In order to have a peaceful society, we have to work together and live in a peaceful way.'

This sentiment was reflected by the facilitators and villagers from both sides who took part in focus groups, who offered numerous comments demonstrating their feelings of goodwill and acknowledgement of similarities with the Other.

In another example of civility, villagers participating in programme evaluation activities expressed desire for increased engagement with neighbouring villagers, explaining that interaction cultivated emergent constructive dialogue and intercommunal trust. They reported a range of improvements to relationships and ability to cooperate:

> 'We have seen many changes, particularly in attitudes. We are happy to see that … the villagers are more aware of community development and willing to work together. And we enjoy working with Muslims, together. Before that, we did not want to work with them. The project had mutual benefit and we hope to work on more projects with Muslims together.'

They identified civility to be in their own self-interest, and that nonviolent processes could resolve conflict.

Participants identified the need to stop using derogatory names as an act of avoidance for everyday peace. At the beginning of the programme, even the facilitators frequently used the derogatory Burmese word for Rohingya and voiced negative opinions of their neighbours. Two years into the programme this term is still in common usage in villages, but the facilitators themselves are avoiding its use and encouraging their fellow villagers to use more respectful identifiers. Some of the facilitators suggest avoiding any labels and just say "we are brothers" (an act of rhetorical solidarity) and highlight that "we are not talking about religion, we are just talking about peace". Commonly used disrespectful terminology is changing slowly, with participants noting that avoiding contentious labels is an easy way for them to promote peace. Another example of avoidance reported by facilitators is where a villager started to complain about politics, they would be reminded to focus on other, more productive topics.

As they continue to work together with their paired village, facilitators' initially negative opinions of their neighbours are beginning to change with facilitators commenting that they like working with their neighbours and they feel safe and welcome visiting the neighbouring village. One of the staff members commented that "the Muslims said they never thought they would see the Rakhine coming to work with them like this and they are very, very happy".

In another act of avoidance, one facilitator planned to work with his paired villages to demarcate safe spaces that were designated as either shared (for both villages) or private (only for the use of one village). He suggested that they would open the children's playground in his Rakhine village so that the Rohingya children and their parents could access it at any time and know that they were welcome. While cultivating the playground as a safe shared space, they highlighted that the religious buildings in each village should be designated as private spaces where residents knew they could avoid the intrusion of their neighbours. Additionally, the villages concluded it would make everyone feel more secure and relaxed if they had a 7pm curfew from each other's villages, noting that people can feel uncomfortable with 'Others' roaming around their spaces after dark and that it could cause tension and conflict. Rather than being a mandated and enforced rule, the idea was that this could be a mutually agreed way of demonstrating respect and care for the residents of each other's neighbouring villages. This is a good illustration of avoidance being a potentially very positive, rather than just negative, practice.

Nine months into the programme, residents in one set of paired villages were presented with a testing situation. A cow was stolen from the Rakhine village during the night. Initially, the Rakhine villagers blamed one of the Rohingya from the neighbouring village. As emotions began to rise, other villagers stepped in to shield and de-escalate the situation. Rather than allowing this incident to ruin the fragile and slowly repairing relationship between the two villages, villagers on both sides consciously decided that renunciation of this incident would be the wisest choice. Convinced by the few villagers demonstrating the everyday peace behaviours, the others involved in the conflict agreed to let this issue go and continue rebuilding their relationship.

Besides constant vigilance for one's own safety, one important aspect of watching/reading is allowing the Other to easily read one's intentions towards them. Facilitators have noted the importance of being open and transparent about their intentions, to enable others to 'read' them. In particular, several noted that they always try to smile and act kindly, and when discussing potential projects they transparently discuss their intentions, budgets, motives and concerns.

Village residents in focus groups mentioned they are better able to understand intentions of residents of their neighbouring villages now, through regular interaction. One Rakhine villager noted of their Rohingya neighbours: "We see them every day now. We have no fear at all. We are also grateful to do trading and selling food with them."

An important part of the programme is an expectation that facilitators will encourage peacebuilding projects and co-design these with residents of the village-pairs. These projects have been difficult to undertake since the onset of COVID-19. However, several early projects provided residents with opportunities to enact practices of everyday peace, demonstrating initial outcomes. The focus of these projects is mutual benefit for residents of each paired village. These can include activities such as poetry competitions, other arts-based events and sports matches; infrastructure projects such as building a health clinic, library or road; or weeding the areas around each other's religious buildings.

As an example, one of these mutually beneficial peacebuilding projects involved building a footbridge over an irrigation canal, to strengthen connections between the Rakhine and Rohingya villages. Residents from both villages were keen to be involved; but when it came to constructing the bridge, the Rohingya grew suspicious and fearful of their neighbours and decided they would not help unless the Rakhine paid them for their labour. The facilitator explained that this bridge was for both villages and everyone had agreed to donate their labour. The Rohingya were unhappy with this and went away. Instead of similarly packing up and going home, the Rakhine villagers stayed and built the bridge on their own. Once the footbridge was complete, the Rakhine villagers showed their Rohingya neighbours and clarified that this was a bridge for everyone to use. They recognised it would take some time for their Rohingya neighbours to trust them and see that their peacebuilding intentions were genuine, so they decided not to keep account of the lack of Rohingya input into the project. This gesture of goodwill was instrumental in building trust, and the Rohingya have agreed to take part in subsequent projects, including plans for a vehicle bridge and a road. With the Rakhine villagers making a first effort towards reciprocity (that is, they displayed neighbourliness without expectation of immediate resolution of the 'debt', which can build into reciprocal neighbourly acts), they were able to move towards a culture of reciprocity with their neighbours.

Over time, paired villages are creating more opportunities to trade with one another and enact the everyday peace behaviour of civility. Now at the halfway point of the programme, the facilitators are noticing numerous changes with Rakhine hiring Rohingya workers as they did before the conflict, and with residents from each paired village regularly conducting business transactions. Staff link these positive outcomes to the engagement that paired villages have fostered through mutual-benefit projects: "The relationships are very improving and we see the changes there. It's not quite like before 2012 yet, but it is improving." Another staff member agreed that "these peace projects offer a chance to restore broken relationships through reconciliation in order to live peacefully again". Notably, the inequalities of Rakhine being more likely to own land and the Rohingya more likely to be their labourers are not being challenged (indicative of a compromise now for the sake of growing more sustainable peace in the longer term), at least not yet, but the everyday peace provides a foundation upon which such inequality may begin to be addressed.

After the start of the latest conflict in 2012, the Myanmar government stopped Rakhine and Rohingya from sending their children to the same schools. Given most schools were located in Rakhine villages, this resulted in many Rohingya children losing access to education. As the programme has given paired villages reasons to re-open communication channels, Rakhine have come to care about the Rohingya's exclusion from the education system. One staff member commented that they have "become friends and have sympathy for each other". Recently, several Rakhine villages taking part in the programme have asked the Myanmar government for permission to allow their Rohingya neighbours to attend the Rakhine schools. The government is currently reviewing this request. As the villagers wait in hope of a positive result, Rakhine teachers are teaching Rohingya children in informal open-air classes. Many Rohingya children from neighbouring villages have joined these classes, and the Rakhine villagers have begun raising funds for Rohingya children to attend the township high school. The fact that the Rakhine people were moved to advocate on their Rohingya neighbours' behalf is a significant act of solidarity and highlights the important and transformational outcomes that can occur as a result of micro-solidarities and actions accumulating over time.

Conclusion

This chapter offers a practical study of how everyday peace can be layered within community development programming. This case study highlighted the potential outcomes that people can achieve, even over the short term, to improve their relationship with the Other and enjoy more peaceful coexistence. Community development offers a strong foundation on which to scaffold an everyday peace framework. Everyday peace can only be enacted from within communities, so community development's focus on locally led initiatives, active participation and subsidiarity provide theory and tools that support implementation of everyday peace practices. Layering everyday peace within community development offers deeply divided societies a realistic 'real-world' approach that addresses conflict issues and attempts to ameliorate them gently, in a way that avoids further harm. Raising villagers' awareness of everyday peace has strengthened people's agency to find solutions to local tensions, simultaneously celebrating the small, everyday peaceful actions they take to promote peace. Over time, these small, micro-solidarities accrue into a situation where deeply divided societies can live side-by-side, if not as friends, at least as functioning neighbours.

Our research suggests an appreciative inquiry-based consciousness-raising (Elliott, 1999; Bushe, 2011), stepping ordinary people through collaborative dialogic processes of unpacking their situation, their intuitive positive responses, engaging empathy for the Other, and formulating further solutions to address the problems specific to their contexts, can open doors for those with limited power to undertake agentic action towards peaceful outcomes. Engaging in processes of consciousness-raising has encouraged villagers to talk together, be open-minded about peace, and enhance empathy. By avoiding certain topics and behaviours, ignoring slights, deliberately acting civilly and working in solidarity, the 12 village pairs have completed over 170 mutually beneficial, community-led projects in the past two years (Kelly and Htwe, 2020). The tangible achievements have provided opportunities to interact and engage across the conflict divide, resulting in both positive development and social outcomes. Interactions provide space to practise and hone everyday peace skills that strengthen their relationships and help move away from rigid conflict identities that define and divide.

Admittedly, these are the best cases, and villages were selected based on pre-existing relatively strong intercommunal relations. Further, a key advantage of an everyday peace approach is that it builds on existing social practices to strengthen their agency. Hence, a more nuanced evaluation would undoubtedly uncover negative events and abuses of power continuing to occur in these communities, despite the everyday peace training. However, our analysis only aimed to examine whether community development programming could be used to operationalise a framework that previously only existed as theory. Operationalisation of this everyday peace framework through consciousness-raising appears to have provided incremental, but tangible, practical benefit.

References

Al Jazeera (2015a) *Breaking Down Genocide in Myanmar*, 28 October, distributed by Al Jazeera Investigates. Available at https://www.aljazeera.com/news/2015/10/28/breaking-down-genocide-in-myanmar

Al Jazeera (2015b) *Genocide Agenda*, 28 October, distributed by Al Jazeera Investigates. Available at https://bulawayo24.com/index-id-news-sc-international-byo-76523-article-al+jazeera+investigation+uncovers+evidence+of+government-led+genocide+in+myanmar.html

Amnesty (2017) '"My world is finished": Rohingya targeted in crimes against humanity in Myanmar', 18 October, Amnesty International.

Aung Nyein Chan (2020) 'Arakan Army meets for talks with Tatmadaw in Wa capital', *Myanmar Now*, 14 December.

Bergh, A. (2010) *I'd Like to Teach the World to Sing: Music and Conflict Transformation*, PhD thesis, University of Exeter.

Bushe, G.R. (2011) 'Appreciative inquiry: Theory and critique', in D. Boje, B. Burnes and J. Hassard (eds) *The Routledge Companion to Organizational Change*, Oxford: Routledge, pp 87–103.

de Certeau, M. (1984) *The Practice of Everyday Life*, Berkeley: University of California Press.

Elliott, C. (1999) *Locating the Energy for Change: An Introduction to Appreciative Inquiry*, Winnipeg: International Institute for Sustainable Development. Available at https://www.iisd.org/publications/locating-energy-change-introduction-appreciative-inquiry

Firchow, P. (2018) *Reclaiming Everyday Peace: Local Voices in Measurement and Evaluation after War*, Cambridge: Cambridge University Press.

Fortify Rights (2016) Supporting human rights in Myanmar: Why the US should maintain existing sanctions authority, *Fortify Rights*, 2 May.

Freire, P. (1972) *Pedagogy of the Oppressed*, Middlesex: Penguin.

Green, P., MacManus, T. and de la Cour Venning, A. (2015) *Countdown to Annihilation: Genocide in Myanmar*, London: International State Crime Initiative, Queen Mary University, University of London.

HRW (2013) *'All You Can Do is Pray': Crimes against Humanity and Ethnic Cleansing of Rohingya Muslims in Burma's Arakan State*, Human Rights Watch, 22 April.

HRW (2017) *Massacre by the River: Burmese Army Crimes against Humanity in Tula Toli*, Human Rights Watch, 19 December.

IOM (2018) *ISCG Situation Update: Rohingya Refugee Crisis, Cox's Bazar, 07 December*, Dhaka: International Organization for Migration, Inter Sector Coordination Group.

Kelly, L. and Htwe, S. (2020) *Year Two Interim Evaluation: The Community Development Education Project, Rakhine State, Myanmar*, Leopold: GraceWorks Myanmar.

Lowenstein, A.K. (2015) *Persecution of the Rohingya Muslims: Is Genocide Occurring in Myanmar's Rakhine State? A Legal Analysis*, Prepared for Fortify Rights by Allard K. Lowenstein International Human Rights Clinic, Yale Law School, New Haven, CT.

Mac Ginty, R. (2013) 'Indicators +: A proposal for everyday peace indicators', *Evaluation and Program Planning*, 36(1): 56–63.

Mac Ginty, R. (2014) 'Everyday peace: Bottom-up and local agency in conflict-affected societies', *Security Dialogue*, 45(6): 548–564.

MSF (2017) *MSF Surveys Estimate that at Least 6,700 Rohingya Were Killed during the Attacks in Myanmar*, Médecins Sans Frontières, 12 December.

Sen, A. (1999) *Development as Freedom*, Oxford: Oxford University Press.

UNHCR (2020) *Joint Government of Bangladesh–UNHCR Population Map as of 30 April 2020*, United Nations High Commissioner for Refugees. Available at https://data2.unhcr.org/en/documents/details/76155

Union of Myanmar (2015) *The 2014 Myanmar Population and Housing Census, Rakhine State Report, Census Report Volume 3–K*, Napyidaw: Ministry of Immigration and Population, Union of Myanmar.

UNOCHA (2013) *Rakhine Response Plan (Myanmar) July 2012–December 2013*, Yangon: United Nations Office for the Coordination of Humanitarian Affairs. Available at http://reliefweb.int/report/myanmar/rakhine-response-plan-myanmar-july-2012-%E2%80%93-december-2013

Ware, A. and Laoutides, C. (2018) *Myanmar's 'Rohingya' Conflict*, London: Hurst & Co; and New York: Oxford University Press.

Ware, A. and Ware, V. (2021) 'Everyday peace: Rethinking typologies of social practice and local agency', *Peacebuilding*, https://doi.org/10.1080/21647259.2021.1997387

Ware, A., Ware, V. and Thein Nyunt, P. (2020) *Community Development Education (CDE) Trainer's Manual Part II: Strengthening Everyday Peace Formation*, GraceWorks Myanmar, Leopold, Australia.

Ware, V., Lauterjung, J. and Harmer McSolvin, S. (2021) 'Arts-based adult learning in peacebuilding: A potentially significant emerging area for development practitioners?', *European Journal of Development Research*, http://doi.org/10.1057/s41287-021-00416-x

Ware, A., Ware, V. and Kelly, L. (2022) 'Strengthening everyday peace formation after ethnic cleansing: Operationalising a framework in Myanmar's Rohingya conflict', *Third World Quarterly*, https://doi.org/10.1080/01436597.2021.2022469

Westcott, B. and Smith, K. (2017) 'Rohingya violence a "textbook example of ethnic cleansing," UN rights chief says', *CNN Edition*, 11 September. Available at http://edition.cnn.com/2017/09/11/asia/rohingya-un-ethnic-cleansing/index.html

Williams, P. (2015) *Everyday Peace? Politics, Citizenship and Muslim Lives in India*, Chichester: Wiley Blackwell.

12

Conclusion: Drawing the threads together

John Eversley, Sinéad Gormally and Avila Kilmurray

Summary

In this chapter we draw together some of the themes from earlier chapters and outline what we think are the foundations for practice in peacebuilding through community development. We consider some of the theoretical foundations; we try to address some of the questions which practitioners on the ground might have about how do you know what needs to be done, how to do it, how long it might take and how you know whether it is working. We also draw particularly on the editors' experience of working in Northern Ireland as well as an appreciation of the importance of grounded community-based peacebuilding approaches supported by the members of the Foundations for Peace Network (FFP)[1] – a network that was co-founded by Avila Kilmurray in 2004.

What is peace and how does it come about?

The contributions in this book draw on very diverse contexts and experiences of working in conditions of violent conflict. However, a common theme is that they reflect Galtung's conception that peace is not simply the absence of open violence (negative peace) but to be sustainable requires the underlying ('structural') violence of economic and social conditions to be addressed (Galtung, 1969). Another common theme which is perhaps particularly reflective of a community development approach to peacebuilding is summed up on the placard displayed in a demonstration in Rio de Janeiro referred to in Chapter 7 (p 130): 'Peace without voice isn't peace.' As Chapter 2 by Ware, Ware and Kelly points out, much community development is concerned with bringing about 'everyday peace'. This entails both a task and process orientation, reflecting the understanding of community development that is presented in the definition of community development adopted by the Community Workers Co-operative, Ireland, in 2006 (AIEB, 2016), that was cited in Chapter 1. When both task and process have to be addressed in the context of open violence, they are invariably more problematic as the underlying causes of conflict may themselves be contested in the eyes of different communities. Understanding the complexity of the nature of the conflict experienced also remains crucial as demonstrated by the situation in the Caucasus – 'neither war nor peace'[2] – and violent conflict in parts of Nigeria is endemic. In addition, Chapter 3 on Colombia uses the term 'confluence' and Chapter 5 on Nigeria talks about 'knitting' to refer to the interaction of political, criminal violence and, for example, violence against women and children.

It is clear from the contributions that there is no guarantee of sustainable peace by achieving signatures on any formal peace agreement. Indeed the PA-X Initiative, based in the University of Edinburgh, Scotland, mapped over 1,500 peace agreements and settlements that were concluded over the period since 1990, in 150 different peace processes, finding that the breakdown rate was 82 per cent for inter-state agreements relating to intra-state conflicts; 14 per cent for intra-state conflicts; and 4 per cent for inter-state conflicts. The PA-X Initiative concluded that peace processes are becoming more complex, requiring multilevel peace processes, which highlight the importance of both inclusive local buy-in and credible leadership by empowered local actors (University of Edinburgh, nd).

Hence, peacemaking is important, but it needs reinforcement and careful nurturing that can be offered by effective peacebuilding. Attention also needs to be paid to the possible roll-back on the terms of peace agreements where future electoral shifts in power may return political leaders who are reluctant to deliver the implementation of the terms agreed, as both Chapters 3 and 10 on Colombia and Northern Ireland. Notwithstanding the very different contexts shared, the contributors to this book identify peacebuilding as both being possible and necessary at all stages of a violent conflict and post-conflict transformation, although the possible forms of interventions may well vary depending on circumstances.

Many of the contributions challenge the idea that peace comes about because it is imposed from above by elites or force and/or it happens only because of the pressure of external interventions. However, again the dynamics of negotiating and navigating peace agreements vary from country to country and at different times. Arguably Nepal, Colombia and Northern Ireland can be seen as experiencing post-war peace as negotiated by elites (that is, state and non-state combatants and elected politicians). Sri Lanka is in a post-war period that came about through one-sided military victory. Meanwhile Chapter 7 on Brazil addressed the impact of violent conflict at a community level in a country that has known war and dictatorship in the past, while both Palestine and Myanmar are currently enduring violence due to occupation and a military coup, respectively. In short, these varied contexts underline the nature of the violent conflict/peacebuilding/conflict transformation continuum. Additional complexity arises given the fact that developments do not move only in one direction but can move forward and backwards as well as experiencing roll-back dependent on the power politics of any specific situation.

Using knowledges

The book illustrates the observation that knowledge of what to do may come from theoretical knowledge (also called propositional knowledge or *episteme*); practical knowledge of the art or craft of how to do things (*techne*); or practical knowledge from experience (sometimes called embodied or tacit knowledge or *phronesis*) which is often the same as indigenous knowledge (Stanton, 2021) or everyday knowledge (de Certeau, 1984; Chapter 2 in this volume). As already pointed out, the perspectives and experiences of the case study authors are highly diverse. Some are community development practitioners, drawing their reflections from grounded experience. Others are approaching the subject from a more academic perspective, reflecting on various studies and evaluations of community development interventions; and then there are those who span the practitioner–academic spectrum, although invariably acknowledging the importance of proactive local engagement and participatory methodologies. The editors feel that there is strength in this diversity to allow for a range of discussion. Many of the case studies acknowledge the need for holistic approaches to be adopted, asserting the importance of flexibility, creativity and the ability to draw on a palette or toolbox of approaches in often challenging, complex and uncertain conditions. Community development tends to emphasise the value of learning from lived experience, drawing on Paulo Freire (1972), evolving theory from reflection, learning through action as argued by writers like Donald Schön (1991).

The authors may be 'insiders' or 'outsiders', academics or activists, but they have in common a shared understanding of community development principles:

- the importance of a value framework;
- the need for intra- and inter-community activism;
- the centrality of local community participation, leadership and decision-making;
- the necessity of inclusion, particularly where exclusion and voicelessness has been a causal factor in the outbreak of violent conflict and/or exists as a result of societal attitudes and norms; and
- the core challenge of trust-building and safe space.

These factors are considered here.

Prioritising local communities

The peacebuilding literature speaks of the 'local turn', but too often the practice does not address the massive centrifugal forces which centralise power at the national and international level. All too often these communities may be enacting programmes and providing a local face, but the major decisions are being taken far away (Mac Ginty, 2015; Paffenholz, 2015; Autesserre, 2021). This is not community development as we understand it.

Reference was made in introductory chapters to the distinction drawn by Peace Direct between:

- locally led and owned initiatives, where local people and groups design the approach and set priorities (external support can assist with resources);
- locally managed, where the approach comes from the outside but is managed locally; and
- locally implemented, which is primarily an approach with priorities set externally and local organisations implement it. (Vernon, 2019: 3)

Applying this typology to the initiatives described in the nine case studies it can be seen that the vast majority are at the 'primarily local ownership' end of the continuum.

When the authors in this volume use 'local' and 'communities', geographically 'local' might mean part of a city or a rural district. However, as Chapter 3 on Colombia highlights, it is not solely community as an administrative unit or defined by ownership. It can also mean a community of practice or experience, or a group of people within such areas (women, young people, and so on). We recognise that communities are not necessarily benign or homogeneous environments. They can be experienced as prisons – which restrict people in any expression of difference or even become sites where those who question generally accepted certainties may endure violence and hostility. They can be fortresses which keep people out – either not letting people in or expelling them because they are perceived as different or with fewer rights than others (Eversley, 2018). Communities, caught in politically contested circumstances and/or politically manipulated, may play a major role in forming the character of the violence, both as against 'other' communities and internally against groups and individuals who question positions taken. A key challenge during times of violence and polarisation is that often minorities and marginalised groups, within communities, such as women, are told, sometimes forcibly, that their needs or rights are less important than those who adhere to dominant political narratives. Part of the value base of community development is to say this is not acceptable. Emmanuel and Gowthaman, in Chapter 6, writing about Sri Lanka, emphasise this point: effective inclusion entails proactive and intentional work that needs to be sustained over time. The importance of such inclusion is reinforced by the value base of community development as articulated by the International Association for Community Development (IACD, 2018).

Building trust requires community ownership and agency

Reference was made in Chapter 1 to Lederach's (2003: 35) four goals of working at personal, relational, structural and cultural change in the interests of peacebuilding. The personal change relates to agency and the importance attributed to empowerment within community development discourse. Ware, Ware and Kelly argue the importance of everyday life as a locus of agency in Chapter 2, noting how a focus on the everyday can bring to the fore practices and narratives that may appear routine and are often taken for granted, but that actually demonstrate the high levels of local agency in the face of abnormal circumstances. The who and what about how that agency is actioned is an important area of analysis as described in both Chapters 6 and 10, on Sri Lanka and Northern Ireland.

Much work on personal change entails creating engagements that allow for deep listening and critical conversations between individuals who have experienced the impact of violence, an approach described by Risal in her case study of work in Nepal in Chapter 8. The potential to use creative approaches to facilitate hearing the experience of 'the other' is a theme that runs through a number of the case studies. In Chapter 11 on Myanmar, Ware, Ware and Kelly speak about the importance of rehumanising 'the other', while being sensitive to differences in ethnicity and identities. One of the approaches adopted in the work in Myanmar was to link participating villages with arts/peacebuilding specialists. Working in a very different context, Chapter 7 outlines how community-based work in Redes da Maré, in Brazil, has invested heavily in arts and culture to both celebrate local identity but also to empower people and enhance their abilities. Currently this includes the Maré Arts Centre, the Lima Barreto Library, the Herbert Vianna Cultural Canvas and the Museu Maré. Use of creative approaches can spark personal agency and shift perceptions by facilitating reflection and challenging strongly held narratives. There is now a substantial literature on the role of arts in peacebuilding (Brandeis University, nd).

In order to build greater trust and understanding both within and between communities, there is also the need to work for relational change. Violent conflict creates a binary narrative. There are the 'in' group and the 'out' group; those that are 'with us' and those who 'oppose us'. There is 'our' 'right' view/interpretation of events and the 'wrong' one. This is not to imply that where binary narratives are present the narrators are equally powerful and the narrative equally legitimate. However, within each group, fear, defensiveness and a sense of loyalty all too quickly demands allegiance to the specific group narrative with critical questioning being seen as being disloyal, collaborationist or at the very least unreliable. Shades of grey tend to be unwelcome and space for exploring difference, limited. This is why the challenges of building relationships and trust within, and between, local communities are so important, albeit difficult.

Relationship-building and striving for trust is referenced in all of the case studies in this book. A number of different approaches are described. This reflects a view, expressed frequently in the chapters of the book and elsewhere (for example, Stanton, 2021), that theory and practice or praxis has to be grounded in the communities in which it is in use. In the Caucasus, discussed in Chapter 4, a more formal programmatic approach was found to be helpful in facilitation of regional networking across conflict divides. On the other hand, many of the other contexts benefited from long-term credible presence within communities or introductions by trusted partner intermediaries. Credible, trustworthy and resilient connections at local community level are important assets in any mapping of asset-based community development in conflict-impacted environments.

The established community development appreciation of the importance of networking and inter-community collective action around mutual concerns and interests (for example, Gilchrist, 2009) has to be considered in the context of the nature of the conflict experienced (for example, the safety of those involved) but also how the purpose of networking is framed. Emmanuel and Gowthaman, in Chapter 6, write movingly of trust-building in the conflict-riven communities of Sri Lanka, stressing the need for solidarity and long-term engagement to build and maintain trust. They also note that relationship-based trust can often be multidirectional, giving the example of trusted relationships with individual agency personnel. The point is further made that trust can be shattered, whether as a result of crises situations or due to organisational imperatives. The issue of trust-building is linked to that of clearly held and communicated values, in the case of Nepal, in Chapter 8, where mention is made of the climate of suspicion arising out of the violent conflict. Risal explains how the building of trust is linked to a sense of groundedness and 'creative hearts'.

The Northern Ireland case study in Chapter 10 sets the question of trust and confidence-building in a social capital frame, identifying community trust and capacity within 'single identity' communities as bonding social capital, while inter-community trust-building – with 'the other side' – is categorised as bridging social capital.[3] In general, bonding social capital is built as a prerequisite to bridging social capital, given the need for communities to have the confidence to engage with those of a different experience and viewpoint than their own. The Myanmar case study in Chapter 11 also refers to this, describing the tentative engagements between Rakhine and Rohingya villages after work had been undertaken in Rakhine villages over the period 2016–18. Reference is further made to the impact of the uncertain macro-political context in which these developments were taking place, as when the military attacked two Rohingya villages and one Rakhine village.

However, the everyday peace indicator schema, and the trust-building work invested, helped community activists to maintain connections.

The work of MATS youth corporation in Cúcuta, discussed in Chapter 3, was built on a very different approach to trust-building. Youth activists used the agency of their own personal life-stories to make connection with marginalised young people involved in drug use. This approach has echoes of the use of personal stories that has been an effective community organising tool used by United We Dream, an undocumented youth immigrant movement in the United States (United We Dream, nd). Trust is drawn from relationships that are modelled on the experiences and needs of the young people themselves[4] and, gradually, built up with other members of the broader community. The 'Story of Me' becomes the 'Story of Us'. The strong emphasis on building relationships within disadvantaged and marginalised communities through a web of interrelated community support services and advocacy is also evident in the work of Redes da Maré in Rio, where, again, programmatic work is rooted in a clear seven-point value statement, with the first being to defend the rights of residents.

Merely stating the importance of building trust and confidence is only the start of the story, the challenges emerge when it comes to the question of who should be included, and even prioritised, in the trust-building process. For example, is it important to build relationships with non-state combatant groups, or indeed, state representatives when active in conflict-affected environments? The answer may well vary according to the results of a peace/conflict analysis of local circumstances. Nonetheless, in many situations the reality is that militants will be family members of community activists and/or residents in disadvantaged local communities. Relationships may well already exist and can be of benefit to enable community action to continue in what may be violently contested areas. The tension is in the assessment of what is coercive community control by combatant parties and what is genuine community inclusion. As many of the contributions indicate, the local community perspective is crucial in arriving at any grounded analysis.

This analysis also needs to be applied to the remit and membership of community networks. Inappropriate network descriptors many serve to alienate communities of a particular identity or political position. In the case of Northern Ireland, O'Prey, in Chapter 10, notes how the differential levels of organised community activism and infrastructure means that communities holding Unionist/Loyalist identities may be less likely to be represented in networking. Given this reality she describes how proactive steps should be taken to build such capacity in the interests of equity and conflict transformation. She details how a 5–10-year programme, supported by the Community Foundation for Northern Ireland, addressed this challenge in practice (Kilmurray, 2012; Feenan et al, 2020: 41–76). O'Prey reiterates the centrality of the community development principles of empowerment, participation and inclusion in this important work; principles that Gilchrist and Taylor refer to as 'core values' – alongside cooperation and shared learning – underpinning community development practice (Gilchrist and Taylor, 2022).

Building trust takes time and a long-term commitment to the larger goal. It is not a quick fix and is not an outcome-driven practice. It also takes skill and the various kinds of knowledge already discussed.

The other important aspect of relationship building that is touched on is that of the relationship between community activists and development workers. Working in the difficult circumstances of the Batticaloa area of Sri Lanka, discussed in Chapter 6, Emmanuel and Gowthaman recognise the importance of the strong relationships of trust built up over time that enabled local community activists to vouch for the credibility of development workers during periods of suspicion and crisis. Acceptance by credible local activists is particularly important in situations where the pressures of violent conflict breed rumour, counter-rumour, suspicion and distrust. All too often survival seems bound up with silences or a whispered aside to one of one's own. In Northern Ireland there is a popular saying from the Troubles: 'Whatever you say, you say nothing', which the poet Seamus Heaney immortalised in a poem (Heaney, 1998: 131). People can still relate to it with a knowing nod. Sotieva and Schofield, in Chapter 4, refer to self-censorship in the Caucasus and Sellick, in Chapter 9, notes the silences that were experienced during her work in Palestine. Relationship building and striving for trust can never be taken for granted. They require constant attention and sensitivity, given that both the macro-context and the nature of participation will inevitably change over time.

Rights-based conflict transformation and community development

The challenges of addressing structural and cultural change as an essential part of peacebuilding can be considered by reflecting on those chapters in the book that refer to the importance of rights-based work as part of the strategies adopted. There is reference to the importance of uncovering truth and delivering justice, despite the highly contested nature of both. Niño Vega, in Chapter 3, refers to critiques of the interpretation of the Havana agreement in Colombia, particularly as experienced by Nasa Indians in North Cauça who understand peace as 'harmonisation' – respecting mandates of human life and nature. Halliru, in Chapter 5, warns against peacebuilding which sees marginalised people as problems rather than as potential partners for change in Nigeria. Risal in Chapter 8, writes about how long it took to implement the promised Disappearances Commission and Truth & Reconciliation Commission in Nepal. Emmanuel and Gowthaman lament, in Chapter 6, the limiting of the Sri Lankan Human Rights Commission and the Commission on the Disappeared. Similarly, in Chapter 10, O'Prey describes how a social justice approach to peacebuilding was an integral part of her work in Northern Ireland. She details how discrimination and a perceived lack of social justice were the basis of a sense of clustered grievance in the late 1960s.

Chapter 7, by Sousa Silva and Malanquini on Redes da Maré, focuses most strongly on a rights-based approach to community action. A key point, which applies to many of the other country contexts included in the book, is the assertion that public security is a human right. There, the everyday reality of the 'pacification' of the favelas through the 'war on drugs' involved the shooting of mainly young Black men. Countering this police logic of repression necessitated the negotiation of a new community narrative – that of the community right to public security and access to justice. Data was collected and shared through a local bulletin; assistance was provided to victims of violence; local people were trained as to their rights; the community was mobilised to respond to incursions by security forces; and strategic partnerships were developed to effect maximum advocacy. A coordinated programme of action was initiated in 2012 under the slogan 'Somos da Maré, Temos Direitos' ('We're from Maré, We have Rights'). This campaign saw the first ever collective lawsuit on public security being heard in Brazil – the Public Civil Action of Maré. Parallel to this exercise in strategic litigation was a children's letter-writing campaign to document and highlight the various incidences of violence that they saw and experienced on their way to, and from, school.

The Colombian case study, in Chapter 3, also reflects how important it is to generate a grounded community narrative to that imposed on marginalised communities by outsiders when talking about challenging the official understanding of acceptance and unacceptable forms of violence. The young people who were dubbed criminals and drug dealers were also those that became community security activists and that safeguarded local public space. This as a result of the community-based work undertaken that enhanced the potential of empowered communities to transform their environments and to challenge various expressions of violence. As Chapter 7 highlights, Redes da Maré makes a point of defending ethnic-racial and gender equality as one of its seven operating principles, underlining the importance of intersectionality in community development (Ledwith, 2020). This is reflected in Redes da Maré's programme of community-based activities, but also in the priority that it places on making racism visible and accountable. The disproportionate number of young Black men killed by the state security forces makes them a priority for community participation and inclusion. Similarly, the MATS youth corporation in Colombia seeks to build the confidence and capacity of the most demonised local youth to contribute positively at community level.

As Risal concludes on the basis of her experience in Nepal, a culture of peace needs to take account of basic human needs.

Questions of voice, identity and memory are all important when considering the importance of cultural change which can challenge widely accepted 'common sense' norms that are often reinforced by official institutional and state narratives. The recognition of the importance of presence and identity forms the core of Chapter 9 by Patricia Sellick on capturing memory in Palestine, where, she holds, storytelling can have a transformative power. Working with young people to record the memories of an older generation of residents in scores of hamlets in the South Hebron Hills, she argues that the act of storytelling fills silences and overcomes singularity. It was found that cultural heritage can contribute not only to sustainable development by strengthening inter-generational chains of connectivity but can also support collective memory and sense of identity. The short film that was produced as part of this programme was later shared with Palestinians in the diaspora (On Our Land, nd). The use of storytelling is a well-established tool in peacebuilding (Senehi, 2009).

In Nepal, Nagarik Aawaz is also acutely aware of the importance of listening to unheard voices – not only of women, but also of Dalits and minority ethnic communities. Risal, in Chapter 8, writes about the centrality of storytelling in terms of people's personal experience, but also reflecting collective community experience. It is often possible to draw out shared values from this exercise. She notes that it is impossible to ignore the past and that the sharing of experiences can actually build greater collective solidarity in the longer term. While this is undoubtedly true, it is by no means guaranteed, and community memory must be approached in a sensitive and ethical manner.

The very dramatic 'insurgent cartography' engaged in by Redes da Maré in Brazil was a means to establish the presence of some 140,000 favela dwellers, who all shared a back history of being ignored and demonised over many years, to such a point that it took direct action and advocacy to get the area officially mapped. As described in Chapter 7, by quantifying the presence of local residents through a participatory community census carried out in 2010 (Redes da Maré, 2010), the exercise also quantified the need for adequate public services, such as schools and health facilities. What is further noteworthy is that the mapping was augmented by the collection of the stories of local people and the related naming of the favela alleyways and streets. For the first time residents had a recognisable address and a history to go with it, thus challenging the official stance that they did not exist.

In the still fraught circumstances of Sri Lanka, the authors of Chapter 6 express the hope that holding fast to memory and records of past atrocities will provide a future platform for accountability and justice, in addition to a recognition of the impact of the conflict on individuals and communities.

Although the remit of official agencies to address these issues has been reduced, community-based recording can still influence the political understanding of future generations. Similarly, in both Myanmar and Northern Ireland the legacy of violent conflict is still raw and remains a shadow over effective peacebuilding. Chapter 3 on Colombia notes the need to challenge preconceptions and the negative 'othering' of particular groups, in this case young people, as being crucial in building community cohesion; while, in a context where fear of losing cultural identity was a key conflict driver, the multiethnic format of the Caucasian Forum of non-governmental organisations (NGOs), discussed in Chapter 4, enabled participants to celebrate their own distinct ethnic identities within a shared unifying identity – another important facet of successful networking.

The nature and role of the state

The focus on structural and cultural change is important given that the state is often part of the problem and may not be able or willing to be part of the solution. In 2011, the International Association for Community Development (IACD) discussed the role of government in relation to community development as being a supporting one: actively facilitating and supporting community development through the provision of information, expertise, guidance and other resources, as appropriate (IACD, 2011: 8). More recent documents from IACD do not describe the role of the state in this way (for example, IACD, 2020). The reality in many of the contexts described in this book are that the state may be unwilling or unable to play such roles or their involvement in this context would be unacceptable. The perceived illegitimacy or ineffectiveness of the state is central to many of the conflicts described. The legitimacy of the state may be accepted by some parties to the conflict but not by others as in Northern Ireland, Nigeria, Sri Lanka or Colombia during the hot phases of conflict, or it may be seen as ineffective, as in Mexico, or unstable as in Nepal. The state may be fragmented or engaged in infighting. It may be unbuilding, destabilising or stabilising (Kaldor, 2019), or disassembling (Sassen, 2008).

In relation to community development approaches to peacebuilding the blurred boundaries between the state and other institutions are particularly important, for example:

- The tendency in the Caucasus of activists to move between civil society and formal political or governmental institutions at various times.
- Civil society organisations and anti-state movements becoming part of the state and paramilitary groups becoming or giving birth to or sponsoring political and community action in Northern Ireland.

- The state promoting an official narrative of the conflict that serves to demonise specific communities while privileging others, thus exacerbating antagonisms.
- The state using its access to and control of resources to augment a win/lose perception at community level, rather than working to promote win/win strategies of mutual benefit.
- The state strongly protecting some interests and civil society organisations and those interests and organisations being deeply embedded in the state.

One of the core attributes of community development is to create opportunities for people to influence decision-making. This can prove to be particularly difficult in situations of violent conflict where policymaking tends to be primarily seen through the lens of the conflict itself. Where the state is under pressure, advocacy to address structural inequalities and inequities can be all too easily presented as an attack on institutions and state structures that are aligned to non-state combatant demands. Consequently, community development skills in thinking through the demands prioritised, the language used and the alliances built are essential if inter-community solidarity is to be maintained.

Holistic community development

The majority of contributions to this book suggest that the most effective strategy is to adopt a holistic approach to community development and meeting community needs. Making the connections between the different levels is a well-established process in community work. As Saul Alinsky put it, 'we organize to get rid of four-legged rats so we can get on to removing two-legged rats' (Alinsky, 1971: 68).

This means analysing the broader picture, which may be ideological and rebranding any negative perceptions people may have, both of individuals and of areas. It is also about analysing people's own perceptions of worth and agency and questioning 'what are we living for', which might include notions of capability or sustainable development (Robeyns, 2016; Harley and Scandrett, 2019). It means making changes in the way economic, political and social institutions work but also how interpersonal relationships are conducted, including questions of exclusion, prejudice, discrimination and intersectionality, and personal introspection (Freire, 1972; Westoby and Dowling, 2014; Ledwith, 2020). This broad range of activities is well reflected in this book.

The work by and with young people around drugs in Cúcuta in Colombia, described in Chapter 3, is a powerful illustration of how very personal experiences can be linked to institutional change: taking away cannabis supply from criminals – and transforming the perception of young people by themselves and others. Arts, sports activities and eating snacks were used as 'tool projects' to introduce bigger themes such as human rights and conflict resolution. This approach can also be seen in the case study from Redes da Maré in Brazil, in Chapter 7, where the need to challenge violence, and to shift the narrative around it, is one pillar of community-based work which also encompasses a focus on education, arts and culture and territorial development. O'Prey makes the point in Chapter 10 on Northern Ireland about the value of 'small wins' – building confidence in terms of both community activism and peacebuilding.

The application of everyday peace indicators in Rakhine State, in Myanmar/Burma, offers a very specific methodology to community-based peacebuilding, based on principles that are explained by Ware, Ware and Kelly in Chapter 11. They argue that community development offers a foundation on which to scaffold the everyday peace framework. The community development tools of local leadership, participation and subsidiarity are held to be supportive of the peacebuilding approach adopted. A trained community development facilitator guides a three-year process which allows for the exploration of sensitive issues through cascade training and discussion. Narratives based on hate speech and stereotyping are critically examined and challenged. Where the work progresses to being inter-community in nature, there is a search for shared issues and priorities, as well as promoting greater understanding of 'the other' community. The example of the virtual exclusion of Rohingya children from school is offered as a point of commonality.

Nagarik Aawaz, in Nepal, discussed in Chapter 8, also adopts a clear methodology in addressing community-based peacebuilding, which building on Lederach's integrated peacebuilding model (Lederach, 1997: 80), starts with identifying priority needs and potential interventions (2–6 months); the provision of short-term training opportunities and forward planning (1–2 years); the design of longer-term social change priorities (5–10 years); and discussion and planning for a generational change vision (20 years plus). O'Prey and many of the other contributors agree. There is also general agreement about the need to be flexible in approach and pace given the uncertainties of the peace/violence context. As Risal points out, the path of peacebuilding is complex and uncertain.

While there is a strong emphasis on working to community priorities that focus on livelihood opportunities and survival in the face of shifting power-holders in an area, a number of the chapters also reference specific conflict-related issues. There is the question of trauma that Nagarik Aawaz addresses, which requires investment in the foundational work of relationship-building and trust, but which also benefits from an understanding that Western trauma management approaches are not the most appropriate in Nepal. A survivor-to-survivor programme is built on a self-help and caring approach. Both Nagarik Aawaz and Emmanuel and Gowthaman's work in Sri Lanka indicate an intersectoral approach to trauma which takes account of domestic and familial violence alongside that caused directly by the ongoing political violence.

The reintegration of ex-combatants is a form of overcoming exclusion, particular to post-conflict situations. It is something that can divide communities, with much depending on the prior community–combatant group relationship. Again, there is evidence to suggest that self-help and community-based initiatives can be most successful if adequately resourced and not seen to be in competition with pre-existing community programmes. Ex-combatants can also be a resource for peacebuilding as having proved their loyalty they often have the social capital to call for alternatives to violence and resist calls for renewal of hostilities. This is referred to in the Caucasus, Northern Ireland and Sri Lanka chapters.

While many community development principles can be applied to peacebuilding at a local level, the pace of the work will undoubtedly vary given shifting political contexts and, as has already been noted, the possibility of a roll-back in commitment to conflict transformation. Whatever the circumstances, however, there are two consistent requirements – the building and maintenance of trust and the availability of safe space. The latter needs to be accessible and secure to facilitate inclusive participation. 'Safe space' encompasses not only the physical environment but also agreement on how engagement will be communicated more widely to avoid misinformation that might endanger the participants.

The process of supporting local communities

John Paul Lederach is associated with the idea of peacebuilding being most effective when it is 'middle-out' with middle-level leadership ('track II actors') holding the 'greatest potential for establishing an infrastructure that can sustain the peacebuilding process over the long term' (Lederach, 1997: 60), though he has also talked about a 'web approach' (Lederach, 2005: chapter 8) and he has given explicit attention to grassroots activists (track III actors). The driving force of community development is a bottom-up perspective. This requires consideration of methodologies that can support and facilitate such approaches as well as introducing new concepts and ways of thinking, particularly as related to peacebuilding and conflict transformation. Chapter 4 on experiences in the Caucasus is in the context of a post-Soviet society. It highlights the contribution of the Caucasus Forum of NGOs (1998–2005). It argues that any distinction between a national civil society 'intelligentsia' and local community development is misleading. In addition to its role as a multilateral platform for dialogue across multiple conflict divides, the role of this network in providing a hub for learning and broadening perspective was found to be crucial. This was alongside its work in developing and delivering specific supportive programmes, such as the 'Forgotten Regions Programme' that prioritised community-based activities in South Ossetia and Nagorny Karabakh and thematic work with marginalised groups, such as ex-combatants.

The contribution from Nigeria speaks to the work of the Niger Delta Development Commission, the Local Empowerment & Environmental Management Project and the Community and Social Development Projects, all designed internationally and funded by the World Bank. This example can be seen as being located at the further end of local management as noted in the Peace Direct schema noted earlier (Vernon, 2019: 3), and stands in marked contrast to a number of the other case studies. Nonetheless, the chapter makes the argument for the need for, and the possibility of, government agencies and more formal NGOs being more responsive to the priorities of the most marginalised groups and communities.

An interesting hybrid mix of external facilitation and internal community connections forms the basis of the methodologies described by Sellick as applied in Palestine, in Chapter 9, and the innovative approach adopted by Ware, Ware and Kelly in Chapters 2 and 11, in applying everyday peace indicators to work with Rohingya and Rakhine communities in Myanmar/Burma. In both cases the importance of community-sensitive and connected local partners was recognised and acknowledged, as is the application of community development principles to what Ware, Ware and Kelly describe as sites of 'intense micropolitical struggle' in Chapter 11.

Finally, the Kathmandu-based Nagarik Aawaz, in Chapter 3, discusses how work with more locally based partner organisations delivers programmes of feminist-inspired conflict transformation work with mainly women and young people in remote communities of Nepal that were most impacted by the protracted violence in that country. Risal also describes how Nagarik Aawaz, as an urban organisation based in the capital, was able to draw on the very local community-based connections forged through the grant-making work of TEWA, a Nepali Women's Fund previously established by Rita Thapa, who was also a founder of Nagarik Aawaz.

Community inclusion and leadership

One important area of support work with local communities is that which focuses on community inclusion and leadership. Chapters 6 and 8 from Sri Lanka and Nepal, in particular, speak strongly to the importance of ensuring inclusion in community development processes as well as supporting community-based leadership. In both cases there is a focus on the specific inclusion of women who have often been previously excluded from local decision-making. It is noteworthy that both chapters reflect a feminist lens.

Risal turns the feminist catchcry that the personal is political, into 'peace work is also not only personal but political as well'. There is recognition from both contexts that women need the safe space and support to challenge the legitimacy of established power relationships and structures as well as to question traditional social norms.

O'Prey, in Chapter 10, also comments on the importance of building resilient community leadership that is inclusive in nature. Her priorities include ex-combatants – mainly men in the Northern Ireland context – as well as women. Unlike in other country situations, women were more visible as activists and leaders over the period of open violence than in the current peacebuilding period, partially due to the increasing formalisation of NGO sector activity encouraged by donors. Consequently, there is a re-emerging need to focus on support for community-based leadership by women, and particularly as exercised by young women.

These initiatives are not talking about leadership as it might be understood in the kind of models put forward for business, the state or politics in the global North (Grint, 2010). It is often a direct challenge to male and masculine, centralised and authoritarian leadership. Rather leadership comes from women and young people teachers, clergy, journalists, lawyers and other human right defenders and clinicians, what Gramsci called free-floating intellectuals, and Bourdieu, Putnam and others have identified as people with social capital (Gramsci, 1971: Scott, 2014). As the Caucasus contribution notes, people who are conscious of multiple identities such as 'mixed families' are often crucial actors, having networks of trust or bridging capital that span the geographic and political conflict divides. The pattern of strong centres adapting or co-opting local structures, processes, traditions and individuals to strengthen central control is one strand of colonial rule, as Halliru's chapter on Nigeria highlights. Community development has not always been on the side of emancipation (see also Eversley, 2018). However, there is another model of emancipatory leadership in community development which reflects the thinking of people like Paulo Freire and bell hooks (Bagula and Green, 2021).

The community leadership described in both the Nigerian and Caucasus chapters may be seen as more formalised and established. However, in Chapter 5, Halliru notes the need to build leadership skills with young people and Sotieva and Schofield recognise the important role of local community leaders both in their own communities and as representatives of their community, in the wider post-conflict region. Reference is also made to the network of ex-combatants and the Caucasian Women's League identified and supported by the Caucasus Forum of NGOs, in the interests of meeting needs and inclusion.

While inclusion, as much as possible, is a priority for all, the question of community leadership raises issues of power and both the need and the ability to question traditional accepted structures and norms. Emmanuel and

Gowthaman write persuasively about the need for alternative community structures to facilitate new inclusive community leadership. O'Prey also refers to this in Northern Ireland, arguing the importance of training and support for community leadership but designed to meet local needs and priorities rather than those dictated by donors or state agencies. Halliru in the case study on Nigeria does, nonetheless, pose challenges to community-based peacebuilding by asking:

- Can peace be achieved mainly by, or led by, action in the area prone to conflict?
- Are conflicts transformed and reconciliation achieved by local action?

These are clearly key challenges to any claim that community development makes a substantial contribution to peacebuilding. One writer described the peace sector in Northern Ireland as 'quite good ... as an ambulance, a stretcher and Valium tablet' but with 'minimal long-term impact' (quoted in Cochrane and Dunn, 2002: 160). While we disagree with this assessment both in the specific context and more generally, we recognise that how effective community development is as an approach in peacebuilding does depend not only on the context, but on the nature of community and political leadership, as well as the key causes of conflict. It also brings into question how the effectiveness of peacebuilding is measured (see, for example, Fisher et al, 2020; Senehi et al, 2009; Ramsbotham et al, 2016; Firchow, 2019).

Community development at all stages of conflict

A powerful conclusion from the contributions to this book is that community development is practised and can be effective at all stages in conflict. As Risal points out, rescue, relief, recovery, rehabilitation and reconstruction are part of, possible and needed for holistic community development during violent conflict (Chapter 8: 101). This includes the importance of community development workers keeping a finger on the pulse of issues of concern to diverse local communities and supporting advocacy around issues of discrimination, prejudice and injustice. Effective community development can play a crucial role in defusing and preventing conflict before it becomes violent in nature. Collating and sharing information on nonviolent forms of protest and action can be particularly useful in averting the use of violence as a default strategy. Where violent conflict is the order of the day there are still interventions that can be considered, as discussed in the following sections.

During the 'hot' phase

- Intra-community building resilience, adaptability and solidarity which is not only focused on a common external enemy; nurturing belief that

developing local solutions to local problems under local leadership is necessary, possible and desirable.
- Inter-community relationship building around common agendas on issues such as the need for better housing, health, education and welfare, and campaigns on poverty and unemployment.
- Meeting basic needs, humanitarian action including creating safe spaces for children and young people.
- Preventing outbreaks, escalation of violence through information sharing, preventing ill-founded rumours and monitoring.
- Monitoring human rights abuses and making contact with agencies tasked to maintain international standards of rights in order to highlight and address abuses.
- Facilitating humanitarian exchange of prisoners of war and identification and return of the remains of the fallen.

An important factor in making interventions necessary and possible is that the violence changes gender relationships. Although there are women combatants and direct victims, much of the violence is by and against men. Women are active in trying to protect male relatives, taking the place of men away fighting or incarcerated, trying to stop the violence or deal with its immediate consequences.

During the 'no war – no peace' phase

The period when open violence has subsided is rarely one of positive peace (Galtung, 1969; Ramsbotham et al, 2016). As Gramsci described: 'The crisis consists precisely in the fact that the old is dying and the new cannot be born; in this interregnum a great variety of morbid symptoms appear' (Gramsci, 1971: 275–6). It has been described as 'imperfect peace … a process between negative peace and positive peace, between the absence of violence and the preeminence of justice' (Muñoz, 2010: np).

Despite rhetoric about a peace dividend, very often many local actors do not see or acknowledge any benefits from the cessation of violence and indeed Ware, Ware and Kelly make the important point in Chapter 2 that peace may well involve some uncomfortable compromises. Community development interventions in this phase might include:

- Meeting basic needs, humanitarian action especially with victims/survivors and internally displaced people (IDPs).
- Helping survivors to be change agents through building their self-esteem and taking initiatives for their rights – nurturing optimism and potentiality.

- Preventing renewed outbreaks, escalation of violence through information sharing, monitoring and potentially locally based peace committees.
- Opportunities to share the past suffering – through dialogue forums that serve to humanise 'the other'.
- Prisoners and ex-combatants: exchanges and/or reintegration.
- Finding missing persons.
- Facilitating the return and resettlement of IDPs.
- Reconciliation work through building trust and finding new identities to create a sense of solidarity.
- Developing community infrastructures and supporting inclusive community leadership.

In addition, the peacemaking phase can offer opportunities for advocacy around structural and cultural change in the context of sustainable peacebuilding. It can also be an opening to call for reframing issues and transforming rules or structures. However, these demands need to be assessed pragmatically in terms of the support they are likely to mobilise and the related impact on inter-community solidarity.

A bricolage[5] of theoretical underpinning

Reference is made in a number of chapters to the principles of community development that have already been discussed in the introductory chapters of this book. Alongside this, there is a reliance by many on the Freirean perspective of conscientisation, a grounded analysis of actors and context (Freire, 1972). This recognises the centrality of local community experience and lived reality; allowing for community-owned narrative that shifts perspective and priorities. Halliru, in Chapter 5, reflecting on community-based initiatives in Nigeria, calls for lifelong learning to ensure ongoing conscientisation. The kind of lifelong learning he is describing is not didactic education filling an empty vessel but drawing out people's internal knowledge and their ability to reflect on experience (Freire, 1972, after Plutarch).

There is also an emphasis on the assets that local community activists and residents contribute to development and peacebuilding. Ware, Ware and Kelly specifically refer to this in building their relationships with Rakhine and Rohingya villages and O'Prey writes about it in terms of work in Northern Ireland, but it is also implicit in many of the other case studies. An additional dimension is offered by the application of a feminist lens, which details the asset of empowering and supporting local women, who might otherwise have been excluded from decision-making.

In terms of peacebuilding and conflict transformation there is frequent reference to Lederach's (2005) framing, particularly his understanding that peacebuilding needs to be long-term and inclusive, with an eye to both structural and systemic change in the interests of social justice and sustainable peace. Reflecting on the situation in Palestine, Sellick's conflict transformation approach, described in Chapter 9, is based on an acknowledgement that where power relations are unequal, storytelling can develop community and increase the solidarity and power within the oppressed group. It is a way of increasing the power of the disadvantaged group so that peacebuilding on the basis of equal power relations becomes possible. In other contexts storytelling may be used as a way of building relationships and trust between an in-group and an out-group or reconciling narratives.

The critique of liberal peace is clearly stated by Niño Vega, in Chapter 3, who asserts the need for a concept of peacebuilding rooted in a decolonial perspective with social justice and community solidarity at its heart. This visioning of peacebuilding, she states, emphasises the 'local turn', using the local experience and perspective as the starting point. The need to decolonise interventions to promote peace or the idea of decolonial peace is increasingly recognised (for example, Fontan, 2012; Cruz, 2021). Ware, Ware and Kelly, in Chapters 2 and 11, take the framing of everyday peace indicators and develop a community-based application for activists working in conflict-impacted villages, thus bringing together community development and peacebuilding approaches in a programmatic manner.

As Autesserre notes (Autesserre, 2021) there is increased international emphasis on policies of localisation, however the World Humanitarian Summit, 2016, and the 'Grand Bargain', agreed between donors and international NGOs that same year,[6] do not seem to appreciate the importance of the 'local turn', let alone community development. Not surprisingly, there is considerable criticism of the lack of delivery on the localisation commitment at national and local level (Emmens and Clayton, 2017). Although a target of 25 per cent of international resourcing was set to be channelled through national and local organisations by 2020, an assessment by Development Initiatives (2021) held that only some 2.1–3.1 per cent of funding was being delivered in this manner. We argue that without consideration of community-based prioritisation of need and solutions international humanitarian aid and peacebuilding will fail.

Finally, there is the all-important question of values and how these can be realised in practice when working in conflict-affected environments. The often complex issues of rights, truth and justice that refuse to be side-lined or ignored by communities either caught up in the vortex of, or emerging from, violent conflict. While the principles are reasonably clear, the practice requires reflection and judgement as well as courage. Equally, however, there is little likelihood of sustainable peace without the essential building blocks of equality, inclusivity and justice. It is in working creatively to help weave the web of relationships and the clarity of message to achieve these outcomes that community development can make its most important contribution in practice.

Notes

1. FFP is a peer network of Community Foundations and Women's Funds currently working in Northern Ireland, Georgia, Sri Lanka, India, Bangladesh, Serbia, Indonesia, Palestine and Nepal, all of which support local community-based development in situations of conflict.
2. A phrase coined by Leon Trotsky in relation to the Brest-Litovsk Treaty of 1918, later used in relation to the Cold War and used in relation to many other peace processes, including Northern Ireland, since (Russian Delegation at the Brest-Litovsk Peace Conference, 1918; Beloff, 1949; Mac Ginty, 2006).
3. Reference is also made to a third category – linking social capital – which is the capacity of local communities to interact with, and influence, institutional and governmental decision-making.
4. An example is given about not involving the police in situations of drug selling.
5. 'Bricolage' refers to the idea of social phenomena emerging from an improvised rather than an engineered process including drawing on myths and legends rather than a rational scientific body of knowledge (de Certeau, 1984). It can also be seen as a contrast between scientific and technical knowledge and practical wisdom (Buchanan, 2018; Stanton, 2021).
6. Some 28 international NGOs and 400 national and local NGOs agreed a Charter 4 Change – https://charter4change.org – in 2016 to be administered by Humanitarian Aid International, Haryana, India.

References

Alinsky, S. (1971) *Rules for Radicals*, New York: Vintage Books.

All Ireland Endorsement Body for Community Work Education & Training (AIEB) (2016) *All Ireland Standards for Community Work*, Galway: Community Work Ireland. Available at http://www.communityworkireland.ie/wp-content/uploads/2016/03/All-Ireland-Standards-for-Community-Work.pdf

Autesserre, S. (2021) *The Frontlines of Peace*, Oxford: Oxford University Press.

Bagula, F. and Green, Z.G. (2021) 'Emancipatory leadership: A working paper', *Medium*, February. Available at https://bagula.medium.com/emancipatory-leadership-ab3654e9e943

Beloff, M. (1949) 'No peace, no war', *Foreign Affairs*, 27(2): 15–231.

Brandeis University (nd) 'The arts and peacebuilding: About the resource library', in *About the Resource Library: Peacebuilding and the Arts: Brandeis University*. Available at https://www.brandeis.edu/ethics/peacebuildingarts/library/index.html

Buchanan, I. (2018) *A Dictionary of Critical Theory*, 2nd edn, Oxford: Oxford University Press.

Cochrane, F. and Dunn, S. (2002) *People Power: The Role of the Voluntary and Community Sector in Northern Ireland*, Cork: Cork University Press.

Cruz, J. (2021) 'Colonial power and decolonial peace', *Peacebuilding*, 9(3), 274–88.

de Certeau, M. (1984) *The Practice of Everyday Life*, Berkeley: University of California Press.

Development Initiatives (2021) *Global Humanitarian Assistance Report*, Bristol: Development Initiatives. Available at https://devinit.org/resources/global-humanitarian-assistance-report-2021/?msclkid=bbb8835fac1f11ecbcc491d4883a36b7

Emmens, B. and Clayton, M. (2017) *Localisation of Aid: Are INGOs Walking the Talk?: Start Network, Actionaid, Cafod, Christian Aid, Tear Fund, Oxfam & Concern*, London: Start Network.

Eversley, J. (2018) *Social and Community Development: An Introduction*, London: Macmillan.

Feenan, S., Kilmurray, A. and O'Prey, M. (2020) *Activism across Division: Peacebuilding Strategies and Insights from Northern Ireland*, Belfast: The Social Change Initiative.

Firchow, P. (2019) *Reclaiming Everyday Peace: Local Voices in Measurement and Evaluation After War*, Cambridge: Cambridge University Press.

Fisher, S., Matovic, V., Walker, B.A. and Mathews, D. (2020) *Working with Conflict 2: Skills & Strategies for Action*, London: Zed Books.

Fontan, V. (2012) *Decolonizing Peace*, Lake Oswego: Dignity.

Freire, P. (1972) *Pedagogy of the Oppressed*, Harmondsworth: Penguin.

Galtung, J. (1969) 'Violence, peace, and peace research', *Journal of Peace Research*, 6(3): 167–91.

Gilchrist, A. (2009) *The Well-connected Community: A Networking Approach to Community Development*, Bristol: Policy Press.

Gilchrist, A. and Taylor, M. (2022) *A Short Guide to Community Development*, Bristol: Policy Press.

Gramsci, A. (1971) *Selections from the Prison Notebooks*, edited by Q. Hoare and G. Nowell-Smith, New York: International Publishers.

Grint, K. (2010) *Leadership: A Very Short Introduction*, Oxford: Oxford University Press.

Harley, A. and Scandrett, E. (2019) *Environmental Justice, Popular Struggle and Community Development*, Bristol: Policy Press.

Heaney, S. (1998) *Opened Ground: Poems 1966–1996*, London: Faber & Faber.

International Association for Community Development (IACD) (2011) *IACD Strategic Plan 2011–2015*, Fife: IACD. Available at IACD_Strategic_Plan_2011-2015.pdf

IACD (2018) *Towards Shared International Standards for Community Development Practice Summary Guide*. Available at https://www.iacdglobal.org/wp-content/uploads/2020/07/IACD_31-Standards-Guidance-Summary-English.pdf

IACD (2020) *IACD Strategic Plan 2020–2024*, Glasgow: IACD. Available at https://www.iacdglobal.org/wp-content/uploads/2020/07/IACD-Strategic-Plan-2020-2024-English.pdf

Kaldor, M. (2019) 'Peacemaking in an era of new wars', in T. de Waal (ed) *Peace: Essays for an Age of Disorder*, Brussels: Carnegie Europe. Available at https://carnegieeurope.eu/2019/10/14/peacemaking-in-era-of-new-wars-pub-80033

Kilmurray, A. (2012) *Then, Now, The Future: Learning as we Go, 1979–2012*, Belfast: Community Foundation for Northern Ireland.

Lederach, J.P. (1997) *Building Peace: Sustainable Reconciliation in Divided Societies*, Washington, DC: US Institute of Peace.

Lederach, J.P. (2003) *The Little Book of Conflict Transformation*, Intercourse, PA: Good Books.

Lederach, J.P. (2005) *The Moral Imagination: The Art and Soul of Building Peace*, Oxford: Oxford University Press.

Ledwith, M. (2020) *Community Development: A Critical and Radical Approach*, Bristol: Policy Press.

Mac Ginty, R. (2006) *No War, No Peace: The Rejuvenation of Stalled Peace Processes and Peace Accords*, Basingstoke: Palgrave.

Mac Ginty, R. (2015) 'Where is the local? Critical localism and peacebuilding', *Third World Quarterly*, 36(5): 840–56.

Muñoz, F.A. (2010) 'Imperfect peace', in N.J. Young (ed) *The Oxford International Encyclopedia of Peace*, Oxford: Oxford University Press.

On Our Land (nd) *On Our Land*. Available at https://www.youtube.com/watch?v=TO9lIusw09w

Paffenholz, T. (2015) 'Unpacking the local turn in peacebuilding: A critical assessment towards an agenda for future research', *Third World Quarterly*, 36(5): 857–74.

Ramsbotham, O., Woodhouse, T. and Miall, H. (2016) *Contemporary Conflict Resolution*, 4th edn, Cambridge: Polity Press.

Redes da Maré (2010) *A Maré que Queremos*. Available at http://itdpbrasil.org.br/wp-content/uploads/2016/05/Relato%CC%81rio-Mare%CC%81-que-queremos.pdf

Robeyns, I. (2016) 'The capability approach', in E.N. Zalta (ed) *The Stanford Encyclopedia of Philosophy*. Available at https://plato.stanford.edu/archives/win2016/entries/capability-approach/

Russian Delegation at the Brest-Litovsk Peace Conference (1918) *No Peace and No War, Declaration*, 10 February. Available at http://soviethistory.msu.edu/1917-2/treaty-of-brest-litovsk/treaty-of-brest-litovsk-texts/no-peace-and-no-war/

Sassen, S. (2008) *Territory, Authority, Rights: From Medieval to Global Assemblages*, Princeton: Princeton University Press.

Schön, D. (1991) *The Reflective Practitioner*, Aldershot: Ashgate.

Scott, J. (2014) *A Dictionary of Sociology*, 4th edn, Oxford: Oxford University Press.

Senehi, J. (2009) 'Building peace: Storytelling to transform conflicts constructively', in D.J.D. Sandole, S. Byrne, I. Sandole-Staroste and J. Senehi (eds) *Handbook of Conflict Analysis and Resolution*, Abingdon: Routledge.

Stanton, E. (2021) *Theorising Civil Society Peacebuilding: The Practical Wisdom of Local Peace Practitioners in Northern Ireland, 1965–2015*, Abingdon: Routledge.

Tambiah, S.J. (2017) 'The anti-Tamil Gal Oya riots of 1956', *Thuppiah's blog*, February. Available at https://thuppahis.com/2017/02/02/the-anti-tamil-gal-oya-riots-of-1956/

United We Dream (nd) *United We Dream*. Available at https://unitedwedream.org

University of Edinburgh (nd) *PA-X-Initiative*, University of Edinburgh. Available at https://www.peaceagreements.org

Vernon, P. (ed) (2019) *Local Peacebuilding: What Works and Why? Summary Report*, London: Peace Direct, UK & Alliance for Peacebuilding.

Westoby, P. and Dowling, G. (2014) *Theory and Practice of Dialogical Community Development: International Perspectives*, Abingdon: Routledge.

Index

References to figures appear in *italic* type;
those in **bold** type refer to tables. References to chapter endnotes
show both the page number and the note number (21 n2).

Local places and events, and the people involved in them,
are indexed under the country that contains them.
Places, events and people of international or general
significance are indexed with their own alphabetical entry.

A

Abkhazia
  Armenian offer of rehabilitation 65–6
  Georgian conflict 62, 67–8, 69–70, 71, 74–5
  Ruslan Gelayev invades 76
activism *see* community: activism
Adaptive Management Approaches 188
aesthetics of violence 44
  see also violence
'Agenda for Peace, An' (United Nations 1992) 6
Alinsky, Saul 220
All Ireland Endorsement Body for Community Work Education & Training (AIEB) 5
Appreciative Inquiry 33, 35
Arendt, Hannah 155
Armenia 62, 65, 71, 74
arts, the 122, 124, 143, 198–200, 213
Azerbaijan 62, 71, 74

B

Bangladesh 191, 192, 194, 196
Berghof Foundation 9, 68
Boko Haram 86, 88, 90–2
Boutros Boutros-Ghali 6
Brazil 117–33
  Access to Justice 127
  Building Code (*Código de Óbras*) 118
  Constitution 118, 128, 131
  Court of Justice 128, 129
  COVID-19 130
  Fachin, Edson 130
  Institute of Geography and Statistics 123
  map *119*
  military dictatorship 121
  Public Civil Actions 128–30
  security forces 121
  Torres, Judge Jessé 129
  see also favelas; Redes da Maré; Rio de Janeiro
Brexit 173
British Council Cultural Protection Fund 163, 164
Buddhism 112, 191, 194
'Building Leadership for Women, Peace, Security and Equity' (Nagarik Aawaz) 146–7
Burma *see* Myanmar

C

Cannabis Awareness Training 52, 53
Caucasian Women's League 73, 74–5
Caucasus 59–78
  commonalities 67
  diversity in 75
  ex-combatants 74
  Forgotten Regions programme (Caucasus) 70
  international and local 72
  map *61*
  women in 75
Caucasus Business and Development Network 73
Caucasus Forum Coordination Council 76
Caucasus Forum of Networks 70–7
  closing down 76–7
  complexities of establishment 72–3
  conflict prevention 75–6
  Forgotten Regions programme 70
  mission 70
  multilevel dialogues 71
  spin-off networks 73–5
  women and 75
censorship 68, 77, 180
charismatic individuals 27
Chechens 62, 67, 76
Chernomyrdin, Viktor 67
children
  abandonment of 146
  Boko Haran 92
  community proposals 54
  exclusion of 89
  exploitation of 52

233

favelas 122–3
  guerrilla recruitment of 45, 86
  international trafficking of 82
  LTTE recruitment 100–1, 108
  Maré favela 129, 131, 217
  playground 203
  police violence 124–5
  Rakhine and Rohingya 203, 205, 221
civil society
  Caucasus Forum and 70, 71, 76
  churches and 15
  concerns of 66
  conflict prevention 76
  dialogue efforts 69, 74
  dispute resolution 76
  Hope Interactive 91
  national elites 73
  peacekeeping and 7
  roles of 18
  ruling class and 59–60
  Soviet intelligentsia 65, 77
  women in 75
cleavages 25, 29
Colombia 40–58
  Administrative Department of Security-Presidential Security Corps 44
  Alvaro Uribe Vélez 40, 44
  Arturo Ruiz Mobile 43
  Association of Indigenous Cabildoes 48
  Campesinas De Córdoba and Urabá Self-Defenses (ACCU) 43
  Carlos Velasco Villamizar Urban Front 43
  Catatumbo, Colombia 43, 51
  Cimitarra Valley 48
  Consultoría para los Derechos Humanos y el Desplazamiento, Colombia (International Displacement Monitoring Centre) 43
  FARC see FARC-EP
  Gaitanist Self-Defence of Colombia-Urabeños 45
  Havana peace agreement 40, 48, 49
  jíbaros 53
  JOLIPAZ 52, 54
  Justice and Peace process (Colombia) 44
  Los Rastrojos 45
  Mancusor, Salvatore 43
  map *42*
  MATS (Youth Analytical Movement for Social Transformation) 41, 50–1, 53–4, 215, 217
  Middle Magdalena 48
  Municipal Prosecutor's Office, Colombia 44
  Santander state, Colombia 42–5, 53
  young people 49–50
  see also Cúcuta
Communist Party (USSR) 60
Communist Party of Nepal (CPN) 134
Communist Party of Nepal (Maoist) 134, 136
community
  activism
    academics and 165
    conferences 70
    contributions 227
    culture and 117, 151, 155
    dependence on 110
    ex-combatants and 179–80
    experience and 4, 20, 98, 177
    financial support 178
    human rights issues 174
    information and 19, 69
    infrastructure 176
    mediation **17**, 154, 176–7, 185, 211
    organised 20, 65
    personal tragedies 108
    relationships 215, 216
    respected people 15, **17**, 187
    safety and security 18, 53, 121, 122, 126, 128, 175
    social capital 181
    space for 12
    state and 131, 219
    sustainability 184
    understanding 2, 187
    women and 110–12, 224
    youth and 215, 217
  churches 15, 184
  communication 145
  conflict and 14, 35, 84, 174–5
  decision making 88
  dimensions of 2, **3**
  education 122–3, 221
  everyday peace and 30, **32**, 49, 194
  families and **3**, 27, 52, 86, 144, 162
  groups 101–7, 144, 148
  hierarchies 102
  identification with 14
  impacts 3
  improvement 4
  infrastructure 176, 178, 181, **182**, 215, 227
  initiatives **17**
  inter-community conflicts 30, 84, 108, 112, 124, 168, **182**, 182
  inter-community relationships
    activities 181
    development of 107, 176, 182, 186, 211
    everyday issues **32**, 33, 221, 226
    ex-prisoners and 179–80
    networking 176, 214
    organisation 177, 179
    problems 185–6
    projects 180
    requirements 178

234

Index

skills needed 220
solidarity 227
interdependence **3**
interests 47, 55
leaders
  commitment 20–1
  dialogue *10*
  families 64
  human capital 181
  inter-community work 176–7
  investment in 187
  national leaders and 64, 65, 77
  role *8*, *10*, 59, 65, 76, 211, 221, 224, 226
  skills 224
  support for 199, 223, 225, 227
  trust in 109, 145, 177, **178**, 210
  truth and 110
  victims 40, 44
  women 20, 98, 104–7, 109, 110, 111–12, 138, 142–3, 147, 224
learning 90
mobilisation 118, 127, 130–1, 217
needs **17**, 174, 175, 180, 220
networks **3**, 60, 105–6, 214, 215
organisations 8, 15, 18, 44, 48, 98, 101, 102, 105, 109, 170, 177
paramilitary groups and 170, 175–6, 182, 222
peacebuilding and
  activism 12
  everyday peace and 25, 144, 209, 221
  ex-prisoners and 180
  financial support 178–9
  inter-community 181
  networks 15
  organisations 18, 138, 177
  perspectives 90
  raising issues 14
  support 189
  values 139
  visions 130–1
  women 91, 107, 138, 148
police and 121, 124–6, **125**, 130, 170
power-holders and 18, 49, 55, 222
problems 52–4
processes 47, 51, 52
relationships 2, 15, 44, 49, 50, 107–8, 112, 214
religion and 89, 112, 170–1
safety and security 118, 121–2, 126, 217
segregation 171
self-organisation **17**
solidarity 46, 151, 155, 176, 228
storytelling and 92, 142, 155, 161, 162, 165, 218, 228
strategies 2, 15, 124, 131
structures 103–4, 108, 225
tensions 15, 108, 181, 182, 183, 184–5

violence and 30, 54, 124, 210
women and
  decision-making **17**
  dialogue 148
  families and 147
  initiatives 142
  inter-community contacts 176
  leadership 20, 98, 105–8, 112
  organisations 91, 138, 176
  programmes 91–2
  safe spaces 144
  targets 86, 91–2
young people and 52–4, 142, 147, 155, 157, 158, 159, 161, 176, 217
community development
  activities **3**
  approaches 98, 101–3, 168, 177, **178**, 187, 191, 201, 220
  aspects 5
  awareness 202
  conflicts and **13**, **14**, **17**, 18, 110, 175, 225
  definitions 3–5
  empowerment 165–6, 188, 213, 215
  everyday peace
    framework for 21, 25, 35–6, 191, 206, 221
    innovations 26, 31, 191–2
    strengthened by 21, 35, 191, 209
    tool for 19
    translation into practice for 191, 193
  justice and 110
  Ledwith on 4
  local leaders and 59, 76–7
  national elites and 60, 111
  necessity for 101
  participation
    approaches **178**
    focus on 36, 90, 206
    importance of 8, 103, 174, 211, 215–16
    meaningful **5**, 5
    promotion of 87, 183, 185, 186
    state and 18, 88
    tool 221
  peacebuilding
    achieving SDGs 9
    approaches 178, 182, 187, 192, 209, 219, 225, 228
    everyday peace and 25, 33, 196
    ex-prisoners and 180
    from below 40, 182
    important element in 45
    shared values 19, 183
    training 198
    women and 91
  practice 52, 91, 168, 191, 192, 211, 216
  principles 123, 192, 211, 215, 222, 223, 227

programmes 192–3, 197–8, 200, 206
rights-based 20, 109, 216–17
role of 1, 9, 12, 79, 91, 93, 225
SDGs and 9
state and 18
storytelling and 162, 164–5, 218, 228
training 198, 199, 221
values **5**, 212
Community Institutions for Peace 48
Community Workers Co-operative (Ireland) 5, 209
Complexo da Maré, Rio de Janeiro
 arts and culture centres 117, 124
 community mobilisation 130
 mapping and naming 123–4
 policing 121–2, 124–6, 128–30, 132
 realities of life in 131–2
 security forces 121
 see also favelas; Redes da Maré
Conciliation Resources (UN) 91
conflict
 analysis 15, 19, 49, 71, 84, 92, 188, 215
 armed
  communities and 52, 142, 174, 191
  data on 127
  ending of 7
  eruption of 64
  escalation of 76
  favelas and 131
  internal 49
  long-term 40
  non-state 1, 21 n1, 40, 125, **126**
  peacebuilding and 138–9, 145
  police and 121, **126**
  prevention of 7, 70
  recommencement of 98, 186
  reduction of 129
  state-based 1, 134
  three-sided 170
  transformation 48
 Caucasus 19, 59–78
 causes
  addressing of 12, 18, 174
  analysis of 15, 140
  impact on peacebuilding 225
  minorities and 99
  response to 138
  revisiting **18**
  structural 81–2
  underlying 145, 209
 Colombia 40–56
 community and
  activism 228
  contribution 3
  impact 2, 79, 147–8, 214, 228
  issues 86
  lack of change 174
  organisations 91, 145, 147–8
  role of the state 137

structures 104
community development and
 addressing 93
 approach to 110
 everyday peace and 191, 201
 importance of connections 214
 interventions **17**, **18**
 stages of 225
 transformation 216
culture and 151
definition 1
dynamics 65, 75, 77, 194, 196
environmental 83
escalation *16*, 76, 92, 175
ethnic 85, 88, 99
everyday peace and 26, 28–36, **32**, 193, 197, 228
factors 2, **13**, **14**, **182**
fatalities 2
impact 2, **3**, 12, 146–7, 176–8, 181, 186, 188, 214, 218, 228
inter-community 84
inter-state and intra-state 1, 210
latent 62, 72, 73, 75
leaders and 64, 65, 88
legacy 171, 175, 179, 186
levels of 12, **13**, **14**
management **7**, 12, 91, **140**
Myanmar 21, 25, 27, 36, 191–206
nature of 8, 12, 210
necessity for 165
Nigeria 79–93
non-state 2, 21 n1
Northern Ireland 168–189
peacebuilding and
 activities 89
 ending 7
 literature 45
 post–conflict *6*, 6, 40
 reconciliation 177
 SDGs and 9
 transformation **7**, 139, 210, 227
phases 15, **17**, 14, 15, **17**, **18**, 168
poverty and 79, 82–3, 102, 174
prevention *6*, 6, 9, 60, 70, 75–6, 225
religion and 84, 85, 88, 170
resolution 8, **32**, 54, 66–7, 69, 74, 87, 200, 203, 221
resources and 82
Sri Lanka 20, 98–113
state-based 1, 202
transformation
 approach 12, 139, 146
 commitment to 222
 communities and 31, 215, 228
 context 168
 description 9, 12
 ex-prisoners and 180
 importance of 55

236

individuals and 144
literature 45
long-term process 142, 148, 227
organisations 139, 223
peacebuilding and **7**, 210
rights-based 216–17
women and 140, 142, 223
types of 1–2, 12
violent
  addressing consequences of 88, 89, 145, 214
  causes 6, 12, 47, 79, 82–3, 86, 90, 117, 138, 140, 211
  communities and 1, 102, 177, 213, 216, 220, 225, 228
  contributors 9
  death rates **126**
  dynamics of 18–19, 45
  escalation 85, 92
  everyday peace and 33, 191–2
  experiences from 15, 209
  impact of 1, 2, 145, 175, 210
  lack of agency in 4, 18
  long-term 50
  nationalism and 78 n1
  nature of 84, 210
  organisations 138–9
  peace agreements 137
  peacebuilding and 1, 6, 7, 18, 55, 138–9, 145, 219
  risk factors **13**, **14**
  stages 7, 210
  stereotypes and 75
  terminology 21 n2
  women and 74, 86, 137–9, 140–1, 143, 144–9
Conflict Analysis Resource Centre 49
conscientisation 35, 118, 227
Coventry University 164
COVID-19
  Maré favela Brazil 130
  Myanmar 199, 201, 202, 204
  Nepal 138
Cúcuta
  Border Block 44
  guerrillas in 42–4
  police and paramilitaries 44
  Venezuela and 42
  violence in 41
  Young Peace Leaders (JOLIPAZ) 52, 54
  young people in 41, 50, 55

D

DDR (disarmament, demobilisation and reintegration) 45
decolonialism 41, 45–8, 48, 55
definitions
  community development 2–5, 209

conflict 1
ends and means 90
everyday, the 27, 28
everyday peace 29–30, 35, 191–3
gender 75, 140
interlocking 83
key terms in peacemaking **7**, 9, 191
Palestinians 156
peacebuilding 6, 40, 48
dialogue
  Caucasus examples 71
  Caucasus forum and 74
  ex-combatants 74
  Georgia/Abkhazi 67–8, 69
  independence of participators 73
  internal and external 66
  International Dialogue Centre 88–9
  international facilitators 68
  Nagarik Aawaz in Nepal 147–8
  neutral mediators 67
  opposing intelligentsias 63
  between religions 88–9
  safe spaces for 72
  Soviet intelligentsia 60
  sympathy and frustration with 69
dispute resolution 60, 69 76
donor priorities 110
  burnout and wellbeing 77
  Caucasus 65, 70, 72
  international 70, 90
  local needs and priorities 225
  NGOs and 224, 228
  priorities of 77, 110
drugs 41, 44–5, 53–4, 126, 131, 217
Dual Mandate 81
Durkheim, Émile 27

E

Elbrus declaration 70
elites
  cajoling attempts of 33
  community leaders and 77
  community level and 25
  everyday and 28
  imposing peace from above 210
  interethnic in Sri Lanka 98–9
  liberal peace and 46, 47
  national elites in Caucasus 59–60, 62, 64, 73
  Nigeria 90
  shades of 65
  Soviet rule and 78
  Track One peacemaking 7
Engels, Friedrich 27
EU PEACE programmes 178–9, 181
everyday peace
  avoidance and 31, 200, 203
  community and 40–1, 55, 205, 206, 215, 223

community development and 19, 21, 25–6, 35, 191–3, 196–8, 201, 206, 209, 221, 228
concept 26, 28–30, 191, 193
conflict and 30, 33, 191
innovations 31–3, 36, 191–2
justice and 34, 194
Nagarik Aawaz **140**
social practices 30, 31, **32**, 34, 36, 192, 199–200, 204, 206
territorial peace and 48
training 198, 199, 206
external organisations 66–7

F

facilitators 67–9, 72, 147, 198–9, 202–5, 221
FARC-EP (Revolutionary Armed Forces of Colombia-People's Army) 40, 42, 43, 49, 50
favelas 117–26
  ADPF das Favelas 130, 132
  history of 118
  Maré 118–19, *120*, 129, 131
  Observatório de Favelas 123
  policing 121
  policy of repression and neglect 126
  protection of life 122
  quality of public services 123
  see also Redes da Maré
fear 25, 107, 144
feminism
  decolonial 47
  generally 227
  Nagarik Awaaz 139, 141, 143, 144, 223
  Sri Lanka as well as Nepal 223–4
  see also women
Foucault, Michel 28
Foundations for Peace Network (FFP) 209, 229 n1
four goals (Lederach) 12, 213
four Is (of oppression) 8, 12
Freire, Paolo
  conflict transformation 9, 12
  conscientisation 35, 227
  consciousness raising 197
  critical consciousness 93
  importance of engagement 79
  learning from lived experience 210
  Redes da Maré 118
  Rohingyas 192
  Sri Lanka 102

G

Gabrielyan, Gevorg Ter 71, 72, 77–8
Galtung, Johan 6, 84, 117, 142, 209
gender 104–8, 140–2
  Caucasus 75
  a definition 140

Nigeria 85
Redes da Maré 217
storytelling 155, 158, 162
violence and 64, 91, 226
Geneva Conventions 154
Georgia
  Abkhazian conflict 62, 67–8, 69–70, 71, 74–5
  Armenian offer of rehabilitation 66
Gramsci, Antonio 224, 226
grounded agency 47
guerrillas 41–5, 49
  see also paramilitaries

H

Heaney, Seamus 216
Heidegger, Martin 28
heritage 163
Hindus 30, 112
Human Rights Commission 109
Human Rights Watch 121

I

India 30, 34
indirect rule 81
INGOs (international NGOs) 46
intelligentsias
  assuming power 63
  Caucasus ethno-nationals 59, 64
  civil society 222
  local 76
  Soviet 60–2, 64–6, 77
inter-group contact theory 67
Internally Displaced People (IDPs) 2, 226
International Alert 71, 72, 77
International Association for Community Development (IACD) 4, 212, 219
International Humanitarian Law 152, 154
invasion 154
Ireland 168
  see also Northern Ireland
Islam 81
  see also Muslims
Israel 151–4, *153*, 164

K

Karabakhs 62, 67
Kilmurray, Avila 209
knowledge, types of 211

L

Latin America 15, 47, 49
  see also Colombia; Cúcuta
Lederach, John Paul
  bottom-up peacebuilding 15
  cycles within stories 156
  effective peacekeeping 222
  four goals and oppression 12
  four phases of peacebuilding 141

Index

importance of local people 139
methods of 91
Nagarik Aawaz and 142
pessimism of sufferers 158
pyramid *8*
on transformation 9
liberal peace 45–6, 47, 55
Local Peacebuilding report (Peace Direct/ Alliance for Peacebuilding) 15
'local turn', the 47, 211–12, 228
long-term commitment 8, 20, 110, 187, 216
Lugard, Lord 81
Lukács, György 28

M

Mac Ginty, Roger 26, 28–32, 45–7
Marx, Karl 27
Mexico 2, 21 n1
missionaries 81, 90
Muslims
 Boko Haran 86
 compulsory charity donations 161
 Hindus and 30
 Myanmar 191, 194, 202–3
 Nigeria 84, 89
 Sri Lanka 112
 Tamil, Sinhala and 108
 Tamils and 99, 101, 112
 Western education and 81
 women 111
 see also Rohingyas
Myanmar 191–208
 COVID-19 199, 201, 202, 204
 everyday peace 191–4, 197
 facilitators 198, 199
 history of Rohingya conflict 194, 196
 map *195*

N

Nagarik Aawaz 138–49
 dialogues 147–8
 establishment of 138
 feminist approach of 143
 foundational principles **140**
 gender and women 140–1
 personal transformation 142
 programmes and partnerships 146–7
 Rita Thapa 138
 safe spaces 144–5, 147
 trauma 145, 146–7
Nagorny Karabakh 62, 70, 71
Nepal 134–50
 casualties of violence 137
 Comprehensive Peace Agreement 136–7
 COVID-19 138
 CPN (Maoist) 134, 136, 137
 Madhesis 136–7
 map *135*

Operation Romeo 136
Palace massacre, ensuing violence and restoration of monarchy 136
political history 134
women in 137, 138
see also Aawaz, Nagarik
networks
 building trust 20
 Caucasus 60, 70–6
 Community Institutions for Peace 48
 drug dealers 54
 Elbrus declaration 70
 Lederach on 15
 Nigeria 86, 91, 92
NGOs
 Caucasus Forum 70, 76; *see also* Caucasus Forum of Networks
 formalisation of 224
 'Grand Bargain' 228
 international peacebuilding 67
 internet and 71
 Lederach 8
 mobilisation 46
 national elite formation and 73
 Progesar 43
 Rio de Janeiro 117
 Sri Lanka 112
 St Egidio 7
 a success story 59–60
 Western style 65
Nigeria 79–98
 banditry 85
 Borno State 91–2
 colonial background 81
 community based approaches 89–92
 diversity 84–5
 farmers and herders 83
 federal structures 82
 government intervention and projects 86–8
 Hausa people 82
 Hope Interactive 91–2
 International Dialogue 88–9
 Lake Chad Basin 86
 Living Standards Survey 82
 map *80*
 Niger Delta 82, 84, 86–7
 non-governmental intervention 88
 patterns of conflict 85–6
 poverty 82
 religion 84, 88–9
 revenue collection 82
 Umuada 91
 violence 84–5
 women and children 82, 85, 86, 90, 91–2
Northern Ireland 168–90
 Belfast 181
 Brexit 173

Britain, Republic of Ireland and 172–3
charitable organisations involved 178–9, 181
civil rights 170, 171, 175
community action programme and lessons learned 181–9
community approaches **178**
community infrastructure **182**
Derry 181
Direct Rule 170, 171, 174
EU PEACE programmes 178–9, 181
Good Friday agreement 171, 172–4, 177, 179, 182
maps *169, 173*
paramilitaries 170, 172, 174–83, 185–6, 219, 222
partition 168–9
policing 173–4
prisoners 174, 179, 179, 180
Protestant and Catholic 170, 171
safe spaces 185, 187
single identity areas 171, 176, 179, 180
Stormont 170
Troubles (the) and its combatants 170, 171–2, 179, 180
victims and survivors 179

O

ordinary people
 academic literature on 29
 elites and 28
 majority do not practise violence 33, 192
 micro-solidarities among 36, 206
 suffering of 144
organised crime 1, 2, 49, 50, 52
Ossetians 62, 67, 71
Other, the
 acknowledgment of similarities 202
 after dark 203
 improving relations with 206
 inferiority of 63
 loathing for 31, 36, 197
 offensive behaviour of 200
 openness and transparency 204
 rehumanising 25

P

Palestine 151–67
 historical context 152
 occupied territories 152, 164
 On Our Land 156
 South Hebron Hills 151–4, 156, 162–5
 two-state solution 163
paramilitaries
 Colombia 40–1, 43–5
 Northern Ireland 170, 172, 174, 177–83, 185–6, 219
 Ruslan Gelayev 76

Sri Lanka 101
 see also guerrillas
Pathways for Peace: Inclusive Approaches to Preventing Violent Conflict (United Nations and World Bank) 2
PA-X Initiative 210
Peace Direct 15, 212, 223
peacebuilding
 approaches
  arts-based 198, 199
  community and 25, 91, 148, 209
  community development and 168, 182, 187, 219, 221, 222, 225
  four-pillars 9
  leaders and 199
  liberal peace 46
  phases of conflict and 15
  social justice 217
  training 188
 arts-based 198, 199, 213
 bottom-up 15, 34, 40, 47, 55
 challenges 12
 change and 213, 216, 227
 community and
  assets 227
  challenges 12, 14, 225
  commitment 45, 47
  culture 221
  experiences 55, 148
  impacts **3**
  information 188
  inter-community 177, 180, 182, 183
  leaders and 187
  organisations 15
  perspectives 90
  programmes 179, 188, 204
  religion 89
  rights 130–1, 174
  social cohesion 25
  solutions 228
  sustainable 144, 182, 187–9
  tolerance 144
  values 139
  women and 91, 107, 138, 145–6
 community development and
  activism 177–8
  activities **3**
  challenges 225
  commitment 183, 187, 222
  conflict and 1, 4, **18**, 18–19, 93, 168, 191
  development 188
  empowerment 18, 93, 213
  everyday peace and 25, 33, 228
  ex-prisoners and 180
  foundations 209
  interacting 1
  leaders and 65
  organisations 168, 182, 192, 219

Index

post-violence 196
power relations 164
SDGs and 9
security 122
state and 219
training 198
women and 140
concepts 1, 6, **7**, 7, 141, 228
conflict and **3**, *6*, 12, 67, 164, 168, 210, 219
conflict transformation and 9, 18, 45, 139, 142, 146, 210, 222, 227
contextual challenges 12
definitions 6, 7
everyday peace 26, 35–6, 197
ex-combatants and 222
innovations 31
liberal peace and 45–7, 49, 67
literature 211
organisations 20, 45, 67, 70–1, 89, 91, 138–9, 140–6
participation 5, 180
peacemaking, peacekeeping and 7, 9, 210
politics of 172
post-conflict *6*, 6, **18**, 112, 141
process 8, 20, 40, 45–7, 50, 55, 79, 138, 140, 145, 183
Smith's palette *10*
state and 8, 40, 88, 138
storytelling and 218
territory and 48
training 198
United Nations 6–7, 9
violence and 3, 55–6, 224
West and 78 n2
women and 20, 85, 91, 138–9, 140–6, 224
youth and 40, 50, 89
peacekeeping *6*, 7, 9
peacemaking *6*, 7, 9, 141, 210, 227
personal presence and involvement 109
personal transformation 138, 142
police
 brutality 85
 operations 121–2, **125**, **126**, 127–31
 paramilitaries and 44
 peacekeeping **7**
 presence 175
 reforms 173–4
 violence 118, 124, **126**, 132, 136, 170
Progresar 43
Putnam, Robert D. 168, 186

R

Rakhines, Myanmar 191–2, 194–8, 201–5, 214, 221
Red Cross 109
Redes da Maré 117–33

'A Maré que Queremos' (Redes da Maré) 123
arts and culture centres 213
community based Public strategy 126–8
Complexo da Maré 117–18, 120, 122, 124, 130, 131
Federal Supreme Court 129
'Letters of Maré' 129
map *120*
mapping exercise 123–4
Maré de Noticias 128
Military Police and Public Defender 129
police violence 124–5, **125–6**
Public Civil Action (ACP Maré) 118, 128–30, 132
Right to Public Security and Access to Justice 125, 127, 129, 130
self-description and values 124
'Sodos da Maré, TemosDireitos' ('We're from Maré, we have rights') 127
strategic objectives 122–3
'Talking about Public Security in Maré' course 128
Textual Production Workshop 128
violence, approaches to 126–7
see also favelas
resilience 92, 101, 111, 112 n1, 176
Revolutionary Armed Forces of Colombia-People's Army (FARC-EP) *see* FARC
Richmond, O. 46–7, 48
Rio de Janeiro 117
 Avenida Brasil 119, 121
 equal rights to access resources 123
 favelas in 118, 119
 Guanbara Bay 118
 housing crisis 118
 police operations 130
 see also favelas; Redes da Maré
Rohingyas 191–4, 196, 198, 201–5
Russia
 Caucasus Forum 70–1 *see also* Caucasus Forum of Networks
 Chechens 62
 geo-political stand-off 60, 77
 South Caucasus 67
 Yeltsin, Boris 63

S

safe spaces
 children and young people 26
 enabling 187
 everyday peace and 26, 31
 facades of normality 192
 importance of 185, 222
 International Alert 72
 Nagarik Aawaz 140, 144–5, 147
 Rakhine and Rohingya 203
 women and 224

241

'Schlaining' process 68
self-censorship 68, 77
Sen, Amartya 12, 112 n2, 197
Seventeen Sustainable Goals 9
Shevardnadze, President 67
single-identity narratives 14
Smith's palette 10
social capital
  bonding and bridging 214
  last remains 26
  mediators 68
  networks and 73
  Northern Ireland 176, 181
  Putnam's theory 168, 186
  Soviet intelligentsia 66
social cohesion 25–6, 33, 88, 192
social practices 28–36
  academic literature 29–31
  awareness of 197
  daily networks of 48
  eight aspects of 193, 200
  everyday life and 28
  everyday peace and 26, 192, 199, 206
  suspicion and 25
  types of **32**
South Hebron Hills 151–4, 156, 162–5
Soviet Union
  censorship 68, 69, 77
  community borders 62–3
  disintegration 59, 62, 67, 78 n1
  governance system 60–1, 65
  ideology 61
  intelligentsias 59–62, 64, 65, 66, 77
  leadership model 73
  role of women 75
Sri Lanka 98–116
  Batticoloa 101, 106, 110, 111
  JSSK 107–8
  Karuna 101
  Land Development Ordinance 106
  Liberation Tigers of Tamil Eelam (LTTE) 98, 99, 100–1, 104, 106, 108, 110
  map *100*
  Sinhalas 99, 106–7, 112
  Tamil Muslim Sinhala Sisters Group 112
  Tamils 98–9, 101, 107–8, 112
  tsunami 103, 105
  war of independence (1948) 98–9
  women 102, 103, 105–7, 111, 113 n3
  Women's Coalition for Disaster Management 106
St Egidio (Mozambique) 7
storytelling 155–62
  Bir Zeit University opportunities 162
  examples 157–62, *160*
  an optimistic act 151
  power through 165

recording life stories 156–7
Sustainable Development Goals (SDGs) 2, 9, 11

T

Tamil Tigers *see* Sri Lanka: Liberation Tigers of Tamil Eelam (LTTE)
terminology 1, 7, 21 n2, 203
territorial peace 48–9
terrorists 1, 136
Things Fall Apart (Chinua Achebe) 85
training
  Caucasus Forum 70
  facilitators 198–200, 221
  NGOs in Caucasus 67
  Nigeria and religion 89
  opportunities for 188
  young people in Sri Lanka 111
trauma
  Abkhazia 67
  causes of 64
  funding for 88
  Nepalese traditions 145–7, 149, 221–2
  Northern Ireland 171, 175
  women 143
  young people 92
trust 109, 214–15

U

UNHCR (United Nations High Commissioner for Refugees) 5, 54, 67
United Nations
  Abkhazia relies on 71
  Conciliation Resources 91
  impact of violent conflict 2
  liberal Peace 45
  peacebuilding as post-conflict strategy 6–7
  Sustainable Development Goals *11*
United Nations Volunteers (UNV) 68
United We Dream 215
Uppsala Conflict Data Programme 1–2
Utstein Report 9

V

Venezuela 41–2, 43, 45
violence
  aesthetics of 44
  alternatives 225
  avoidance 31–3, 193, 197
  causes **3**, 6, 84
  community and
    activism 174–5
    addressing 47, 49, 221
    challenges 98
  everyday peace and 30, 55
  ex-prisoners and 180
  impacts on 2, **3**
  innovations 117–8

Index

issues 86
mobilisation 130
peacebuilding and **3**
pogroms 99, 112
role in 212
security 124, 131, 217
support for victims **178**
women and 105, 112
youth and 41, 53–4, 55–6, 92, 217
community development and **13**, 15, **17**, 45, 93, 101, 168, 175, 196, 226
conflict and 3, 6, *16*, **17**, 144
conflict transformation and 12, 48
criminal 1, 41, 49, 53–4, 120–1, 131, 210
cultural 84, 85, 148
definitions 1, 200
documentation of 217
everyday peace and 26, 29–34, 36, 55, 192, 197, 199
fear and 25
grounded agency 47
impact of
 challenges 98
 conversation about 131–2, 144, 213
 damages 19
 families 108
 individual and collective 144, 145
 issues 176
 liberal peace and 55
 mobilisation 126, 130
 reflecting on **18**
 rural areas 136
 single identity areas 171
 state and 130, 132
 women 138, 223
 youth 138, 223
internal 2, 82, 85, 86
nationalism and 59, 62–4
organised 1, 49
paramilitary 43–4
peacebuilding and 3, 55–6, **7**, 45, 107, 196
police and 118, 120–1, 124–6, **125**, **126**, 130, 132, 136, 170
political 1, 41, 85, 146, 210, 222
prevention of **7**, 226
risk factors **13**
social cohesion after 25
state and
 backing settlers 154, 165
 community 124–5
 local response to 122
 non-state and 1, 83, 105, 175, 194, 196, 210
 sanctioning of 99
 security policy 117, 130
structural 6, 29, 64, 82, 84, 117, 138, 144, 148, 193, 209

women and
 activism 224
 community and 102, 105
 discussion about 105
 domestic 103, 105, 105
 experiences 91, 107, 141, 146
 gender relationships 226
 ignoring of 85
 initiatives 142
 measures against 82
 sexual 106, 140, 143, 147
 workshops 89
 youth and **17**, 19, 49–50, 53–4, 82, 92, 217

W

West Bank 152
Williams, Philippa 29–30, 33, 34
women
 Caucasian Women's League 73, 74–5, 224
 FFP 229 n1
 Hope Interactive 91–2
 minorities and the marginalised 212
 Nepal *see* Nagarik Aawaz Nepal
 Nigeria 82, 85, 86, 90
 safe places 224
 Sri Lanka *see* Sri Lanka: women
 violence and gender relationships 226
 volunteering 175–6

Y

young people (youth)
 adults and 82
 Borno Coalition on Democracy and Progress 92
 communism and 136
 Cúcuta 40–1
 drug use 215, 217, 220
 explaining histories to 111
 favelas 122–3, 125
 feminism and 223
 Latin America generally and Colombia 49–56
 letters to judges 125
 Nagarik Aawaz 138–9
 negative images 219
 NGOs and 71
 Nigeria 82, 88–90, 92
 paramilitarism problems 180
 researchers (Palestine) 156–7
 safe spaces 226
 storytelling 157, 161–2, 164, 165
 teaching leadership 224
 those on the margins 56, 88, 90
 vulnerability 186
 women volunteers 175
 Youth Peace Platform 92

www.ingramcontent.com/pod-product-compliance
Lightning Source LLC
Chambersburg PA
CBHW071155070526
44584CB00019B/2794